Reflections of a
Would-Be Anarchist

Reflections of a
Would-Be Anarchist

Ideals and Institutions of Liberalism

Richard E. Flathman

University of Minnesota Press

Minneapolis • London

An earlier version of chapter 7 appeared in *Political Theory* 24, no. 1 (February 1996): 4–32. Copyright © 1996 by Sage Publications, Incorporated. Reprinted with permission.

Published by the University of Minnesota Press
111 Third Avenue South, Suite 290
Minneapolis, MN 55401-2520

http://www.upress.umn.edu

Printed in the United States of America on acid-free paper

Library of Congress Cataloging-in-Publication Data

Flathman, Richard E.
    Reflections of a would-be anarchist : ideals and institutions of liberalism / Richard E. Flathman.
       p.   cm.
    Includes bibliographical references and index.
    ISBN 0-8166-3061-5 (hardcover : alk. paper). — ISBN 0-8166-3062-3 (pbk. : alk. paper)
      1. Liberalism.   2. Pluralism (Social sciences)   3. Authority.
4. Rule of law.   5. Police.   I. Title.
JC574.F58   1998
320.5—dc21
                                           97-26577

The University of Minnesota is an equal-opportunity educator and employer.

10 09 08 07 06 05 04 03 02 01 00 98 99   10 9 8 7 6 5 4 3 2 1

The illumination of incongruities is not tantamount to the solution of problems arising from a relatively closed conceptual and empirical context. It only answers the question of how these incongruities come to appear, that is, what completely different intentions lead to such contradictions, incomprehensible as they are to systematic thought. We must let the contradictions stand as what they are, make them understood as contradictions, and grasp what lies beneath them.

—Hannah Arendt

Contents

Acknowledgments   ix

Introduction   xi

PART I   IDEALS

1 / Strains in and around Liberal Theory: An Overview from a
Strong Voluntarist Perspective   3

2 / Liberality, Idiosyncrasies, Idiolects, and a Little Beyond: Ortega y Gasset,
Proust, and Wittgenstein on Liberality   17

3 / The Good or Goodnesses of Polity and Polities à la Liberalism:
Plurality Rather than Unicity, Singularity beyond Plurality   31

PART II   INSTITUTIONS

4 / Ruling, Rules, and Rule Following: Mainstay or Mirage, Miracle
or Misfortune?   49

5 / Liberalism and the Suspect Enterprise of Political Institutionalization:
The Case of the Rule of Law   79

6 / The Ideas, Ideals, and Practices of Liberalism and the Institutions
and Institutionalisms of Police and Policing   105

7 / Liberal versus Civic, Republican, Democratic, and Other Vocational
Educations: Liberalism and Institutionalized Education   137

Notes   165

Bibliography   187

Index   195

Acknowledgments

It is a pleasure to express my gratitude once again to Bill Connolly and Kirstie McClure for their contributions to my thinking, writing, and teaching. They have provided acute comments on all of the chapters that follow, and my conversations with them, across a wide and continually changing range of themes, texts, and issues, are invaluable to me. I am equally indebted to the superb graduate students who now are or recently have been participants in the political theory program at Johns Hopkins University. In courses, seminars, and personal conversations I have explored with them many of the theories and topics discussed in this book. It is accurate to say, I believe and indeed hope, that they disagree more than they agree with the views here expressed. But I am confident that they, jointly and severally, will readily discern the considerable impact of their thinking on my reflections. The numerous more particular intellectual debts that I have incurred are recorded in the notes to the several chapters and in the bibliography.

Final revisions and editing were done under the hospitable and engaging circumstances provided by a visiting professorship in the Jurisprudence and Social Policy Program of the University of California at Berkeley. Special thanks to Rod Watanabe for his innumerable kindnesses. Yet more special thanks to Carrie Mullen and her editorial associates at the University of Minnesota.

Four of the chapters have previously been published, and all of the others have been presented to various conferences, symposia, and the like. I have revised the original versions of each of the essays, in some cases substantially. In doing so, I have tried to diminish but not entirely eliminate a certain amount of reiteration that occurs in and among them. The chapters address closely related themes and issues, responding to and drawing on formulations that I continue to find engaging and provocative. In addition, they approach these materials from a perspective that, I hope, lends a degree of unity to the several discussions. Although my imagined and wished-for ideal reader would work through the volume from cover to cover, I believe that, if read together with the introduction, each of the essays can be assessed on its own terms. (In the few instances of repetition, as distinct from reiteration, in the later chapters I signal the beginning of the repeated material. I have allowed one repetition of several paragraphs to stand for two connected reasons. First, the materials in question are integral to both of the chapters in which they appear. If I had eliminated them from the second of the two presentations, the latter would be diminished. Second, we are all familiar with the idea that ideas and their formulations take on different colorations according to the settings in which we encounter them. I think, and was encouraged to continue to do so by an anonymous reader of the manuscript, that the materials that appear in both Chapters 4 and 5 will read in importantly different ways in the two contexts. Although in literal terms they are repetitions, from a performative perspective they differ importantly.)

The previously published materials, reprinted with the kind permission of the original editors or publishers, are as follows: Chapter 1, which appeared in *The Liberal Political Tradition: Contemporary Appraisals*, edited by James Meadowcraft (Edward Elger, 1996); Chapter 3, which appeared in the *Cardozo Journal of International and Comparative Law*, (Winter 1996); Chapter 5, which appeared in *The Rule of Law*, edited by Ian Shapiro (New York University Press, 1994); and Chapter 7, which appeared in *Political Theory*, vol. 24 (February 1996).

Introduction

As prelude to identifying and generalizing over the concerns and themes specific to this work, it may be appropriate to say something concerning the wider question of the role of the mode of inquiry and reflection—that is, political theory and political theorizing—of which the following essays are intended to be examples. What tasks should political theorists set for themselves, what objectives should they pursue?

It is widely agreed that political theorists, especially those who are also scholars and teachers, have the responsibility to transmit understanding of and sustain critical reflection concerning the rich tradition(s) of which they are most manifestly the heirs. Self-conscious, orderly, and not infrequently systematic reflection concerning the political and its relationships to other dimensions of human affairs has been a valued feature of human experience for several millennia. These rich traditions, however, remain alive, indeed continue to be culturally available to us in any significant sense of the term, only to the extent that political theorists of our own day study, teach, and write concerning the texts in which those traditions are primarily located and expressed. Contributing to this objective is one of my purposes in this work, an aim pursued most explicitly in Chapter 1 but also (especially with respect to comparatively recent theorizings) at intervals throughout the book.

But there are potent objections to this view, particularly to the argument that *political theorists* should pursue the objectives just discussed. Why should those with this self-conception engage in these activities of retrieval, rehearsal, and reinvigoration? There are numerous arguments to the effect that the modern, late-modern, or postmodern time abounds in characteristics, perhaps especially political characteristics, that are not only unprecedented empirically but were not anticipated or so much as imagined by earlier practitioners of political theory. Worse, the reflections of the preponderance of these dead (and predominantly white/male) thinkers can now be seen to have been governed, even if sometimes unwittingly, by presuppositions that are now regarded as vulgar prejudices. It may indeed be valuable to know where we came from and how we got to where we now are—if only to avoid previous mistakes—but it is the task of historians not of political theorists to provide these genres of information and understanding.

Despite what I said in the two preceding paragraphs, the following pages are not uninfluenced by these and kindred objections (albeit the distinction between "historians" and "political theorists" is replete with difficulties). I do hope to help keep alive critical awareness of past political and related thinkings, but my primary objectives in attempting to do so are "presentist" in a stronger sense than that in which Michael Oakeshott and others correctly insist that the historian's past is always the "present past," is always a construal or interpretation of the past from one or another currently operative perspective. In Oakeshott's terms, my engagements with earlier theorists are in the mode of the practical not the historical past; they are concerned with the bearing of past thinking on present theory and practice.[1]

Stating my reasons for adopting this orientation will help to articulate the central concerns and themes of the following chapters. As I now read them, the earlier political thinkers discussed in these pages understood political theorizing to have two primary objectives (that is, two objectives in addition to maintaining, in part through either explicit or implicit commentary on their own predecessor political theorists, the tradition of critical political thinking). The first of these was to imagine or envision, and to articulate in the most attractive terms they could muster, *ideals* worthy of human pursuit. In this dimension of their theorizings, their concern was to identify and vivify the largest and especially the highest aspirations appropriate to human life and human affairs.

As with numerous of the political theorists of our own time, some among these earlier thinkers—Plato and Aquinas, Hegel and Bentham are leading examples—thought that this task required the discovery and elaboration of ideals that are "for everybody" (Nietzsche) at least in the sense that all human beings should accept and endeavor to achieve them and hence that all human institutions and relationships should be governed, finally, by the objectives that the ideal identifies. Although differing importantly with one another, each of them promoted *an* ideal, a unified and highly substantive teleology that, while allowing the need for a diversity of contributions to the idealized final end or good, was to provide the motivating and as possible the directing purpose of human conduct. By contrast, other thinkers who also never wavered in their commitment to the "idealistic" dimensions of their theorizing—Aristotle and Marx at their best; Montaigne, Hobbes, and Nietzsche throughout are examples—rejected this monistic view. We can say of them that they sought to imagine and articulate a multiplicity of ideals that would, severally and variously, inspire the diversity of individuals and societies of which they thought humankind does or should consist. Alternatively and in my judgment more perspicuously, we can say that each of them had a conception of *the* ideal for humankind but that their conceptions were formal or adverbial in character, not only allowing but inviting and celebrating a changing diversity of substantive realizations.

A bit later in this introduction, and at greater length in Part I, I associate myself with the second of these two forms of idealism and present a formal and adverbial conception of the ideals I regard as appropriate to liberalism and a liberal polity. First, however, a word concerning the second of the two objectives of political theorizing that I anticipated above. Although concerned with the actualities of political life, this second dimension is not effectively captured by widely drawn distinctions such as between normative and descriptive studies or between idealist and realist approaches. The focus in this regard, rather, is on marked and repeated patterns and tendencies that give continuing organization, direction, and implicit or explicit justification to substantial numbers of the members of politically organized societies. More particularly, my focus is on those patterns that are produced and sustained by what I call *institutionalizations* and *institutionalisms*.

In these of their inquiries and reflections, numerous of the most celebrated political theorists have sought to understand the genesis of the patterns they had observed and attempted to use those and related understandings to explain continuities and changes in political and related institutions and institutionalisms. Aristotle is clearly engaged in this enterprise in several of the books of the *Politics*, Machiavelli pursues this aim in the *Discourses* and other works, and the activity is especially prominent in Montesquieu's reflections on differing regime types, in the various works of Benjamin Constant, and in Marx's analyses of feudal and especially capitalist formations. In its primarily interpretative/explanatory forms, it is of course a staple of political science studies from the late nineteenth century to the present.

Influenced by the example of "genealogists" such as Friedrich Nietzsche, Michel Foucault, Michael Oakeshott, and their followers (especially William Connolly), however, I want to underline what I call—albeit I am not satisfied with the characterization—the critical purpose and thrust of studies of institutionalizations and institutionalisms provided by political theorists such as those I have just mentioned.[2] It is explicit that the primary aim of *soi-disant* genealogists is critical as distinct from descriptive/explanatory. Of course they identify and describe tendencies and patterns that strike them as salient in their time, and they attempt to explain those patterns in part by uncovering and recovering the historical sequences (above all the ideational sequences—of which what I am here calling institutionalisms are subsets) in the course of which and out of which those patterns emerged. By understanding both where we are now and how we got here, they hope to gain critical leverage on present patterns and arrangements. Thus they identify and describe, interpret and explain, but they do so for the purpose of assessing the merits and defects of the characteristics and tendencies that they find to be predominant.

As a conceptual/theoretical matter, of course, the foregoing paragraph effects no clear distinction. As any number of critics of empiricism have long since established, there is no such thing as a purely or antiseptically descriptive/explanatory inquiry or reflection. And although some inquirers and thinkers restrict themselves to quite recent historical and practical pasts, neither is there any such thing as a non- or ahistorical inquiry or reflection. (These two points, it is perhaps unnecessary to say, are intimately related.) As a matter of self-understanding and self-conscious purpose, however, there is an important distinction here. There are many students of politics (and of every other subject matter) whose objective—if I can put it this way—is to be as objective as possible, to reduce to the minimum the influence of their own "subjective" values and preferences on their descriptions, analyses, and explanations of political actualities. They of course aim to be "critical" in the sense of observing minutely, of giving close attention to the concepts and methods they use, of seeking counterexamples to the generalizations-cum-explanations that seem initially plausible to them, and the like. Not a few of them, moreover, are of an "improving" or "reforming" outlook. Following the example of predecessor thinkers such as Bacon and Bentham, they think they can "get it right" as to how and why things are as they now are, and they also think that when they have done so it will be perfectly, objectively, clear whether and if so in what ways those things should be changed.

As my invocation of the genealogists should make clear, these are not the primary senses in which I am saying that political theorists take a critical approach to institutionalizations and institutionalisms. Rather, resolutely and relentlessly in the case of the genealogists and skeptics such as Montaigne, at their best moments in theorists such as Aristotle and Montesquieu, Constant and Marx, these thinkers regard institutionalizations and institutionalisms with a wary, a skeptical eye. In a term that I use in the title of Chapter 5, they regard the enterprise of institutionalizing human conduct and consolidating institutions with institutionalisms (established, authoritative ideologies) as "suspect." They deny neither the prevalence nor the necessity of these features of human affairs, but they are sensitive to and critical concerning the ways in which they constrain and confine, normalize and homogenize what might otherwise be a more abundant, a richer, diversity of arrangements, activities, and sensibilities. They are or seek to be critical not merely in the senses discussed above but in Marx's sense of directing their critical attentions to the "roots" of the realities and ideas of institutions and institutionalisms.

I adopt and attempt to sustain such a stance or approach in Part II. My endeavor to do so largely explains the phrase "would-be anarchist" in the title of this volume. Institutions consist primarily of more or less articulated and interrelated nodes or amalgams of rules and norms (and rule makers and enforcers) that are accorded authority by those who accept them or who submit to their governance. And where they are stable and effective in organizing and governing human conduct, institutions are typically supported (legitimated) by a higher-order—that is a somewhat more abstract—array of principles and beliefs that are more or less widely treated as authoritative and that form the kinds of constellations that I am calling institutionalisms. These among the features of institutions draw the attentions of political theorists who are critical in the sense just discussed. In my own case, critical attention to these characteristics has heightened the attractiveness of positions that are anarchist (or, more radically, antinomian) in that they deny that any arrangement or rule, principle or person, can deserve standing as having authority or as being authoritative.[3] It is in part for this reason that I think of myself as a would-be anarchist—that is as someone who would like to be an anarchist. But I am a "would-be" anarchist because I accept the view briefly stated above that institutionalizations are both necessary and desirable and also accept (albeit with more reservations) that institutions can be viable only if they are supported by institutionalisms.

It is hardly necessary to say that this combination of views leaves me, as both a theoretical and a practical matter, with and hence in substantial difficulties. These difficulties are abundantly on display in the remainder of this book. I think it is impossible to resolve them completely; the task, rather, is to show why the tensions and dissonances arise and to look for strategic and tactical moves that make them creative while keeping them within manageable bounds.

But my self-conception as a would-be anarchist owes yet more to the ideals of liberalism as I have come to imagine and articulate them. The obvious point here is that one can be critical in the foregoing strong sense only if one has criteria by which to judge institutions and institutionalisms. As I read the political theorists that I admire and have tried to follow, the criteria they employ for this purpose are provided primarily by the political and related ideals that they have envisioned for their societies or for humankind generally. For example Montaigne, Constant, Nietzsche, and Oakeshott all promote ideals of self-making, self-overcoming, and self-enactment, and the most important question they ask concerning institutions and institutionalisms is whether or in what ways the latter contribute to or obstruct attempts to pursue and partially realize those ideals. The ideals promoted by Aristotle, Machiavelli, Montesquieu, and Marx are very different, but these thinkers also advert to their proposed ideals in assessing this or that society, polity, or set of arrangements.

I hope these remarks help to explain the sequencing of the essays that follow. Of course the substance of the essays depends on the character of the ideals I try to imagine and promote and on the interaction between those imaginings and the various institutions and institution-alisms that I critique in Part II. As to the former, readers of my recent publications will know, at least generally, what to expect. I argue that the highest ideal of liberalism is individuality understood as self-making or self-enactment. I also argue that pursuit of this ideal requires an abundant social and political plurality and, essential to both, the widest possible freedom of action. In the essays that make up Part I, I try to expand on and more especially to embellish these elusive but to me quite beautiful ideas.

As already suggested, I have not found the extant literatures of anarchism particularly helpful,[4] but I expect that readers of these essays, perhaps particularly those who read the essays in Part II, will understand why I want to associate myself with the general ideas and ideals of anarchism and antinomianism.

In order to assist readers who want to select among them, I conclude this introduction with condensed accounts of the main concerns and themes of the chapters that follow.

Chapter 1 was originally written for a conference and subsequent volume that attempted to identify and assess main tendencies in recent and especially contemporary liberal theory and practice. My discussion, which precedes from the perspective for which I argued in a previous work (Flathman, 1992), is primarily organized by a distinction between "agency-oriented" and "virtue-oriented" liberal theories. I argue for the former as intensified by what I call *strong voluntarism*.

Chapter 2, versions of which I have presented at a couple of conferences, aims to develop somewhat further the notions of agency, individuality, and voluntarism through use of the ideas of idiosyncrasy and idiolects. One of its central themes, which in various modulations reappears in Chapters 4 and 5, concerns the ways in which the shared languages necessary both to thinking and to interpersonal communication constrain or circumscribe thought and action and, often at the same time, open up possibilities that are not only unexpected but unpredictable. Here as later I draw primarily on Wittgenstein for an understanding of language, on the novels of Proust for examples of the idiosyncratic and the idiolectal, and on Ortega y Gasset for an understanding that links these notions to the idea of liberality.

Chapter 3 continues these themes, but more in that register of social and political theory that concerns itself with the possibility and desirability of unity or homogeneity and the ways in which these characteristics of a society contribute to or diminish the possibility of a radical form of plurality that—echoing the notions of idiosyncrasy and the idiolectal—I term *singularity*. I contend that the "goodness*es*" of a liberal polity reside primarily in its capacity to engender and sustain the continuing arrival, alteration, and disappearance of singularities.

Turning in Part II to institutions and institutionalisms, in Chapter 4 I examine what I take to be the fundaments of these notions, that is the ideas of ruling, rules, and rule following. Although I agree with Wittgenstein, Derrida, and others that there is something miraculous—that is something of which it is very difficult to give a systematic or even any very orderly account—about these prevalent features of human affairs, I concede that the social, political, and legal phenomena most commonly signified by the ideas of ruling, rules, and rule following are indeed mainstays of organized, more or less stable political societies. But I also argue that the institutionalisms that have developed around these ideas have greatly exaggerated both the possibility and more particularly the desirability of subjecting human conduct to rules and ruling. Owing importantly to the influence of these ideologies, which treasure and promote values such as orderliness and predictability, commonality and rationality, ruling, rules, and rule following frequently present themselves as human misfortunes. I should add that the difficulties mentioned above, the dissonances and tensions in and among the positions I take, are at their most severe in this essay.

Chapter 5 addresses the same issues and concerns, but this time with respect to that particular instance of ruling, rules, and rule following that goes by the name of the rule of law. I argue for both the occasional reality and (albeit tepidly) the desirability of arrangements and practices that are commonly conducted under this rubric. But I also argue that ideologists of the rule of law—for example Hayek and his followers—are confused about the conditions of its possibility, make unwarranted claims concerning its efficacy, and significantly overestimate its desirability. Toward the end of the essay I consider an ideal or imagining of a rule of law society, namely Michael Oakeshott's, that seems to me to be at once more realistic concerning possibilities and to offer a much less onerous vision.

Philosophically or theoretically, Chapter 6 is strongly continuous with Chapters 4 and 5 but is addressed to yet more particular questions concerning institutionalizations of the police power and policing. At once importantly indebted to and in some disagreement with the seminal work of Michel Foucault on these topics, I examine and for the most part reject the empirical applicability (I am tempted to say the ontological credibility) of familiar distinctions such as those between "Anglophone" and "Continental," "protection" and "service" conceptions (institutionalisms) of police and policing. In actuality, I claim, all attempts to provide police protection against criminality lead to expansions of the conception of the police power and significant enlargements in the range of police activities. If I am correct concerning these alleged actualities, a liberalism inspired by the ideals sketched above must be deeply wary of the institutions of policing and of institutionalisms that magnify or glorify their role in society.

In part for this reason, in one important respect I then attempt an about-face and argue that we ought to do our best to resist service and *Polizeistaat* ideologies, ought to struggle to maintain an understanding of policing that restricts it as narrowly as possible to providing protections against criminal conduct. In making this argument I understand myself to be continuing my efforts to recover and reinvigorate critical appreciation of the thinking of Thomas Hobbes.

The organization and thematics of Chapter 7 should be evident from its cumbersome title. I distinguish liberal conceptions of education from liberal moral and political theories, but I argue that the liberal understanding of the former, as distinct from vocational conceptions, is complementary to moral and political liberalism and is the understanding of education appropriate to a liberal political order. The contrast between liberal and vocational educational thinking and practice is, I believe, widely familiar. I devote a few pages to explaining my understanding of it, but these efforts are primarily preparations for my contention that the various forms of specifically political education I oppose are vocational rather than liberal. This argument depends importantly on the Aristotelian view that citizenship is an office in the state and in that sense is a vocation for which one is trained and otherwise prepared (it is not a vocation in Max Weber's sense of a calling). If Aristotle and I are correct in this regard, it follows that education for citizenship, most especially education for modes of citizenship regarded as necessary to particular types of political regimes, is vocational education. Elaborating this argument leads me to some general remarks about government, the state, and politics. Here as in my reflections about the police and policing, some of my liberal friends are likely to think that I have associated myself with some pretty unsavory views.

The book stops rather than comes to a conclusion. There is no end to the activity of imagining and articulating the ideals of liberalism, and there are innumerable institutions and institutionalisms that require continual critical assessment. Thus political theorizing, understood as an often tense interaction between idealistic and critical thinking, is an activity vital to liberal societies and polities.

PART I
IDEALS

1 / Strains in and around Liberal Theory: An Overview from a Strong Voluntarist Perspective

The recent theoretical literature in and around the ideology of liberalism is profuse, rapidly burgeoning, and sharply conflicted.[1] Contemporary discussions reenact a by now richly diverse history of moral and political reflection.[2] Complicating matters further, both recent writings and the tradition they continue are refractions of disputes in the wider and yet more controverted domains of general opinion and public policy. In the hope of making some overall sense of these multiplicitous phenomena, I begin with and then explore the deficiencies of a rough but I hope serviceable distinction between "agency"- and "virtue"-oriented liberal theories. This exploration will identify a few characteristics common to nearly all liberalisms, but its more salient outcome will be to underline that there is no liberalism as such, that the term refers to a diverse, changing, and often fractious array of doctrines that form a "family" only in the most extended of Wittgenstein's famous uses of that term (1953, paras. 65–81). I suggest, moreover, that we extend the family further by appropriating into it elements from modes of thinking usually and on the whole rightly regarded as a- or illiberal.

AGENCY LIBERALISM

Liberal theories of this type foreground a number of interwoven elements. Of these the most important is the individual person as actor,

3

initiator, producer, creator. Theorists of the agency liberal persuasion are more interested in action than in thought. They do not deny that reasoning and reflection can and should play a role in action, but they stress that most forms of action involve elements distinct from thinking. Their philosophical and empirical psychologies foreground less exclusively cognitive or ratiocinative elements or forces such as desire, intention, imagination and will. As classically formulated by Hobbes (1962c), in the agency liberal view reason is a "scout" for the passions and desires; it neither can nor should aspire to be their master.

Echoed more or less audibly by later thinkers such as Benjamin Constant (1988), John Stuart Mill (1951), Raymond Aron (1957), Isaiah Berlin (1969), H. L. A. Hart (1962), Stuart Hampshire (1983, 1989), and Bernard Williams (1985), the theory of action and of reason prevalent in agency-oriented liberalisms manifests a distinctive combination of attitudes or judgments, a combination that many critics—from both within and without liberalism—think is internally conflicted or otherwise unacceptable. On the one hand, agency liberals are confident concerning the capacity of human beings not only for self-movement but for self-definition and for what Michael Oakeshott (1975) calls self-enactment. Given tolerably favorable circumstances, human beings are able to identify and act to obtain desired objects and objectives, form and execute intentions, adopt and pursue ends and goals. In the course of doing these things they develop and sustain personalities or characters that distinguish them one from another. On this construal, agency liberals idealize individual human beings as restless, pulsating sources and loci of singular ideas and ideals.

On the other hand, liberal thinkers of this orientation manifest a certain skepticism. Although not dogmatic or programmatic skeptics in any technical epistemological sense, they doubt the power of reason or mind to arrive at general truths, especially general truths concerning morals and politics.[3] At the same time, they fear the effects of attempts to subjugate thought and action to a rigorous rule of reason.

Agency-oriented liberals are, both descriptively and normatively, theorists of individuality and of other modes of plurality. It is at once a fact and a good that human beings form desires for a large and shifting variety of objects, adopt and pursue a wide and changing array of purposes, value and disvalue a fluctuating diversity of persons and things. Descriptively, these diversities and this flux, certainly forces tending to produce and sustain them, are observable in all human affairs.

These sources of energy and divergence can be contained or stifled in varying degrees by social and moral, political, and legal forces and devices. But attempts to suppress or control them commonly provoke resistance that testifies to the persistence and power of diversifying impulses and desires in human thinking and acting.

Numerous facts about human beings and their affairs are indifferent from a moral or otherwise evaluative standpoint; numerous others are bad or evil. But for agency-oriented liberals, two connected considerations recommend the judgment that the human characteristics and proclivities I have been mentioning ought to be valued and encouraged, even celebrated.

Most important, it is either exclusively or primarily by acting on passions and desires, and by pursuing ends and purposes chosen to satisfy passions and desires, that human beings are able to obtain what they themselves regard as goods and to avoid what they judge to be harms or evils. In language frequent in agency liberal discussions, desire fulfillment or satisfaction is the only or the chief means of and to well-being. Hobbes adopts the first, stronger view. For him, good and evil consist exclusively in the satisfaction or frustration of actually and perhaps occurrently experienced passions and desires. "Felicity," the only overall end or good of human life that Hobbes recognizes, consists exclusively in more or less regular success in obtaining the objects of the passions and desires.[4]

Most agency-oriented liberals take the second and weaker view. They affirm or at least entertain a possibility that Hobbes rejects, namely of criteria of value that are partially independent of desire. If, for example, someone desires to become a slave, and does so for its own sake rather than because of a circumstantial judgment that slavery will maximize her desire satisfaction or felicity, Mill and perhaps Constant appear to think that this desire and hence its satisfaction are bad in themselves or because they are virtually certain to diminish well-being. Likewise but more insistently, Judith Shklar (1984) and Richard Rorty (1989), whose thinking is at once importantly within but also against agency-oriented liberalism, argue that the impulse to be cruel to others, and hence acting on that impulse, is unqualifiedly bad or wrong. More generally, a variety of recent thinkers (e.g., Elster, 1979; Hare, 1981; Scanlon, 1982; Griffin, 1986; Raz, 1986; Sen, 1987), who for present purposes can be classified in the same way as Shklar and Rorty, argue that occurrent desires are sometimes "adaptive" or otherwise distorted such that their satisfaction results in ill- rather than well-being. And Shklar, Stuart Hampshire, and Jean-François Lyotard (1991; Lyotard and Thebaut, 1992) contend that there are certain minimal requirements of justice that must be respected and hence ought to be enforced regardless of the present distribution of desires. Even if they don't manage to say it with Hobbes's resounding aplomb, however, all of these thinkers agree with Hobbes's assertion that "as to have no desire, is to be dead: so to have weak passions, is dullness" (1962c, chap. 6). A multiplicity of desires and desire satisfactions is the necessary albeit not the sufficient condition of human well-being.

It is also a fact that desires and purposes frequently conflict, and this further fact warrants the inference that legal and other restrictions must sometimes be placed on attempts to satisfy desires and achieve purposes. Equally, hopes and fears, beliefs and values sometimes converge or complement one another. Because these latter eventualities may enhance the prospects of present and continuing gratifications, efforts can and should be made to harmonize, or at least mutually to accommodate, the desires that occur both within and among individuals and groups. But this observation brings us to the second consideration supporting a favorable evaluation of the sources of subjectively based individuality and various other forms of plurality. Diversity, dissonance, and even conflict between and among desires enlivens and invigorates those whose desires they are. Whatever other effects doing so may have, experiencing dissonance, disagreement, and conflict animates what Mill calls the "meaning," for or to me, of my beliefs and values and thereby also animates my individuality. And the competitions that disagreements stimulate often energize capacities for effective action and hence for mutual as well as self-gratifications. There is no individual and certainly no collective *Summum Bonum*, but the prospects for individual and collected felicity are heightened rather than diminished by dissonance, divergence, and even strife.

The features discussed thus far are core commitments of agency liberalism. The other elements commonly found in theories of this type, some of which I now briefly discuss, should be understood as corollaries of or supplements to their conceptions of agency and action and their strongly favorable valorization not only of plurality but especially of that extreme form of plurality that is individuality.

Just as agency liberals are not dogmatic skeptics, so they are neither anarchists nor radical antinomians (albeit their emphasis on individuality likens them to individualist anarchists and their disposition to a certain incredulity makes them receptive to the rule skepticism of antinomians). In the hope both of containing destructive forms of conflict and enabling mutually advantageous forms of cooperation, agency liberals promote rational or reasonable patterns of interaction and accept that principles, rules, and established practices sometimes contribute to these objectives. But all such constraining and directing devices are or ought to be adopted for the sake of the felicity of individuals. If or to the extent that principles and rules, duties and obligations disserve felicity, they should be altered, revoked, and if necessary disobeyed. Perhaps most important, there is a tendency among agency-oriented liberals to view principles and rules as primarily (to borrow yet another term from Michael Oakeshott, 1975) adverbial, as concerned less with ends and purposes, rights and duties, and more with the manner in which or the sensibility out of which each individual does whatever she chooses to do. If there is a primary political virtue it is civility, and there is a good deal of emphasis on moral virtues (or *virtùs*) such as magnanimity and fastidiousness, courage and free-spiritedness.

The notion of equality has a fundamental place in agency-oriented liberalism, but it is first and foremost equality in the sense articulated by Hobbes's notion of the Right of Nature. Every individual ought to be accorded standing as an end-defining and end-seeking agent. The very fact that I have chosen an end or purpose is reason for thinking that it is a prima facie good for me to achieve it. If others are disposed to prevent me from doing so, the burden of justification falls on them. If stated as a principle rather than a right, this becomes what I have elsewhere called—perhaps tendentiously—the Liberal Principle (Flathman, 1987, 1989).

Looking ahead a bit, it is true that something like this notion of equality is also prominent in the thinking of virtue-oriented liberals such as T. H. Green (1986), Leonard Hobhouse (1964), John Rawls (1971, 1993), and Ronald Dworkin (1977, 1978). In the views of these latter thinkers, every agent is entitled to that respect from others necessary to sustain her self-respect and hence her capacity to define and pursue a conception of her good. This notion of equality can even be associated with the "recognition" that Hegel (1977) says we all crave or ought to crave. But in the virtue liberal formulations I am now discussing, equality, respect, and recognition are deeply conditional. I am entitled to standing and respect as an agent only if my desires, goals,

and purposes meet the criteria of justice, of reason, or of like standards. Recall what Rawls famously (or infamously) says of those "who
find that being disposed to act justly is not a good for them": "their nature is their misfortune" and is no reason for the more favorably en-
dowed to hesitate before punishing them for their failings (1971, p. 576).

Liberty or freedom of thought and action is also fundamental to
agency-oriented liberalism. Liberty is understood as "negative" rather
than "positive" in Berlin's sense (or "modern" rather than "ancient" in
Constant's diction) and notions such as "forced to be free," "perfect
service is perfect freedom," and "you shall know the truth and the truth
shall make you free" are regarded as at once oxymoronic and repugnant. Liberty, however, is an instrumental not an a priori and certainly
not an unqualified good. It is chief among what Rawls (in the most
important of his agency liberal moments) calls the "primary" goods
(1971), a good that one must enjoy in order to satisfy effectively whatever desires one may have and in order to pursue whatever ends and
purposes one may adopt. Thus agency-oriented liberals allow the necessity of restrictions on liberty, but they are as congenitally wary of
such restrictions as they are skeptical of foundationalist accounts of
liberty or its value.

Hobbes and perhaps Montaigne are protoliberals of the agency
type or orientation. In the early history of liberalism as a named idea
and force the chief examples of agency orientation are found in Humboldt (1993), Constant, and parts of J. S. Mill (especially his emphasis on
individuality and on meaning as distinct from truth). Among more recent thinkers, the most prominent representatives of this mode of liberal thinking are Aron and Berlin, Hart and Hampshire. George Kateb's
promotion (1992) of a liberal individuality deeply indebted to Emerson
and Whitman represents a distinctive and distinctively engaging variant
of agency liberalism, as does the in some ways similar thinking of Will
Kymlicka (1989). There are obvious objections to classifying thinkers
such as Jean-François Lyotard as liberals of any sort, but elements of
agency-oriented thinking are evident in the latter's work with Thebaut,
Just Gaming (1992), and especially in *The Inhuman* (1991).

VIRTUE LIBERALISM

In the second type of liberal view, virtue liberalism, life is or can be just
and humane, is or can be appropriate to humankind, only if or to the extent that all public and much private thinking and acting are governed

by beliefs that are arrived at under the discipline of intersubjective reason or "deliberative rationality." In a good, just, or humane—hence in this view liberal—society the interpersonal standing of the most operative or controlling beliefs will be underlined or augmented through procedures that inscribe those beliefs in principles and rules that have legal or otherwise authoritative standing. The most basic of these disciplining norms either are not instrumental at all (as in Kant, 1948) or have deontic standing sufficient to withstand (in reason if not in wayward fact) the pressures and temptations of fluctuating desires and interests.

For virtue liberals, ends that are shared or in common are superior to those that disaggregate or divide, and some ends (and hence some desires, intentions, and so on) are—as in Kant and Rawls—categorically inadmissible. There is a realm that is properly "private," but the scope of the private domain is to be determined by public reason and is properly susceptible to delineation and discipline by public procedures and processes. In the public domain, reason, deliberative rationality, and reasoned justification, and the principles and norms that are their favored yield, are to govern. Passion, desire, and interest must submit to the discipline of reason and reason-based principles and rules. Moreover, for virtue liberals the distinction between public and private is deployed to circumscribe the authority of the state and law but not the authority of reason and morality.[5]

In virtue liberalism there is typically more emphasis (than in agency liberalism) on substantive or material equalities and on the conditions and arrangements that create and protect such equalities, an emphasis that is particularly pronounced in late-nineteenth-century "New Liberalism" (Freeden, 1978) and in the welfare state liberalisms that are importantly the heir of the former. There is also more enthusiasm for democracy, the latter understood less as a form of *cracy* or rule (which is how agency-oriented liberals, most of whom favor but do not enthuse over democracy, tend to regard it) than as a "way of life" (Dewey, 1927) or a preferred mode of collective action and governance. These tendencies are especially prominent among thinkers such as James Fishkin (1983) who identify themselves as liberal democrats.[6]

Among earlier writers usually classified as liberals, the thinking of Locke (1960) and Kant, Hegel as interpreted by Shlomo Avinieri (1972) and importantly by Charles Taylor (1979), Rousseau (who in my judgment is no liberal at all), and the utilitarian, empiricist-scientistic and protosocialist parts of Mill all manifest the characteristics of virtue liberalism. The classic proponents of this version of liberalism are Kant, T. H. Green, and Leonard Hobhouse. Among contemporary thinkers, John Rawls and Jürgen Habermas (1984) are the most influential representatives of this orientation. The large literatures affirmatively influenced by these two thinkers give their versions of virtue liberalism great prominence in recent discussions.[7]

For Rawls, justice is the first virtue of a politically organized society. The principles of justice, arrived at by a combination of rationality and reasonableness, have "absolute weight" vis-à-vis all other considerations. All questions concerning the "basic structure" and "constitutional essentials" of politically organized society are to be resolved by "public reason" (1993).

It is true that these virtue elements in Rawls's thinking (as with Habermas's) coexist with other features that are arguably more agency oriented in character or tendency. In Rawls's case, the chief example is that his first principle of justice accords to each citizen such rights to the "basic liberties" as are consistent with all other citizens having the same rights. This principle generates duties or requires virtues, but only in that it is both a duty and a virtue to respect the rights of others. Again, Rawls insists that there is a rationally irreducible plurality of conceptions of the good and appears to argue that, outside of the basic structure, choices among such conceptions should but need not be disciplined by justice or public reason. In company with his recent arguments that even justice should be "political not metaphysical" and ought to seek no more than an "overlapping consensus" on beliefs and values (1993), these features of Rawls's theorizing distance him from Green and Hobhouse and from more uncompromisingly virtue-oriented contemporaries such as William Galston (1991), Amy Gutmann (1980), and Steven Macedo (1990), all of whom share Habermas's view that, ideally, no domain of thought and action would be exempt from the requirements of deliberative rationality and morality.

But Rawls is unwavering in his insistence that justice must take precedence over all considerations that compete or conflict with it, and he clearly thinks that both fair and stable cooperation depends on strict adherence to the principles of justice that ought to govern the basic structure. More ominously, as his apprehensions about stability lead him (most emphatically in 1971, book 3) to "thicken" his theory of the good and otherwise to concern himself with the development of moral character, the agency-oriented elements in his thinking give way to moralistic and indeed to moraline formulations (tendencies prominent in the New Liberal British thinkers and also pronounced in Habermas's thinking).

On my reading, the types of thinking that I have delineated under the rubric "virtue oriented" dominate contemporary liberal theorizing, particularly in the United States. I cannot survey all of the literatures that lead me to this generalization, and it is yet more obvious that I cannot attend in adequate detail to the many differences among thinkers of this general tendency. Important theories such as those of Joseph Raz (1986), John Charvet (1981), and T. M. Scanlon (1982) share some of the characteristics I have mentioned, but also depart importantly from the pattern I have sketched. James Griffin (1986) and Amartya Sen (1987), in their own ways, can be read as seeking a harmonization of what each takes to be best in agency- and virtue-oriented liberalism. Recent attempts to move liberalism closer to classical republicanism (e.g., Ackerman, 1989) continue but also effect important changes in virtue-oriented liberalism. If Michael Walzer (1983) is regarded as a liberal, his work shows the affinities, already evident in T. H. Green, between virtue liberalism and communitarianism of the kind now associated with writers such as Michael Sandel (1982) and Charles Taylor (1989). As with *liberalism* itself, *virtue liberalism* is a family resemblance term, and the dispute between virtue liberals and communitarians is a family quarrel (see Honig, 1993).

A THIRD TYPE? IS THERE A RIGHTS–ORIENTED LIBERALISM?

I must at least notice the objection that my schema largely ignores a major characteristic of or tendency in liberal thinking. The emphasis on individual rights in Locke and Kant, Rawls and especially Dworkin might suggest that we should classify these thinkers as rights oriented rather than as proponents of virtue liberalism in the tradition of Green and Hobhouse or on the model of Habermas and Galston, Gutmann and Macedo. The analogous emphasis on rights in agency liberals such as Kateb and Kymlicka might suggest a similar reclassification.

If we look at Natural and Human Rights thinkers such as Thomas Paine (1953), Robert Nozick (1974), and especially Alan Gewirth (1978), we find that rights are held to have a standing independent of the good and of the virtues or *virtùs* that are necessary to realizing the good. If these thinkers are liberals (doubtful in the cases of Paine and Nozick but not Gewirth), completeness would require the further category of rights-oriented liberalism.

Of the many and difficult questions that arise here (perhaps especially those that concern the place of rights in utilitarianism), I confine my remarks to reiterating the view, most frequently discussed with respect to Hegel's criticism of Kant, that these allegedly strict deontologies are either purely formal and hence empty or are thinly veiled teleologies and virtue theories. If we ask *why* rights are promoted by Locke, Kant, Green, Rawls, and the others I have classified as virtue liberals, we see—or I have satisfied myself that I see—that it is because a properly selected and protected array of rights enmeshes the members of a society in a scheme that stabilizes and otherwise serves justice and other virtues. I cannot adequately defend this argument here, but it may take some support from the fact that most agency liberals are more guarded or qualified in their enthusiasm for rights than are Kant, Rawls, and Dworkin. (If there is an exception to this last generalization it concerns the enthusiasm of agency-oriented liberals for the "liberty type" right [Hohfeld, 1923] that Hobbes calls the Right of Nature. Most analysts of the concept of rights deny that this is a genuine right. Their objections echo Hobbes's own view that, because everyone has this "right," and because the goods it serves are subjectively defined, the only affirmative duty entailed by the right is to acknowledge equality in the sense discussed under the first heading above.)

AGENCY LIBERALISMS, VIRTUE LIBERALISMS, AND STRONG VOLUNTARISM

Both agency and virtue liberalisms presuppose and endorse a weak form of voluntarism, a version of that doctrine that consists primarily in a distinction between chosen and intentional actions on the one hand and causally explainable movements or behaviors on the other. And some virtue theories—such as Kant's in the moments at which he emphasizes Will as a necessary activating agency in conduct—move, formally, toward strong voluntarism. But these moves are compromised by other elements in virtue-oriented theories, elements that are resisted by agency liberals and rejected by strong voluntarists and willful liberals.

On the one hand, virtue liberal theorists tend to be impressed by the weaknesses of agents that are unaided and undisciplined by public reason, that is, by the constraints of reasoning that shows itself to be intersubjectively valid by being articulated in designated public forums following agreed procedures and canons of argumentation. The persons who predominate in virtue liberal theories (especially in those recent examples of such theories that promote the welfare state—Rawls, Habermas, Raz, Gutmann, and Galston are good examples) need not only a lot of help but a good deal of discipline and control. At a minimum, these persons need the protections and other advantages provided by living in company with associates who are for the most part just and otherwise virtuous. And most persons also need more affirmative forms of assistance, material and otherwise.

In these respects contemporary virtue liberals have been influenced by Left and Right critiques of liberal societies and perhaps also by difficult-to-classify critics such as Michel Foucault (1980). Even if the abilities and arts of agency are valued—all theories that can usefully be called liberal value these abilities and arts to some extent—the confidence that Hobbes, Humboldt, and Constant have in the capacity for such agency is at once diminished and feared. Without a good deal of public help, most human beings deteriorate into what Oakeshott (1975) calls the individual manqué and perhaps deteriorate further into that ressentiment-laden creature that he calls the anti-individual.

In the latter mood, so to speak, virtue liberals want weak voluntarism so as to be able to ascribe responsibility and to justify censure and punishment. This is of course the Nietzschean critique of weak voluntarism. Weak voluntarists impute freedom of will sufficient to warrant ascription of responsibility and hence blame. But their voluntarism is insufficient to allow them to celebrate self-enacted individuality and the deviance and disobedience that, as weak voluntarists-cum-virtue liberals see it, are too often the yield of such individuality.

WILLFUL LIBERALISM

If there is or could be such a thing as willful liberalism, it is or would be an accentuation and intensification of agency liberalism.

Willful liberals place yet greater emphasis (greater than, for example, agency liberals such as Mill and Berlin) on the irreducible diversity of divergent, incommensurable, and perhaps interpersonally or intersubjectively inexplicable goods, ends, and especially ideals. Rather than Reason, its chief emblem is Will construed as largely or at least finally mysterious.

This cardinal feature of willful liberalism is obscured by the insistence of late-nineteenth-century strong voluntarists such as William

James (1968) and Nietzsche (1955, 1956, 1967, 1974)—and, later, of Oakeshott and Berlin—on the prevalence of homogeneity and conformity, of the masses, the herd, the tyranny of the conventional and the majority. The individuality and plurality that these thinkers treasure are assured only in the sense that human beings harbor a potential for them. But this potential has been largely annulled or crippled by moraline doctrines such as Christianity, Kantianism, socialism, and, yes, the virtue, welfare, and democratic liberalisms that purport to value and to serve it. Thus this latent possibility must be freed, must be fought for (importantly by contesting the doctrines just mentioned). This leads thinkers such as William E. Connolly (1991) and Chantal Mouffe (1993) to insist on the agonal character of Nietzschean, pluralist, and other strong voluntarist doctrines. But it also leads them to a greater faith in democracy than I and most strong voluntarist liberals are able to sustain. As I suggested earlier, numerous agency liberals follow Max Weber in emphasizing the *cracy* part of the internally dissonant concept of democracy, and some of them follow Hobbes in fearing that its *demo* part enhances the dangers of the *cracy* that it legitimates.

In these respects willful liberalism has affinities with libertarianism and especially with various strains in romanticism. The notion of liberation from state and other forms of power is reminiscent of libertarianism and even of individualistic anarchism, and the notions of self-making, self-enactment, and self-fashioning have manifest affinities with major tendencies in romanticism and expressivism.

These comparisons, however, are seriously misleading. As against libertarianism, especially in the recent American and British formulations that identify with so-called classical liberalism and promote laissez-faire or market economies, strong voluntarists from Montaigne and Hobbes to Nietzsche, James, and Oakeshott are interested in the making of lives not in the making of livings. They find the economistic character of much libertarianism dreary and dispiriting.

The strong voluntarist attack on romanticism is less widely appreciated. In Nietzsche's phrase (1967), strong voluntarists view romanticism as a form of "letting go," as a lack or want of discipline.[8] The discipline strong voluntarists favor, moreover, must begin with quite rigorously impositional social and cultural training, with what Nietzsche calls "preparations" and what Oakeshott speaks of as schooling (1989, 1991) that engenders fluency in the various "languages" that have evolved into modes of experience or traditions of thought and sensibility. In this respect there are important continuities between the strong voluntarists and Wittgenstein's account of the ways in which "agreements in judgment" get established, agreements that allow of "knowing how to go on" in various practices and activities but also provide the settings in which and the materials out of which disagreements in opinion, often unresolvable, emerge (1953, paras. 241–42). The view, mistakenly attributed to strong voluntarists such as Nietzsche, that self-enactment is done in isolation or solitude, that one makes oneself and one's life out of materials entirely of one's own creation, is a serious misunderstanding. The Nietzschean free spirit attempts to achieve distance from society and especially politics, but it is a "pathos of distance" and the "pathos" part of this formula testifies to the fact that the free spirit remains deeply, albeit never complacently or even comfortably, situated in a tradition, culture, and society.

The strong voluntarist ideals of individuality and self-enactment require that over time initial social and cultural training and discipline be transformed into self-discipline, must give way to that "self-overcoming" that is a necessary condition of free-spiritedness. To the extent that such a transformation is achieved, homogeneity and commonality, dependency, conformism, and ressentiment concerning remaining differences and inequalities are replaced by diversity and individuality disciplined by adverbial *virtùs* such as civility, magnanimity, and fastidiousness.

As with the work of all true artists, the arts of self-making require a never to be permanently stabilized combination of discipline and invention; discipline grounded in familiarity with the past and the present together with invention that departs from past and present configurations in unpredictable and often initially incomprehensible ways. In part because the specific forms of discipline necessary to self-making are importantly similar to those promoted by *virtù* theorists such as Machiavelli, we might call willful liberalism "*virtù* liberalism." For reasons that probably don't need to be stated, we do better to call it virtuosity liberalism—virtuosity in the making of lives.

Willful or virtuosity liberalism, and hence strong voluntarism, is essential to a recognizably liberal society at least in the sense that I have elsewhere called minimal (Flathman, 1992). There must be a substantial number of associates who for the most part "take care of themselves," who do not need to be "cared for" by others or by society. And there must be associates who, by cultivating virtuosities such as civility and especially magnanimity, care for others in the sense of not inflicting themselves harmfully or destructively on the latter.

Beyond this necessary minimum, willful or virtuosity liberalism is a form of idealism, a radically individualized version of what is now called—often misleadingly—perfectionism.[9] As such, it cannot be imposed, perhaps cannot even be socially or politically cultivated. Nietzsche declares himself an Argonaut of his idealism, not its evangelist and certainly not its drill instructor. Insofar as he "teaches" his idealism, he does so by example and more particularly by inspiriting writing not by direction or imposition. This understanding seems to me to be true to what is best in the liberal tradition.

LIBERALISM AND PUBLIC POLICY

Willful or virtuosity liberalism provides no recipes, decision procedures, or logarithms for the making of public policy. It bears upon but is radically indeterminate concerning virtually all of the major issues that now animate public life in more or less liberal societies. But I must leave aside this huge question (and hence much of the literature currently being produced by *soi-disant* liberals and their ideological opponents). So as not to end this essay on a banal note, I nevertheless hazard the observation, prompted in part by my reading of the works of Lyotard, Hélène Cixous and Catherine Clément (1986), and Luce Irigaray (1985), that the ideas and ideals of willful or virtuosity liberalism have a particular pertinence to thinking currently being pressed by the oppositional forces most important to the liberal societies of our time—that is, the racial, feminist, and gay and lesbian liberation movements.

2 / Liberality, Idiosyncrasies, Idiolects, and a Little Beyond: Ortega y Gasset, Proust, and Wittgenstein on Liberality

My objective in this and the following chapter is to embellish the ideals of agency-cum-willful-cum-virtuosity liberalism, thereby developing somewhat further an alternative to currently dominant formulations of liberal theory and ideology. More specifically, I want to foreground the notion of liberality treated as an individuating *virtù*. In pursuing this objective, I take my sometimes conflicting inspirations largely from Wittgenstein and kindred thinkers who have moved questions about language and meaning to the center of their investigations and reflections. My discussion begins with languages and language games, dialects and idioms—that is, with the more or less widely shared commonalities that are the usual vehicles of and may appear to be the conditions necessary to our thinking, speaking, and acting. But by urging attention to the notions of idiosyncrasy and especially of idiolect, and in connecting appreciation for idiolects with the *virtù* of liberality, I underline contrary tendencies in order to valorize diversities and incompatibilities within, between, and outside of the commonalities of languages and language games.

The variety of liberal political theories or doctrines is well known. As discussed in part in the previous chapter, in the academy we are accustomed to distinctions and disputes within and among deontological, contractarian, rights and justice-oriented versus teleological, consequentialist, and utilitarian conceptions; we regularly encounter various neutralisms, dialogisms, and other proceduralisms; we are familiar with virtue and common good versus agency-, liberty-, and individuality-oriented doctrines. In more common parlance we have tax-and-spend welfare state liberals, classical or free market liberals, civil libertarian liberals, liberal feminists, and numerous variants of each of these. We also have a variety of doctrines and dogmas that are adjacent to but in varying respects in agreement and conflict with this or that formulation of *soi-disant* liberalisms. Communitarians, democratic and market socialists, libertarians, republicans, and participatory democrats embrace some of the ideas and ideals commonly claimed for liberalism as they distance themselves from what they respectively take to be the ideas and ideals definitive of or dominant in liberalism or the liberal tradition "as such." In this perspective liberalism is a many-splendored thing and is part of a yet more diversely splendorous milieu or tradition.

I yield to the temptation to think of these doctrinal and ideological tendencies as differentiated idioms or dictions within language games characterized by a larger rather than a smaller number of family resemblances. This latter characterization, although at first sight emphasizing the diversity within liberalism, implicitly underscores the confining, circumscribing unity that too often marks it. Of course this claim has been contested. John Pocock, for example, has argued that "liberalism" is primarily a construction of twentieth-century Whig historians and ideologues, a concoction (we might say a confection) that, so far from being rooted in a unified and continuous tradition, has little or no distinct standing in the plentiful array of political languages that he has studied (see, e.g., his "Authority and Property: The Question of Liberal Origins," in Pocock, 1985). In shriller tones, Alasdair MacIntyre asserts that what has been taken to be liberal language and discourse is in fact a mere babel or cacophony that, if it can be understood at all, consists of nothing better than an endless "series of denials," a series that has, predictably in his view, eventuated in destruction of the possibility of mutually intelligible discourse (1971, p. 283; see more generally MacIntyre, 1981).

Although skeptical of the tendency of Pocock's and Pocockian views to marginalize liberalism, I leave their historicity to others better prepared than I to assess them. But one part of Pocock's argument—namely that the "liberal tradition" is at best a *salade* of divergent languages or dictions—is grist for the mill I would like to set agrinding.

That is, I want to take from Pocock the thought that liberalism contains possibilities too little in evidence in discussions currently conducted under such rubrics as *liberal, liberal theory*, and the like. I also think that MacIntyre's asseverations, if taken as descriptions of historical, sociological, or ideological actualities, are for the most part hyperbole, but I argue that a condition *akin* to that which he so balefully laments would, were we to accede to it, constitute the closest thing we can hope for by way of realizing the daunting but inspiriting prospects projected and propelled by liberalism and the ideal of liberality at their distinctive best.

Just below, I comment further on the recent tendencies and countertendencies in and around liberalism. By way of identifying the direction in which I intend those comments to go, I invoke some phrases from José Ortega y Gasset's *The Revolt of the Masses* (1932), phrases of which (given their surroundings in this and other of his works) I am perhaps inordinately fond.

Ortega y Gasset celebrates liberalism as "the supreme form of generosity"; liberalism proclaims "the right by which the majority concedes to minorities and hence it is the noblest cry that has ever resounded in this planet" (pp. 83–84). Rather than merely celebrating or brandishing these words, I think a bit about the ways in which the themes they announce repay unpacking, critiquing, and surpassing.

If we take Ortega y Gasset's "the right" to mean "concessions" that majorities, at their discretion, may make or choose not to make, the "cry" he says is resounded by liberalism is "noble" (we might better say magnanimous) because liberal majorities have the power and perhaps the authority to refuse the concessions he celebrates. The liberal majority is generous, liberal, and even noble because those who form it could if they would repress the expressions, concerns, and objectives of minorities.

On this reading, Ortega y Gasset might be said to identify liberalism with the *virtue* that Aristotle calls liberality (1953, book 4). Alternatively, but to my mind carrying more promise, Ortega y Gasset aligns liberalism with liberality taken as a voluntaristic *virtù* rather than a rationally compulsory or required *virtue* and perhaps equally with those other *virtùs*—for example, civility, magnanimity, fastidiousness and courage—that are promoted by thinkers such as Machiavelli and Montaigne, Nietzsche and William James, Oakeshott and Arendt (all of whom are, like Wittgenstein, famous liberals!).

Construed in this latter fashion, Ortega y Gasset's apothegm is a promising beginning, a start toward a liberalism that would give pride of place to these and related *virtùs,* to sensibilities that cannot be demanded and that, while sharing names or signifiers, have numerous and diverse significations and instantiations.

Coming back to the most prominent formulations of liberal doctrine and dogma, we might take Ortega y Gasset to be talking about the virtue commonly called tolerance or toleration. If we do so, it could be contended that his remarks identify the closest thing to a core ideal or value that gathers the various formulations and manifestations of liberalism as political idea and force. Certainly a disposition to tolerance and institutionally enforced practices of tolerance are at or close to the center of the thinking of liberal theorists from Locke and Kant, Mill and Green to Rawls and Dworkin. Oddly, but revealingly and disappointingly, however, the *virtù* of liberality is little discussed in the most prominent texts of liberal theory and ideology.

At the risk of offering boring commonplaces, I assemble a few reminders of salient features of recent liberal literatures. Contractarian (e.g., Rawls), communicative competence (e.g., Habermas), and other deontological theories plight their troth to Kantian-style rational principles and the rights and duties allegedly grounded in or established by such principles, thereby giving liberalism a strongly legalistic and otherwise imperatival character. Utilitarian liberals profess to identify ends or goods that nature or history, rationally conceived and appropriated, show to be proper to or for all human beings and all organized human communities. Bentham and his followers reason back from rationally required ends to arrangements, institutions, and policies that are, if not the *right* means to those ends (implying that all other means are *wrong*), at least good or even the best means of pursuing them (implying that all other means are bad and to be avoided). Virtue-oriented liberals from T. H. Green to Gutmann, Galston, and Macedo can be located on both sides of the deontology-teleology divide, but they share with the views just mentioned (and with communitarians, republicans, and strong democrats) a marked tendency to privilege a definite, insistently delimited inventory of ends, purposes, and ways of achieving them. As with the deontologists, virtue-oriented liberals are big on duties and obligations. Distrustful of rationalistic calculations, they look to socialization, training, and (what they are prepared to call—on this point, see chapter 7) education to inculcate the habits and dispositions that, following Aristotle, they regard as the only reliable means of bringing about the dutiful conduct necessary to achieving the ends that reason privileges. And they are as ready as the deontologists and utilitarians to supplement, as is judged necessary, their favored means with criminalization and punishment.

Relating these remarks to my concern with languages and idioms, all of these liberal voices demand definite and disciplining ways of thinking and speaking. Some among them, Rawls and Rorty for example, do encourage ironic or otherwise dissonant and idiosyncratic performances in what they call the nonpublic or private domain. But when matters become truly serious, when concern reaches to the fundaments of a just or well-ordered society and polity, they too treat idiosyncrasy as deviance. They vigorously combat languages and dictions that fracture what Rorty calls solidarity or that depart from the norms of what Rawls calls public reason and reasonableness. Their objective is to unify and normalize the members or citizens of what they call liberal societies or polities. If or insofar as they can be said to display or promote liberality, they do so only in respect to those forms of thought and action that they regard as publicly and politically innocuous.

Although at first blush odd or incongruous, it is in fact predictable that these conceptions or attitudes show up in liberal thinking about protest, civil disobedience, civil refusal and resistance. Consider from this perspective the treatment accorded such figures as Socrates, Jesus, and Gandhi, Martin Luther King Jr. and Nelson Mandela. In Urmson's terminology (1958), these are saints or heroes in that their thinking and acting go beyond the requirements set by conventional law and morality. But they are, if sometimes belatedly and always no more than partially, accommodated within the frame I have been discussing. This feat is accomplished in two ways. First, whereas the thinking and acting of figures such as Jesus, King, and Mandela surpass established demands and expectations, they are said to do so in ways that are intelligible within the terms of, even are recognizably implicit in, the conventions of liberal thinking. Second, the likes of Socrates, Jesus, and Gandhi are required to witness, and praised for witnessing, their acceptance of conventional principles and rules by submitting to penalties applied and enforced in the name of the latter.

In this interpretation, we can say that these at first blush deviant ideas and movements are no more than mildly idiosyncratic supplements to agreeably rationalist and regularian conduct. And we can thereby claim that they make valuable contributions to a liberal polity. But we should also note that it is unsurprising that rationalist deontologists, teleologists, and virtue theorists tolerate—of course so long as they stay within the limits I have described—such idiosyncrasies. In Rawlsian terms, so long as we are in the domain of nonideal theory, and insofar as we have the good luck to find ourselves in a society that is "nearly just" by the criteria of ideal theory, there is cogent (albeit not always convincing) reason for making and sustaining such accommodations. Nevertheless, convinced as, say, we Rawlsians are of the rationality of our own views, and perhaps convinced as MacIntyre is that reason and its truths are all that stand between us and mutually destructive chaos, we can tolerate but will hardly exult in the presence of ways of speaking, thinking, and acting that transgress the principles, norms, and rules that ought to inform and discipline speakings and other actings. Concessions, tolerances, and accommodations, rather than being made out of liberality, will be *faute de mieux*. Just as in Rawls's formulations there is no justification for civil disobedience or conscientious refusal in ideal theory and would be none in a perfectly just society, if we could do better than concede, tolerate, and accommodate so we should.

Returning to Ortega y Gasset, his talk of "conceding" may appear to have the qualities just discussed. But if we read his use of this notion through the lens of his emphasis on nobility, he presents himself as less grudging, less rueful, than are the arguments for toleration advanced by rationalist liberals and their republican, communitarian, and strong democratic brethren.

A liberality-infused or -oriented liberalism of the kind that I am trying to discern in Ortega y Gasset (and that I think is more explicit in thinkers such as Constant and occasionally Mill, in Aron, Berlin, and Hampshire) would not merely accept or tolerate, out of necessity, but welcome and encourage speakings and actings that deviate from the forms of language and modes of conduct that unite the majority, the herd, the generality of folks or of a *Volk*. If Ortega y Gasset can't quite bring himself to celebrate deviance, at least his liberalism eschews the claim to a reason, to a truth, or to any other privileged standpoint on the basis of which to condemn or to regret instances of deviance.

This is a beginning, a movement toward a liberalism that promotes and celebrates not unifying, normalizing reason, justice, or virtue, but individuating *virtùs* such as liberality and generosity, magnanimity and courage, *virtùs* that enable the welcoming and celebrating not only of idiosyncrasies but genuine singularities, not only dictions, dialects, and marginal argots but salient idiolects.

Toward what would, should, such a liberalism be liberal, generous, and magnanimous? In the face of what idiosyncrasies and idiolects would, should, liberals of this sensibility be welcoming and magnanimous rather than merely tolerant?

Ortega y Gasset's talk of "concessions" appears to put him in that large company of pluralist liberals who claim to treasure diversities but do so only insofar as the latter are encompassed within or subtended by unity. Idiosyncrasies are to be conceded to, but only if they can be located in a widely shared configuration of values and beliefs, only to the extent that they are intelligible in the terms of a common form of life featuring agreements in judgment sufficient to sustain agreements in opinion and hence shared language games, practices, and institutions. In David Truman's (1957) now neglected but still important formulation, a plentitude of interest groups is to be welcomed, but only so long as there is the actuality or genuine possibility of "potential groups" that, should strident conflict or, worse, mutual unintelligibility rear its head, coalesce and defend the criteria, norms, and protocols that give unifying meaning to political life. (Analogous but yet more potently homogenizing views are prominent in the works of British and Continental pluralists such as Green and Bradley, Barker, Laski and Lindsay, Durkheim, Jaures and Duguit. Nor are such views absent from recent and apparently more radical pluralists such as Mouffe, Laclau, and even Baudrillard.)

To go beyond Ortega y Gasset, Truman, and most of the liberal theorists thus far discussed, we must, as a first step, think of Ortega y Gasset's "minorities" not exclusively or even primarily as assembled and more or less perdurant groups but as minorities of one, as individual and individuating persons.

In attempting to do so, it will be prudent to begin by recognizing that in all instances intelligible to us, minorities of this more individualized kind will be participants in a tradition and culture, a society and polity, and will be more or less competent practitioners of various of the language games of which such traditions and cultures primarily consist. In the great preponderance of instances they will also be members of various of the more circumscribed groups on which Truman and his pluralist predecessors and successors have focused their attentions.

There may nevertheless be respects in which individuals are inassimilable to, will resist or attempt to resist subsumption under, the concepts and categories that inform and organize the main features of cultural, social, and political life.

Because I am trying to think in the Wittgensteinian terms of languages and language games, this thought is what attracts me to the notion of idiolects. As further preparation for addressing this notion, I shift briefly to a narrower, more empirical register.

The greatest glory of the American political culture and polity—namely, the First Amendment-type rights that it affords—implicitly supposits for self-enacting, individuating, self-overcoming, or free-spirited individuals. Whether or to whatever extent this culture celebrates the presence of individualities (it sometimes does, often doesn't), it officially "concedes" to them in that it accords those persons and groups who manifest them the right to express themselves as they are moved to do, to associate or not with others as they see fit, to practice or not such religiosities or irreligiosities as they judge convenable to themselves. These pronounced if often betrayed features of American tradition and practice, I argue, are comprehensible only on the supposition that there will be not only much diversity, idiosyncrasy, and deviance but also mutually unintelligible thinking, speaking, and acting.

In support of this claim, I issue the reminder that the notions of concession to or tolerance of diversity and idiosyncrasy are redundant where there is the confident expectation of unity, homogeneity, and hence agreement. Insofar as First Amendment rights are legally and politically consequential, they presume not only the possibility but the likelihood of disagreements that are durable and even intractable. Admittedly, the further argument that First Amendment rights posit the more radical possibility of mutual unintelligibilities is less easily made. When we say that we disagree or are in conflict with others we at least claim to understand these others, hence, for example, to know what counts as respecting and enforcing the rights accorded to them. But how are we to go about deferring to and protecting forms of speech and conduct that we cannot so much as understand?

The difficulty of answering this question points, finally, to the limited value of my American example and more generally to the tension or dissonance between the language of rights and duties and that of liberality and other *virtùs*. It may nevertheless repay us to tarry a bit with the example and the jural or deontological language, the language of rights and duties, that it represents. How much do we have to understand of or about a religious or moral, ideological or artistic view, or for that matter a mathematical or scientific one, in order to respect and protect the rights of those who hold it to express and otherwise to act on it? If jurally required to say that a ritual or belief is religious, and hence that its adherents are entitled to the right to free exercise or to immunity to conscription, attorneys general and judges may be obliged to claim that they understand the ritual or belief well enough to render this judgment. As an operative of or referee for NEH, NIA, or NIMH, I may be obliged to declare that a proposal is or is not humanistic, artistic, or scientific. In these ways, the language of rights propels at least some who participate in it to classifications or subsumptions that purport to have a cognitive, rational, or interpersonal basis.

Are you and I under any such compulsion? Are prosecutors and judges and bureaucrats? From the standpoint of those dominant forms of liberalism discussed above, it is an advantage of rights-, entitlement-, and other regularian-oriented practices that we and sometimes they are often under these forms of duress.

Nor am I prepared categorically to reject or object to these features of the liberalisms that are predominantly our inheritance. I remind myself that if American culture were not characterized, at least in part, by the features and tendencies just rehearsed it is possible but not likely that I as an American would be trying to present the position that I endeavor to develop in these pages. I might even agree that our rights-oriented and hence judgment- and judgmentalism-demanding political culture, because it engenders the *virtue* of close to the same name, diminishes the need for the *virtù* of liberality.

These remarks about America might be extended to the Wittgensteinian terms of art in which I have cast parts of the foregoing remarks. If meaning is in language, and if language rests upon or is largely constituted by agreements in judgment and opinion, then it is so much as possible to argue for a liberality that extends to idiosyncrasy and deviance only because these ideas and values already have an established place in judgment and opinion. Confronting these arguments and the paradoxes they appear to generate may help me to move from idiosyncrasy to idiolect and to a more abundant notion of liberality.

As to America, the traditions and practices I have mentioned are anything but seamless. Notwithstanding the absurdities of "originalists" such as Bork and "right answerists" such as Dworkin, the slightest familiarity with constitutional and related hermeneutical and applicative activities leaves no doubt that constitutional and legal traditions and texts not only leave open but themselves open up large spaces for diversity and disagreement. There are plenty of demands for conformity in the name of established or otherwise dispositive principles and rules, but they are viewed by civil libertarian liberals as deviant in their repressiveness. The sharply conflicting interpretations advanced by the likes of Justices Warren and Brennan are regarded by "centrists" and "right-wingers" as ahistorical absurdities and jural/political/moral enormities. We might say that, at the level of language and thought if not of legal and political actualities, there is plenty of room for idiosyncrasy.

Against this partly warranted but overly complacent view, various figures we might term skeptics say that, despite its apparent commonalities and continuities, there neither is nor could be anything but idiosyncrasy, and, consequently, that there neither is nor could be anything worthy of that name. Idiosyncrasies or the idiosyncratic are always by contrast with and hence under the sign of the normal, the ordinary, the expected. And if you agree with Proust (not to mention a plethora of thinkers now more widely read and influential in political theory circles) that "il n'y a pas un idée qui ne porte en elle sa refutation possible, un mot le mot contraire [there is no idea that does not carry in itself a possible refutation (of itself), no word that does not imply its contrary]" (1992, p. 183), you are likely also to think that this or these contrasts are in reason spurious and to agree with the likes of Nietzsche and Foucault, Lyotard and de Man, that the commonalities on which they presume—to the limited extent that those commonalities in fact obtain—are due not to the operations of shared reason but to coercion or to unthinking, even if mutual, submissions and submissivenesses.

At the level of epistemology, metaethics, or Lyotard's metanarratives, I agree with Proust. (Most of the liberal theorists mentioned above write as if skeptics from Sextus to Cicero to Montaigne to Pascal to Hume and up to the emotivists and deconstructionists never put pen to paper.) I also agree with Wittgenstein (hence in large albeit nuanced respects with Foucault) that the "agreements in judgment" that subtend and inform agreements in opinion are incomprehensible apart from coercive "trainings" (as Wittgenstein calls them). But these views leave open the question of what stance we should adopt, what sensibilities we should cultivate, in respect to such agreements.

Rorty agrees with Proust, perhaps with Wittgenstein, and possibly even with the descriptions (but not the evaluations) of Foucault. The most recent Rawls, adopting the "method of avoidance," refuses to engage with the more radical elements in Proust, in Wittgenstein-Foucault and their ilk, thereby implicitly conceding the possibility that his Lockean-Kantian rationality and Hegelian-Deweyan reasonableness can provide no cogent response to them. But both Rorty and Rawls are, evidently, deeply anxious about what they take to be the consequences of any widespread influence of these skeptical views. Hence both of them (and the following remarks could easily be generalized to most of the other liberal thinkers discussed or mentioned above), affirm, champion, and, each in her or his own way, seek to consolidate what they respectively but not very differentially take to be the already achieved "settlements" of the societies and polities that they call liberal.

As already admitted, to the extent that these accounts and characterizations of the liberal settlements are accurate, they are not settlements that I am prepared to disparage. Featuring as they do commitment to a tolerance and a pluralism that, while insistently circumscribed, are generous by the standards of virtually all available diachronic and synchronic comparisons, supporting as they do those estimable rights that I have briefly discussed above, they are hardly to be disdained. In the language of the title of this chapter, they both leave and make spaces for individuating idiosyncrasies, spaces that have to be welcomed by any proponent of a liberality-oriented liberalism.

Proponents of such a liberalism, however, need not and should not rest content with this response. They can and should go beyond toleration and respect for rights to liberality and magnanimity toward idiolects.

In what from this perspective are his best moments, Proust helps us (more than does Ortega y Gasset) to make this movement. The most unforgettable characters in Proust's *Recherche* (more so, to me, than the *heros* himself, certainly than Albertine) are the Baron de Charlus and Françoise (the housekeeper of the *heros's* family). In respect to both, Proust, who returns to these two figures and their ways of speaking and acting again and again, shows himself fascinated by the possibilities that he has found within or created out of established language games. Of noble birth and aristocratic social connections, Charlus is partly of German, partly of provincial French extraction. He is more than capable of a refined upper-class Parisian French, and at what he judges to be appropriate moments he restricts himself to it. At intervals, however, he infuses and inflects his performatives with elements that are alien to that idiom and hence often difficult for his auditors to understand. Because he is an active homosexual and sadomasochist, his speech acts also make use, willfully as I am inclined to say, of the argot of a social and cultural *sous-monde*. The speech acts of Françoise have, again willfully, specifically different but generically analogous characteristics. She learned, was trained, to speak in Provence. The performatives Proust assigns to her are a mélange of the Provençalese patois; the argots of the servants, artisans, and shopkeepers of Combray, Paris, and Balbec; and borrowings from the haute bourgeoisie and the decayed aristocrats for whom she works. If Proust more readily attributes to Charlus knowledge and intention of what and why he is saying and doing, it is clear that, as with Charlus, Françoise uses her speech acts to make as well as to disclose what she has thus far become.

Proust details the respects in which the speakings—hence on the Wittgensteinian/Austinian view that he powerfully anticipates—the thinkings and actings of Charlus and Françoise are at once partly intelligible and unmanageably puzzling to their auditors and interlocutors. Returning to Socrates and Jesus, King, Gandhi, and the question of idiosyncrasy, Proust shows (rather than tells) how idiosyncrasies can be understood and to that extent accepted despite departing conspicuously from the rules and conventions of dominant language games and forms of life. Shifting to an alternative but complementary language, as Proust presents them Charlus and Françoise exemplify what Foucault calls "local resistance" to the constellations of micro, capillary, or pastoral power that largely constitute cultural, social, and political life.

From time to time Proust's *heros* shows his annoyance, even his exasperation, with the troublesome, irritating characteristics of Charlus and Françoise. But for present purposes the more salient feature of Proust's presentation is his acknowledgment (I take the term, which is by contrast with knowledge or understanding, from Wittgenstein via Cavell) of respects in which Charlus and Françoise go beyond the distinctive, the deviant, and the idiosyncratic to the unique, the singular, and the idiolectical.

Here again, and unsurprisingly, irritation and sometimes anger occasionally show themselves. Charlus says things that the *heros* puts down as childish in their stupidity. Because the *heros* is continuously dependent on the services provided by Françoise, he is yet more angered when he cannot comprehend those of her ways of speaking, thinking, and acting that impede or frustrate his desires and intentions.

More deeply, however, Proust makes his *heros* loyal to and deeply appreciative of these two characters. When others (especially Mme Legrande and Morel) turn against Charlus, the *heros* excoriates them for their insensitivity, born as he sees it of their blind submission to what they take to be the prescribed modes of speaking and acting. And his own sharpest words for both Charlus and Françoise are reserved for those occasions when they themselves become mimics, when they allow the idiolects they have fashioned for themselves to give way to or lose themselves in the established, the conventional, and the prescribed.

What is an idiolect? *Merriam-Webster's Collegiate Dictionary*, tenth edition, defines it as "the language or speech pattern of one individual at a particular period of life." According to the *OED* (supplement, vol. 3), it is "the linguistic system of one person, differing in some details from that of all other speakers of the same dialect or language"; this is illustrated with the following quotation from one B. Bloch: "The totality of the possible utterances of one speaker at one time in using a language to interact with other speakers." I would not myself know how to go about identifying "the totality of the possible utterances" of a Charlus, a Françoise, or any "speaker" other than a parrot. Nevertheless, taken together with the emphasis both dictionary definitions give to singularity, Mr. Bloch's concluding words usefully underline the point that Charlus and Françoise are "interacting" with others. And insofar as their interactions occur in or by means of their idiolects—that is, in something recognizable as language—their performatives, rather than being "private" in the deep sense that Wittgenstein famously argues is a linguistic impossibility, must in principle have meaning for some number of others.

I conclude this chapter by considering whether there are interactions that are "meaningful" in ways that cannot be communicated in language. But before venturing onto this inherently perilous terrain, let me first note that Proust anticipates Wittgenstein in surrounding the latter's "in principle public" with a great deal of circumstantial but highly practical doubt and uncertainty. Of course Charlus and Françoise (to say nothing of Gilberte, Albertine, Andree, and especially the *heros* himself) deliberately deceive and mislead others (and themselves). But in order for these schemings to succeed, their addressees must grasp what the words mean in the sense of getting the message that Charlus and Françoise want them to receive. Not infrequently, and sometimes because of the idiolectal character of the words used, the message does not transmit. In narrating these misfires, the *heros* claims to understand the "real," roughly the speaker-intended, meaning of what the several parties say and do, thereby serving as witness to the "publicness" of the language they use. As we would expect from the skeptical passage I quoted earlier, however, Proust the narrator behind the narrator not only frequently has the latter mistaken about what has been said but shows *himself*, the master narrator, to be in uncertainty concerning the meanings of the statements that he has put into the mouths of his characters. If we mean by a *recherche du temps perdu* the attempt to artic- ulate memories/constructions/inventions, to put them into words that as needed can in turn be explained by other words, then we search for but are fated *de n'y trouve pas*.

But this is not to say that Proust's search was in vain. If he was often left in uncertainty as to the literal, the public, meanings of the words of Charlus and Françoise, in putting those very words into their mouths he enacted idiolectal individualities that, in another sense of meaning, were immensely meaningful to him. *Recherche* can be rendered as "quest," and Proust's quest was, in the best sense of the term, quixotic. It was the quest not to find but to make himself.

Wittgenstein says that notions such as transubstantiation and im- maculate conception are incomprehensible to him (1969, e.g., para. 239). More generally, he argues that every attempt to articulate an ethic falls into unintelligible nonsense (1965, passim). But he has a deep ad- miration for those of religiosity, and he says of *attempts* at religious and ethical talk that they "document . . . a tendency in the human mind which I personally cannot help respecting deeply and I would not for my life ridicule it" (1965, p. 12). As with Proust's "concessions" to Char- lus and Françoise, Wittgenstein's admiration for what he cannot under- stand manifests, or rather embodies, the *virtù* of liberality.

3 / The Good or Goodnesses of Polity and Polities à la Liberalism: Plurality Rather than Unicity, Singularity beyond Plurality

In this chapter I address, from the perspective of the ideals of liberalism as I conceive them, questions concerning the criteria by which the quality of polities should be assessed. To repeat briefly, liberalism as I envision it is committed to the ideal of individuality and hence self-enactment as formal but not substantive end and to the widest possible freedom of individual action as a necessary but not sufficient condition of effective pursuit of this ideal (Flathman, 1987, 1989, 1992, 1993).

Some will think that this conception-cum-idealization fates my discussion to irrelevance or worse. If our concern is with the good or goodnesses of that collectivity here called the polity, focusing on the disaggregating values of individuality and individual freedom would seem to be an encumbrance if not a distraction. If I had let this objection have sway, I could not have written this chapter and perhaps not this book. But I try to make, at least obliquely, some responses to the objection as I go along and I speak to it somewhat more directly toward the end of the chapter.

The bulk of my discussion concerns ideas and issues that are brought to mind by the words that follow the colon in this chapter's title, "plurality rather than unicity, singularity beyond plurality."

I

Setting "singularity" aside for the moment, we might say that, at the level of liberal doctrine, the movement from unicity to plurality has long since been completed. It is easy to associate unicity and related terms such as homogeneity, commonality, and perhaps community with moral and political ideologies and regimens that are (or seek to become) internally monolithic and unswerving in their commitment to an ordered if not a unified system of beliefs and values. Unicity calls to mind totalizing or at least potently authoritarian understandings and institutions that are widely regarded as the antitheses of liberalism. Virtually all self-identified liberal thinkers accept what John Rawls calls the "fact of pluralism" (1993, introduction); they further agree that this "fact" distinguishes liberal from non- or antiliberal societies. In a more explicitly evaluational register, from Constant and Tocqueville through Mill and Green to Berlin and Rawls it is difficult to find anyone of liberal self-designation who does not promote an abundant plurality of "conceptions of the good" and "plans of life" as well as the plethora of groups, associations, and parties that are commonly regarded as the empirical yield and complement of these ideas. The moral and political ideas and ideals of unicity or commonality, certainly in their more aggrandizing versions, would seem to be in remission if not in disgrace among liberal thinkers. In the contrast between unicity and pluralism, liberalism appears to stand resolutely for, perhaps is even to be equated with, pluralism.

Regarding this contrast and this movement, I make two connected arguments. The first is that the appearance that liberalism has rejected unicity in favor of pluralism is misleading; in fact leading liberal thinkers and much practice widely regarded as liberal continues to pursue various versions of unicity or homogeneity. My second argument is that liberalism ought to prefer pluralism to unicity but that, rather than contenting itself with this progression, it ought to go on to promote what I will be calling singularity. In order to prepare both of these arguments, I give preliminary consideration to the concepts of unicity, plurality, and especially singularity.

There are three different but connected uses of the word *singularity* each of which alerts us to ambiguities and disagreements in liberal thinking and practice. The first of these concerns comparisons *among* various past and present political polities or regimes. Sparta was singular among the city-states of ancient Greece and Calvinist Geneva stood out from the other polities of late-Renaissance Europe. Albania under Enver Hoxha, Cuba under Fidel Castro, Singapore under Lee Yuan, and contemporary Iran all invite similar characterizations. Internally these regimes are striking examples of actual or avidly sought unicity as distinct from plurality. Owing importantly to this very fact, however, there are respects in which these regimes instance singularity and therefore add to global political plurality. They are distinctive among and hence multiply the diversity of organized political actualities. Perhaps it is for this reason that many liberals, as indicated by their frequent use of the languages of national self-determination and of anti-imperialism, agonize over forceful interventions in the affairs of polities such as China, Iraq and Iran, Haiti, and Cuba.

Of course liberals condemn or at least disdain such regimes for their suppression of domestic or intraregime pluralism. In making these judgments, liberals promote not only plurality but singularity in a further sense that is conceptually related to but empirically and politically distinct from the one discussed thus far. Liberals favor and promote polities that are at once internally pluralistic and singular in the distinctive character of their internal diversities. In this second sense (easily the most salient in the canonical texts of liberal political theory), the concept of singularity refers primarily to the extent to which the several groups and associations that jointly compose a single regime are mutually distinctive. It is desirable that polities differ from one another, but it is at least equally important that they all be internally pluralistic.

I don't need to remind you of the intensely practical difficulties of harmonizing or even accommodating these two values or ideals of liberal thinking. Regimes such as, say, China and Syria are singular in the first sense and contribute to global political plurality, but their rulers do all that they can to avoid or suppress internal diversity. Should liberalism support or at least accommodate them on the first ground or should it condemn and otherwise act against them on the second?[1] I return to these questions below, but I want first to introduce a third sense of singularity that might help us to resolve, or at least to achieve an improved perspective on, the conflicts between the two senses thus far distinguished. By way of transition I remark that singularity in the first two senses may be little more than another way of talking about pluralism, not much more than a rhetorical flourish within a discourse that is regarded as liberal because it is pluralist.

II

I begin my exploration of the third sense of singularity on a negative note. To the limited extent that the term *singularity* actually appears in recent discourse in and around liberalism, it is frequently invoked to reinforce the judgment that a liberalism that prefers pluralism to unicity ought to oppose singularities that go beyond those supplied and supported by inter- and intraregime pluralisms. More emphatically, there is much in past and present liberal discourse that presses us to construe singularity in a further sense as totalizing and hence to dismiss it as incompatible with pluralist liberalism. I refer in particular to the tendency to associate singularity with a concept—namely individualism—that pluralist liberals as well as critics of liberalism disdain on both empirical and axiological grounds.

Individualism can be said to feature or to promote plurality over unicity in the weak sense that it (individualism) makes physically distinct individual persons the fundamental unit of moral and political thought and practice. This conception of plurality has been disdained as puerile by antiliberal thinkers from Hegel and Bradley to recent communitarians such as Charles Taylor and Michael Sandel. It has also had a decidedly bad press among liberal thinkers from Tocqueville through T. H. Green and Leonard Hobhouse up to recent liberals such as William Galston. Individualism in this sense has been derided as at once naive and dangerous. It is naive in its failure to recognize the ways in which each of us is and must be what we are because of our historical and cultural circumstances and involvements. And it is dangerous in its tendency to engender "mass" societies consisting of persons most of whom—despite being physically distinct—think and act alike and are unified in the repugnant senses signaled by notions such as herd behavior and the tyranny of the majority. In ways that its alleged proponents (Hobbes and Locke, Constant, Mill, and Berlin are frequently if erroneously mentioned) may or may not have intended or realized, individualism is incompatible with a more than superficial pluralism and hence with liberalism understood as a form of pluralism that is at once sociologically realistic and morally and politically robust.

As regards individual*ism*, I largely agree with this view. All versions of liberalism that have resources adequate to engender and support resistance to orthodoxy or uniformity insist upon the reality and argue for the value of diversities that have a deeper grounding than the mere physical separateness or biological distinctiveness of individual human beings. I cannot form a conception of who I am or of who I might hope to become without attention to my historical, cultural, or socio-logical inheritances and circumstances.

Should we therefore equate liberalism with factually more realistic and axiologically more robust forms of pluralism? More pointedly, should we expunge from liberalism and its conception of the good polity strains of thought and practice that, by these criteria, are naive and dangerous? Tempting as it is, the answer to these questions cannot be a simple affirmative. The reason it cannot, finally, is that liberalism ought to go beyond unicity, pluralism, and individualism to individual-ity. To see why, we need to consider difficulties with intra- as well as interregime pluralism.

There are well-documented forms of intraregime pluralism that institutionalize or otherwise consolidate tendencies and intensify forces that liberalism must abhor. For Montaigne and Hobbes the illiberal form of pluralism in question was primarily the abundantly attested to reality of mutually intolerant and internally repressive religious sects; for Constant it was the same plus movements inspired and driven by fanaticisms such as those promoted by Rousseau, Danton, and Robespierre. Earlier in our own century the usual examples of such misbegotten forms of plurality were various corporatisms and syndicalisms; then but more emphatically now it is ethnicity, gender-, nationality-, and other ascriptively based groups that act toward one other—and often toward their own members—much as did the religious sects that Montaigne and Hobbes feared and contemned.

These last remarks may bring us closer to my initially stated concerns. Intraregime pluralisms of the objectionable kinds I have just mentioned confront liberal polities with severe practical difficulties and liberalism with a critical intellectual challenge. By recognizing and endorsing "the fact of pluralism," liberalism affirms the inevitability and desirability of diversity and disagreement, competition and contention. But liberalism is neither anarchism nor libertarianism. It would be no worse than an exaggeration to say that contemporary liberals continue to be haunted by the prospect of the kinds of civil disorder in reaction to which liberalism and liberal settlements are often said (e.g. by Rawls) to have emerged. And much of liberal practice, in particular its rule-making, institution-building, and educational practices, continues to be devoted to fending off or at least containing such evils.

In the terms I have been using, these anxieties and apprehensions confront liberal thinking and practice with the question of how to distinguish a "reasonable pluralism" (Rawls, 1993), or viable or tenable pluralisms (Mouffe, 1993, among numerous others), from illiberal species of this genus. As Rawls ever so daintily puts it, pluralist liberalism, concerned as it properly is with freedom and equality and justice, rights and self-respect and self-esteem, must also convince us that it can solve the problem of "stability." It is in trying to solve this problem that a quest for unicity resurfaces in liberal thinking.

Distinctive in its details, Rawls's response to the problem of stability is of a kind familiar from Locke and Kant, and from Green and Hobhouse up to recent neo-Kantian liberals such as Dworkin and Nagel, Habermas, Gutmann, and Galston. The basic idea is that at least some especially consequential domains of thought and action can and should be subjected to the power and duty of disciplining reason. For Rawls, a reasonable pluralism is one in which most if not all participants accept, even if on differing (but "overlapping") grounds, principles of justice that must be respected regardless of differences among individual and group conceptions of the good. Although it is asserted that, outside of the basic structure grounded in these principles, individuals and groups may pursue their life plans as they see fit, this freedom is subject to the proviso that projects incompatible with the principles of justice are categorically disqualified. Indeed Rawls goes so far as to contend that arguments promoting such projects should be accorded no standing in public discourse. Because the principles that inform the basic structure are reasonable and consonant with the rational (hence consistent with or rather constitutive of individual autonomy and self-respect), those who refuse to subscribe to the principles can nevertheless be subjected, justifiably, to their discipline. The stability of a "reasonable" pluralism is achieved through the establishment and, as necessary, enforcement of a core of unicity or uniformity.

Of course no form of liberalism has entirely eschewed, or could entirely eschew, reliance on some degree of commonality among those who compose a politically organized society. From Constant and Humboldt through (the best parts of) Tocqueville and Mill to Berlin, Hampshire and Mouffe, liberals suspicious of Lockean and Kantian, Rawlsian and Habermasian strategies have nevertheless joined in the search for ways to contain the actually or potentially dangerous excesses of pluralism. But they have not done so by appeal to an imperatively unifying rationality or reasonableness.

How should a liberalism that takes its bearings from the thinkers just mentioned proceed? What tasks should it set itself and by what criteria should it assess its own performances?

III

One possibility is suggested by the recent work of a thinker, John Gray, who may once have identified with liberalism but has recently become one of its most caustic critics. With neo-Kantians such as Rawls, Dworkin, and Nagel primarily in mind, Gray objects that the currently most influential liberal thinkers are blind to the salient realities of contemporary political life. In "the real human world" the "special attachments" of race, religion, ethnicity, and gender are "essential to our identities." "[H]uman beings think of themselves . . . as being constituted by their histories and their communities, with all their conflicting demands." The "practices of exclusion and subordination [are] constitutive of every community human beings have ever lived in." Because liberalism is incapable of recognizing or responding to these realities, to the facts of pluralism as they really are, Gray claims that liberalism has become a "political nullity" (1992a).[2]

As I have argued above, this assessment of the historiography and political sociology informing past and present liberalisms is badly overgeneralized. In company with the communitarians and republicans whom he sometimes favorably invokes, Gray underestimates liberal awareness of the facts of pluralism. More particularly, he fails to appreciate its anxieties concerning the difficulties that arise from those facts. But let us set this objection aside and ask instead where an enhanced political realism of the kind he favors would take us.

On this type of view it is the primary task of political theory to register and respond to the "realities of political life." Political theorists should eschew rationalist and idealistic attempts to distinguish a reasonable or tenable pluralism from that pluralism of special attachments with which, Gray asserts, we are primarily confronted. If political theory should venture beyond recording truths about human affairs, its task is the admittedly difficult but more modest one of finding ways of "balancing competing claims of similar validity, [of] finding a *modus vivendi* among forms of life that are irreconcilable, and [of] mediating con-

flicts that can never be resolved" (Gray, 1992a, p. 15). The *fact* of inter-
and especially intraregime pluralism is what matters.

Along with liberal thinkers such as Hobbes and Constant, Berlin
and Hampshire, I have considerable sympathy for the idea that the primary aim of *politics* should be to sustain a modus vivendi among competing and conflicting groups, that *in politics* we ought to resist the temptation to attempt to transform ourselves or others into different and
better people. But this judgment, and the "facts" about human affairs
that partly support it, are the beginning not (à la Gray) the end or culmination of their thinking. On the one hand, the liberal thinkers I have
just mentioned have attached great significance to further "facts" that
make few appearances in the kind of thinking that Gray represents.
More important, they reject the view that liberalism is restricted to or
exhausted by the question of what can and should be done through
politics and government.

I return to the "further facts" below. But let us first ask whether
political realism implies that liberals should endorse the particularizing
identifications of race and gender, nationality and religion. Let us say
that we follow Gray and his realist and communitarian allies in eschewing neo-Kantian rationalist individual*ism* à la Rawls. If we do so, are we
then obliged to justify or at least to resign ourselves to the hatred of
Serbs for Croat Muslims, of Turks for Kurds, of Hutus for Tutsis, or
Oxford dons for football yobs?

Liberal thinkers such as Hobbes and Constant, Humboldt, Berlin
and Hampshire, are committed to an ideal of individual*ity* that must be
distinguished from the notion of individual*ism* discussed above. They
appreciate the ways in which each of us is who we are primarily because of our involvement in particular traditions, cultures, societies, and
groups. For various and especially for defensive political purposes, they
are keen to sustain these forms of identification and association. But
(in company with non- or aliberal theorists such as Nietzsche, William
James, and Michael Oakeshott) they join Tocqueville and Mill in their
intense awareness of the often confining, homogenizing, and stultify-
ing effects of group memberships and involvements. They are fervent
in their concern over the ways in which such memberships and identifications work against individual*ity*. We can easily imagine their worries over the ways in which some Muslims attempt to impose their
views on Copts and Kurds, some Serbs on Croats, some fundamental-
ists and evangelicals on Catholics and mainline Protestants. They are or

would be equally distressed by the pronounced tendency of Muslims to demand conformity from other Muslims, of Kurds and Croats to tyrannize over their kinsman, of the leaders of self-styled Christian sects to domineer over their own followers, by the insistence of some feminists that women close ranks against men.

Let's say that we agree that there are forms of pluralism that are obnoxious and repugnant. If so, how should such evaluations be expressed and implemented? One possibility, which prefigures the demand for unicity expressed in neo-Lockean, neo-Kantian, and other liberalisms that promote the power and duty of reason, is enunciated by the old socialist notion of the commanding heights. We seek (let us assume, generously, that we do so through more or less democratic means) to take command of the authority and power provided by established political institutions and institutionalisms and from those heights we suppress forms of pluralism offensive to us. We employ constitutionalism, the rule of law, police power, institutionalized education, and various educative policies (physical and mental health and welfare, criminal law and penology) to produce a populace and a polity that present a reasonable pluralism, a polity that is good by our standards. And we may go on to use—as that liberal democracy called the United States of America has repeatedly done—the political and other resources of that populace and polity to impose acceptance of the same standards among populaces and polities other than our own.

It is improbable in the extreme that understandings and strategies of the kind I have just described will disappear or even significantly diminish among us. In our century these views and proclivities were most powerfully promoted by far Left and far Right forces, but by now they are deeply embedded in our political culture (as is manifested by the fact that both centrist liberals such as Rawls and self-styled realists and conservatives such as Gray and Reagan have, each in her or his own way, unreflectively accepted them). Something akin to these views, moreover, may well be implicated in the very notion of polity and of a world divided among a multiplicity of polities. If our primary identification is as citizen or subject, and if we hold the polity of which we are a member largely responsible for our well- or ill-being, we have powerful motivations for attending to its policies and practices. And because "our" polity or nation is bound to be affected by the policies and practices of other polities or nations, it would be imprudent if we took no concern with "international" affairs and relations. From this perspective, those political scientists who celebrate and promote political apathy and submission to an elite have gotten hold of the wrong end of the political stick.

These observations are pertinent to some of the most urgent and distressing problems and tendencies of our day. They do not, however, settle the question of the spirit in which we, especially those of us who are liberals, should approach the political aspects of our lives.

Consider the striking phenomenon of nostalgia for Stalinism, Titoism, colonialism, imperialism, and the Cold War. It is plausible to think that the evidently widespread regret over the passing of these ugly political formations is due to the extent to which they contained excessive or unreasonable pluralisms. "Evil Empire" though it was, Stalinism effectively suppressed ugly and destructive ethnic and nationalist forces. Titoism did the same in the extended territory that was briefly known as Yugoslavia and that has now become the very emblem of the need for unicity. Imperialism and colonialism, widely or at least officially condemned, did the same in the Middle East, Asia, and Africa. In the West, the Cold War was repeatedly invoked to justify surveillance and criminalization of a host of ideas and activities taken to be not only alien but treasonous. In short, in the name of what I have called unicity, severe restrictions were imposed on diversities regarded as "unreasonable."

These remarks deserve to be underlined. Nostalgia and fear lead many to hanker for the Soviet Empire abroad and to favor continuation or reinstitutionalization of Cold War mentalities and policies at home. Unicity is essential. Neo-Kantians hope to achieve it by philosophical argumentation. If it cannot be achieved in this allegedly benign way, it should be imposed by law and coercion (e.g., through huge enlargement of police forces and prison facilities, great expansion of the number of capital and life-imprisonment offenses, and perhaps—in abject imitation of the vulgar phenomenon of Singaporism—the subjection of spray painters to rattan caning).

Are these the alternatives?

I do not share the judgment that they are. Stalinism and Titoism and imperialism were far worse than the undeniably horrific conflicts that have succeeded them. The Cold War and its mentalities were invoked to license severe restrictions on valuable political thinking and activity. Singaporism represents cold warism yet more emphatically internalized.

For a brief period we were treated to talk about a "new world

order," a regimen that would leave the brutalities of Stalinism and Titoism, imperialism and the Cold War behind. But what was "new" about
this "order" was that it was to be imposed by one superpower rather
than by two. It was of course predictable that lots of disorder, and lots
of local but brutally imposed orders, were of no interest whatever to
the superpower in question. Again and again the boastful trustees of
this superpower averted and continue to avert their glance from events
that went and that go beyond the disorderly to the horrendous. Although less widely predicted, it also quickly emerged that this "power"
was a lot less "super" than had been expected or imagined. The attempts of this superpower to impose order, even on weak and deeply
dependent states such as Panama, Somalia, and Cuba—to say nothing
of more potent states such as Iraq and Iran—produced about the same
results as had its numerous earlier attempts to do so in Vietnam, in Leba-
non, and, for decades, throughout the Caribbean and much of South
America. While often greatly increasing the misery of the peoples in
question, the superpower in question failed utterly to achieve its stated
objectives. The phrase *new world order* is now heard about as often as,
say, the word *Eurocommunism*.

I don't regret the passing of this impertinent notion and I wish that
the thinking and acting that it signals would disappear as well. As I allowed above, lots of terrible things are happening in Eastern Europe
and throughout the former Soviet Empire. But from the standpoint of
liberalism as I conceive it they are less terrible than actions that were not
only commonplace but institutionalized under that empire and no more
terrible than events that repeatedly occur throughout much if not all of
the world (including in the American empire and in America itself).

IV

Having rejected both rationalist, unicity-seeking liberalism and the realist
and communitarian views that are offered as alternatives to it, I end by
returning to the conception of liberal ideals with which I began. What
stance should individuality- and freedom-seeking liberals take toward
the problems I have been discussing? Would, could, such a liberalism
help to resolve or at least to ameliorate the difficulties before us?

The most heartening feature of liberalism is its commitment to
that extreme but inspiring form of pluralism that is the cultivation and
celebration of individuality. To quote José Ortega y Gasset once again,
in its best moments, "liberalism . . . is the supreme form of generosity;

it is the right by which the majority concedes to minorities and hence it is the noblest cry that has ever resounded in this planet" (1932). But the minorities to which such a liberalism asks majorities to concede are not ethnic, religious, national, and other ascriptively designated groups (and not "interest" groups or associations) but rather, first and foremost, those minorities of one that individual human beings sometimes make themselves into. The plurality that such a liberalism cherishes and promotes is that far more radical multiplicity and diversity that Nietzsche calls self-overcoming and that Michael Oakeshott calls self-enacting individuality.

Such a liberalism, which I call *willful*, values a plurality of groups and associations. A pluralism of this latter kind can enable cooperation and hence the effective pursuit of such objectives that, from time to time, show up as shared or common; it can enrich the inherited stock of beliefs and values among which choices can be made and it can supply alternative languages in which to conceive new ideas and ideals; and it can provide a diversity of perspectives from which to assess and, as necessary, oppose received opinions and practices.

But an individuality-affirming liberalism is also wary of the tendency of the members of groups to enforce common identifications and ends upon one another. A pluralism constituted by groups, particularly groups defined by ethnic, nationalist, and other ascriptive identifications, has widely attested and quite powerful impositional and conformity-demanding tendencies. These unpalatable characteristics are most familiar in situations of intense *inter*group competitions and conflicts. If we are defined by our opposition to they or to them, we are likely to think that our successes or triumphs depend on our unity and concerted action. In such circumstances, *intra*group disagreement and certainly dissent, idiosyncrasy and certainly deviance are seldom welcomed and frequently treated with great severity. If we define ourselves by opposition to they or to them, we are apt to think that we can remain what we distinctively are, can maintain the identity that we cherish, only if we sustain uniformity and solidarity amongst ourselves.

In recent reflections on identities that are defined by gender and sexuality, Judith Butler continues and extends the (to my but not to her mind) quintessentially liberal concern over these prevalent but lamentable phenomena. Butler also goes some distance toward identifying ways in which this concern should be enacted. Partly agreeing with Gray and with the best moments in communitarian thinking, she observes:

Doubtlessly crucial is the ability to wield the signs of subordinated identity in a public domain that constitutes its own [e.g.] homophobic and racist hegemonies through the erasure or domestication of culturally and politically constituted identities. [But] . . . insofar as it is imperative that we insist upon those specificities in order to expose the fictions of an imperialist humanism that works through unmarked privilege [e.g., the rationalist humanisms of Locke and Kant, Rawls and Habermas] there remains the risk that we will make the articulation of ever more specified identities into the aim of political activism. [Rather than succumbing to this temptation] . . . every insistence of identity must at some point lead to a taking stock of the constitutive exclusions that reconsolidate hegemonic power differentials, exclusions that each articulation was forced to make in order to proceed. This critical reflection will be important in order not to replicate at the level of identity politics the very exclusionary moves that initiated the turn to specific identities in the first place. (1993, p. 118)[3]

The trajectory that Butler projects, while sharing the rejection of rationalist universalism, is importantly incompatible with the agenda suggested by the political realisms I have discussed. There are two dimensions or directions in which this is the case.

The first of these concerns one of the "facts" alluded to above, a "fact" that is prominent in liberal theorizing at its best but hardly mentioned by realists and communitarians. This fact is the more than merely empirical reality that states are fundamentally nonvoluntary associations and that the governments that rule them claim the authority to do so, as they judge necessary, by physical compulsion and other forms of coercion. Even if, by some miracle, those who have command of state authority and power use them to pursue the purposes Gray or other self-styled realists recommend, even if, by the further miracle anticipated or hoped for by communitarians, the results produced are approved by all or most of those affected, the outcomes will be tainted by the setting in which and the means by which they were pursued and achieved.

These are not conclusive reasons against looking to the state and politics to abate or ameliorate conflict. But the miracles I have just tried to imagine are not often going to take place and are least likely to do so in settings dominated by "special identifications" of the kind that realists and communitarians are keen not only to acknowledge but to endorse and promote. The second dimension concerns the fact that government and politics will continue to consist largely of attempts by those of special attachments and commitments to use state authority and power to impose their values on those who do not share them (Bosnian Serbs against Muslim Croats, Tutsis then Hutus and then again Tutsis in Rwanda, the adamant opposition of the National Rifle Association to the banning of assault weapons). If we must use the state and state power to control or diminish such contentions and strifes, we should do so *faute de mieux*, in a spirit of regret—certainly of caution—rather than in the belief that the lessons of history somehow require this of us.

But liberal political theory need not or rather must not restrict itself to the question of what the state should and should not do. Nor need it confine its attention to what should and should not be sought by way of homogeneity of political and moral outlook and practice. Liberal thinkers who disavow rationalist and other unicity-seeking projects have not justified or resigned themselves to currently existing group identifications and patterns of interaction. Through argumentation and more especially through inspiriting writing they have promoted "adverbial" (Oakeshott) *virtùs* such as civility, courage, and magnanimity. These *virtùs* speak to the manner or style in which one does whatever one chooses to do, leaving questions of ends and purposes, aspirations and ideals to be decided by groups and more especially by individuals. It is first and foremost through the cultivation of these qualities of character that this kind of liberalism addresses the question of unicity and viable pluralism. The virtuosities that these thinkers prize do place constraints on thought and action; they subject thinking and acting to a severe albeit a largely self-imposed discipline. To the extent that they are accepted and enacted they take us beyond mutual accommodation or tolerance to that welcoming, that celebrating, of diversity that Nietzsche associates with "free-spiritedness." In the absence of qualities of these kinds it is difficult to see how individuals and groups can live with one another. Or rather it is difficult to see how they could do so without submitting to a brutally imposed order.

These *virtùs* call upon and hence promote individuality in at least two complementary ways. They do so, firstly, because they promote qualities of character closely akin to those that are necessary to the formation of ends, purposes, and ideals. Secondly, they do so because the requirements they promote cannot be written into rules or programs, cannot be reduced to a set of deontic principles. One can be civil and courageous, magnanimous and generous in a wide variety of ways.

These last remarks underscore respects in which liberalism both should and should not be regarded as an idealism and even a utopianism. In a powerfully pejorative use of these terms, idealists and utopianists are disdained because they are animated by goals that exceed not only the actualities but the aspirations of actual communities. (Invocations of the perdurant realities of "special attachments" are saturated with this charge.) Against it, liberals in the tradition of Constant and Berlin claim that the possibilities that exhilarate them can be espied— even if dimly—in human affairs as we already know them. In Heideggerian terms, human being exceeds and cannot be reduced to human experience. In the terms of a prominent advertising slogan, liberals summon us to be the best that our awareness of our being tells us we might become. A sharp and ineliminable discrepancy between ideal and salient actuality is essential to this liberal stance.

Liberalism thus conceived differs profoundly from the collectivist and rationalist ideologies to which the terms *idealism* and *utopianism* are most commonly applied. The ideals that animate it, the possibilities that it envisions, go far beyond collectivism and pluralism to a radical form of self-enacting individuality that I want to associate with the term *singularity*. It of course follows that liberal ideals are always and necessarily underdetermined, can never be reduced to formulae or rules. But this is at once their beauty and their strength, their inspiring but also their realistic character.

There is much more that can and should be said concerning this conception of the good or rather the goodnesses of the liberal polity, but I must conclude. I do so by quoting one of the best, one of the most distinctively liberal, passages in all of political theory. The features of liberalism I have foregrounded will exasperate not only rationalist neo-Kantians, not only realist and communitarian pluralists, but all human beings who are

> disconcerted unless they feel themselves to be upheld by something more substantial than the emanations of their own contingent imaginations. This unresolved perplexity teases the monistic yearnings of the muddled theorist, it vexes a moralist with ecumenical leanings, and it may disconcert an unfortunate who, having "lost" his morality

(as others have been known to "lose" their faith), must set about constructing one for himself. . . . But it will reassure the modest mortal with a self to disclose and a soul to make who needs a familiar and resourceful moral language . . . to do it in and who is disinclined to be unnerved because there are other such languages to which he cannot readily relate his own. (Oakeshott, 1975, p. 81)[4]

PART II

INSTITUTIONS

4 / Ruling, Rules, and Rule Following: Mainstay or Mirage, Miracle or Misfortune?

Along with promoting the ideals of individuality and freedom, willful or virtuosity liberalism accepts, even if warily or with a certain sense of resignation, both the reality and the necessity of government, of law, and of a partly rule-governed politics that takes its focus from the existence of the established authority of government and law.

The combination of these ideals and the acknowledgment of the necessity of authority, of law, and other rule-governed practices creates a tension within liberalism, a stress or strain that is my primary concern in this chapter and through much of Part II. The idea of established authority, and of politics as a mode of interaction distinct from a chaos or a war of some against others or of all against all, brings with it concepts such as institutions, offices, and procedures, notions that are incomprehensible apart from the ideas of ruling, rules, and rule following. It seems to follow that ruling, rules, and rule following are and must be mainstays of a liberal polity. But if, as rule skeptics from Ockham, Montaigne, and Hobbes to the Legal Realists, Critical Legal Theorists, and postmodernists have persistently argued, ruling, rules, and rule following are figmental, if they are mirages rather than realities, then a liberal polity is an impossibility and the ideals of willful liberalism unattainable.

On the other hand, or rather at the same time, institutions and institutionalizations, hence ruling, rules, and rule following, appear to be inimical to the ideals of free, creative, self-determining individuality. Connoting if not entailing ideas such as regularity and predictability, subsumability and uniformity, obedience and submission, the darker, illiberal resonances of these notions are dramatized but surely not entirely misrepresented when we think, for example, of institutionalizing persons, of rule-fetishizing institutions such as prisons, asylums, and numerous families and schools, of conscripting persons to the regimenting disciplines of police or military duties—even when we think of those who willingly plight their troths to the nomian dominions of monastic orders, sects, or sectarian parties. From the perspective of the liberal ideals as discussed in Part I, it is miraculous in the sense of inexplicable that the human beings liberalism posits and idealizes submit themselves to and impose upon themselves such regimens. In another register, it has to be regarded a misfortune not a blessing that members of *soi-disant* liberal societies so frequently do so.

In short, the topic of ruling, rules, and rule following exposes uncertainties and ambivalences in liberal thinking and practice. Liberal suppositions and idealizations make rules and rule following at once necessary and impossible, desirable and regrettable. I cannot hope entirely to dissolve or obviate these tensions and dissonances. I do try to abate them by arguing that ruling, rules, and rule following, as such as it were, cannot do as much *for* us as their most insistent promoters (who I call, perhaps tendentiously, *regularians*) would have us believe. As commonly represented and championed (for example, by traditional grammarians, musicologists, and arithmeticians as well as by legal absolutists, theorists of the rule of law and of constitutionalism), rules and rule following are indeed a mirage. Grammatically correct speaking and writing, fault-free musical composition, computations that do not draw red marks on homework assignments in courses in arithmetic—these widely sought desiderata, as well as notions of strict, closely determinative constitutional and legal prescriptions and proscriptions, suppose characteristics that no set or system of rules can of itself possess. But if this argument is cogent, it also shows that fears concerning what ruling, rules, and rule following can do *to* us are also exaggerated. In a phrase taken from the thinker, Wittgenstein, on whom I draw most extensively, if rules and rule following take us to or away from any destination they do so by the elbow not by the throat.

I should say at once that there are at least two inferences that do not follow from the arguments I present. The first is that ruling, rules, and rule following are merely mirages and hence cannot be among the mainstays of our affairs and activities. Understood as complex and fluctuating gestalts, practices, and rhetorical genres, ruling and rules are integral to much of what we think and do. The rule-governed aspects of our affairs are, nevertheless, importantly surprising, puzzling, even miraculous. As ordinary or mundane as it is, from a normative perspective the propensity of human beings to organize and direct their present activities by reference to rules adopted or promulgated at a previous and of certainty different time is disturbing and should not be uncritically accepted or promoted. Ruling, rules, and rule following are not generally, certainly are not invariably, a blessing on humankind. As construed and promoted by regularian thinking and practicing, as demanded by illiberal and too often self-appointed liberal thinkers governments and societies, rules and rule following are frequently a plague upon us. The question here is whether there are understandings of these devices that do or would allow them, nevertheless, to be among the mainstays of rather than the curses afflicting a liberal society.

In searching for such an understanding, one that is appropriately skeptical but neither dismissive nor passively nihilistic, I try to think about and from that salient feature of human affairs, language, that has become a focus of much thinking about human beings and their activities. Language is widely regarded as the very exemplar of the rule-governed and hence the regular. The teachers of English grammar of my early education and of other languages in my later days thought of language as, properly, rule-governed in respects that are at once extensive and quite strict. Just as spelling bees are founded on the assumption that there are and that there are known by some to be correct ways to spell all or nearly all of the words of the language in which the contest is conducted, so when teachers "correct" the grammar of the written and spoken performances of their students they presume upon an established, an authoritative, set of rules concerning the conjugations of verbs, the agreement of nouns, adjectives, and pronouns, and the like. Of course persons of this persuasion recognize, lament, and attempt to subdue the errant character of much actual language usage and many linguistic performances. But these critical judgments and interventions are intelligible, indeed conceivable, only on the regularian assumption that there are already established rules that distinguish between correct and incorrect, right and wrong, good and bad performances.[1]

Given the centrality, or rather the indispensability, of language to politics and to law and political governance, it comes as no surprise that attempts have been made to transfer regularian assumptions and norms concerning language and linguistic performances to constitutional, legal, and more generally institutional and political thinking. In order to assess these efforts, I briefly discuss reflections of Montaigne and Hobbes and respond at greater length to the thinking of Wittgenstein, Derrida, and Oakeshott.

I

In returning at many places in his *Essays* to the ways and means by which human beings commmunicate with one another, make their thinking and to that extent themselves at least partially intelligible to one another, Montaigne introduces themes that will be important throughout this discussion. On the one hand, he affirms the reality and promotes the desirability of implicit, background, or otherwise unself-conscious dispositions or tendencies that produce and sustain various commonalities and continuities in human affairs. Observers who notice these regularities can characterize them as rules, but it is important to Montaigne (as it was to Hume and followers of Hume such as Hayek and Polanyi), that these conventions are not only uncodified but seldom explicitly formulated. Anticipating an important Wittgensteinian distinction to be discussed below, conduct "accords with" but does not "involve" these "rules."

As Montaigne sees it, in the entire absence of such "agreements in judgment" (Wittgenstein), promulgated or otherwise formalized ruling, rules, and rule following would be impossibilities. But Montaigne also thinks that tacit conventions need to be supplemented or augmented by explicit, conduct-prescribing rules and commands. The virtue of rules of the latter kind, however, is also their vice or weakness. Because they must be formulated in words or other communicative devices— devices that are inherently ambiguous and inveterately subject to abuse—invoking or relying upon them often exacerbates rather than relieves the uncertainties and conflicts that precede and motivate their promulgations. "Most of the sources of the disorders of the world are grammatical. Our lawsuits are born only out of the debate concerning the interpretation of the laws; and most wars, out of the inability involved in not knowing how to express clearly the conventions and treaties of princes. How many quarrels, and what important ones, have been produced in the world by doubt concerning the meaning of this syllable: *hoc!*" (Montaigne, 1959, p. 60). Nor are these difficulties likely to be entirely remedied:

> There is no meaning or appearance . . . that the human mind does not find in the writings which it undertakes to examine. And out of the clearest, purest, most perfect utterance [written or spoken] which is possible, how much falseness and lying has not been drawn? . . . There is no prophet [or founder or legislator] . . . whom you cannot make say anything you wish, as was the case with the Sibyls; for there are so many manners of interpretation that it is difficult for an ingenious mind, by an oblique or direct interpretation, not to find on any subject something which seems plausibly to serve its purpose. (pp. 98–99)

These remarks of Montaigne are in the spirit of thinking about language that began no later than Plato and that was intensified by Montaigne's more explicitly skeptical ancestors such as Sextus Empiricus and Cicero. They also anticipate the perhaps more resolutely skeptical thinking of recent deconstructionists and postmodernists. In order to pursue the implications of his remarks for my present topics, I first consider analogous views of Hobbes.

Hobbes's largely undeserved reputation as an insistent and optimistic regularian has deflected attention from his agreement with but deepening of Montaigne's views. Hobbes never entirely gave up the ideal, represented for him by geometry, of speech and writing that are transparent and unequivocal. But language itself, or rather the services or benefits that we do and must ask of it, works relentlessly against realizing this objective.

As Hobbes sees it, there are deep-going reasons for this at once unwelcome and welcome fact. The original or basic use of language is to "mark" perceptions and thus to inscribe them in memory and otherwise to stabilize them. In the never entirely surpassed Adamic moments of his thinking, Hobbes insists that this process of marking is entirely arbitrary, that there is no inherently intelligible relation between the marks used and the perceptions to which they are assigned. For this reason, because perceptions are of radically diverse and continuously fluctuating phenomena, and because our perceptions are further multiplied and confused by unruly passions the "objects" of which vary radically within and among persons, "there is scarce any word that is not made equivocal by divers contextures of speech" (Hobbes, 1962a, chap.

5, p. 199). The marks that we invent and use, "besides the signification of what we imagine of their nature, have a signification also of the nature, dispositions, and interest of the speaker" (1962c, chap. 4, p. 40). Most if not all language is doubly ambiguous; along with often communicating something between or among us, it is likely to confuse or deceive us twice over.

As language develops, as those who use it move from marks for particular perceptions to the invention of words that classify kinds or classes of perceptions (a development necessary to the formulation and following of rules), the minimal discipline and uniformity that perception and the passions impose on language diminish further. Although these losses or deficits in mutual intelligibility are to some extent made good by convention, as language becomes more abstract not only the possibility but the likelihood of mutual misunderstanding increases apace.

Hobbes admired arithmetic and geometry primarily because their rules are "certain" in the sense that everyone who knows, and thinks according to, the established rules of these disciplines will necessarily arrive at the same mathematical conclusions. But the certainty of rules and rule-governed conduct in this respect depends on the rules being "certain" in another, namely the entire "perspicuity" of the definitions that mathematicians have stipulated for the terms out of which their further "ratiocinations" are formed. Transposed to the register of political and legal thinking, this thought suggests that the ideal of certainty is one that politics, government, and especially law can and ought to strive to achieve. In promulgating positive laws, sovereigns should define the terms in which their subjects will thereafter think and act. Perspicuous laws provide a clear and settled basis on which the members of a commonwealth can regulate and regularize their interactions.

But Hobbes himself casts deep doubts on this possibility and—of greater interest here—on the desirability of more than approximating it.

Words being necessary to the formulation and promulgation of laws, all words being subject to ambiguity and the multiplication of words therefore compounding ambiguity, the legislator's prospects of achieving perspicuity in laws are less than bright.[2] However satisfied the legislator may be (in her own mind, as we might put it) with her reasons for thinking a law needful, she can have no assurance of making either those reasons or the law itself clear to her subjects. A perfect law is an impossibility, a good law and hence a good system of laws extraordinarily hard to achieve.

Turning briefly from mirage/mainstay to miracle/misfortune, does Hobbes regret and want to ameliorate this state of affairs? No doubt this is one of his hopes. But our concern with the advantages and disadvantages of ruling, rules, and rule following presses us to consider whether the following remarks should be regarded not merely as descriptive generalizations about rules and rule following but as Hobbesian *prescriptions* concerning communicative behavior. In using words "we limit them not to ourselves, but leave them to be applied by the hearer" (1972, chap. 5, p. 199). "It is . . . always to be supposed, that he which intendeth not to deceive, alloweth the private interpretation of his speech to him to whom it is addressed" (1962a, I, chap. 13, p. 244).

Hobbes's chastened and chastening thoughts on these topics brought him neither to solemn despair (passive nihilism?) nor to an apparently frisky but actually febrile gamesmanship (active nihilism?). He did what he thought possible and desirable to clarify and otherwise improve language, thought, and the rules that are at once the supposition of all language and the condition and yield of much thinking. Out of his commitment to an ideal of individuality that is difficult if not impossible to reconcile with obsessively regularian thinking, he also extended to all of humankind his view that "philosophers . . . had always the liberty, and sometimes they both had and will have the necessity, of taking to themselves such names as they please for the signifying of their meaning."[3]

II

Neither Montaigne nor Hobbes denies that there are rules of various kinds, and neither rejects the view that there is much conduct that is properly regarded, whether by those whose conduct it is or by others who judge it, as faithful to or in contravention of established rules. Moreover, both of these thinkers clearly believe (albeit with important qualifications that must be largely ignored here) that wide subscription and generally faithful conformity to rules of various kinds often makes human affairs go better. The skepticism regarding rules that emerges powerfully from their thinking concerns, rather, the illusion that rules speak adequately for themselves, that rules, once promulgated or adopted, can themselves determine the conduct of those to whom they apply. Against this view, Montaigne and Hobbes argue that rules, ruling, and rule-governedness become mainstays of human affairs only if and only to the extent that rule followers as well as rule makers speak and otherwise *act* to, for, or against the rules that apply to them.

Many will think that this argument turns rules and rule following into a mirage, certainly that it annuls the possibility that these devices can be used to achieve control over and give direction to human affairs. If rules themselves don't determine the conduct of those to whom they apply, if the latter make up their own minds as they go along, as it were, in what sense do the rules actually rule conduct?

In fact, the accounts I have been considering have the potential both to diminish and to enhance the respects in which the making and following of rules affords distinctive purchase on thought, action, and moral and political interaction. On the diminution side, those who are convinced of something like Montaigne's and Hobbes's view, but who nevertheless place high value on regularity and predictability, may attempt to achieve and sustain the latter desiderata by promulgating *beliefs* that give definite content to and otherwise buttress some number of rules. (A currently prominent example would be the attempt to inculcate the belief that the Framers of this or that provision of the U.S. Constitution had a definite and properly determinative intent concerning its meaning and the frequently associated attempt to inculcate the belief that the intent of the Framers could and should govern present and future constitutional and legal practice.) To the extent that such attempts are successful in supplementing the rules in question, regularity and predictability may be maintained despite or even because of ambiguities in the rules "themselves." These successes, however, may be at the expense of values such as self-control and -direction.

On the other hand, wide acceptance of views such as those of Montaigne and Hobbes might diminish the incidence of rote, mechanical, mimetic, or otherwise submissive behaviors. To the extent that individuals and groups, whether rulers, rule followers, or both, recognize that interpreting and judging are necessary to rules and rule following, attentive and self-critical thinking and acting will be legitimated and otherwise encouraged. Some will think—as I have suggested Hobbes thought—such a development to be a good in itself, one that more than compensates for any loss in uniformity and calculability that may accompany or be produced by it. Others will argue that rigid insistence on "the letter" of this or that rule is likely to be self-defeating because it will result, sooner rather than later, in dislocations greater than those produced by a more circumstantial and adaptive approach to rule making and following.

The definiteness and credibility of these last thoughts are deepened by a number of the numerous recent thinkers, in particular Ludwig Wittgenstein and Jacques Derrida, who have followed Montaigne and Hobbes in focusing on the language in which ruling, rules, and rule following do and must occur. These thinkers, and more especially Michael Oakeshott, also help us to appreciate that conditions, further to ruling, rules, and rule following "themselves," are equally necessary if practices featuring rules are to produce either (or both) the goods or the ills commonly associated with them.

In what some regard as the more comforting moments in his post-*Tractarian* thinking, Wittgenstein advances a variant of the view that we often do "know how to go on" with our language games, do succeed in conducting practices and in sustaining institutions that prominently feature rules and rule following. He also promotes a version of the view that often we think of ourselves as having "no choice" but to go on in a particular manner; that our conventions, rules, training, and the like allow us one and only one action, judgment, or conclusion. In these aspects of Wittgenstein's thinking, regularity, certainty, and predictability are salient features of our practices and activities; they cannot be understood apart from the role that rules, ruling, and rule-governedness play in our affairs.[4]

Remarks such as I have quoted in the foregoing note elevate rules and rule-following to an enormously important place in describing, understanding, and assessing human activities. If action occurs exclusively or primarily through or in language, if language has meaning, and if in the absence of rules language has no meaning, it would be difficult to exaggerate the importance of rules and rule-governedness in human affairs. Rules and rule following are mainstays in that they introduce into human affairs not only observable regularity but meaning or intelligibility, steadiness, and mutual confidence.

Rules and rule following are also blessings in that they enable both retail and wholesale assessments of actions and actors, performances and performers. Reading a for the most part well-formed student paper, I point out that this word is misspelled, that here one should use *who* not *whom*, *that* not *which*. Going over the bill for repairs to my car, I note that six, not seven, should have been carried from the second to the first column of numbers. Finding numerous such mistakes, I suggest that the student enroll in the remedial writing course or perhaps that the cashier be cashiered. And should we encounter someone who has been taught arithmetic (English grammar, *The Chicago Manual of Style,* Robert's Rules of Order, what is and isn't said at department meetings, dinner parties, or in the locker room) but who "goes on obstinately getting different results . . . when he does a given multiplication [etc.] . . . then we should declare him abnormal and take no further account of his calculations" (Wittgenstein, 1956, p. 112) (urge him to take up vocational education, campaign against his reelection, deny him tenure, ostracize him socially) or perhaps declare him to be a "lunatic" (1964, *Brown*, p. 30) or "a fool and a heretic" (1969, p. 611).

This picture of the place of rules and rule following, while not false, is seriously incomplete and misleading. The features of our affairs that it highlights cannot be sufficiently explained, understood, or assessed by reference to rules and rule following "as such," and they coexist with quite different characteristics that remain not only despite but importantly because of the prominence of rules and rule following among us. At the risk of imposing an organization that Wittgenstein self-consciously avoids (1953, preface), we can distinguish among (1) the preconditions or suppositions of all rules and rule following, (2) the elements that typically do and very often must accompany and complement these or those rules and rule followings, and (3) the many features of human affairs that are outside of and in some respects incompatible with rules and rule following.

In discussing the considerations I gather under 1 above, Wittgenstein frequently uses the concept of "nature"; he speaks of "general facts of nature," "natural history," and the like. For example the many activities that involve measuring depend on the durable qualities both of what we measure and of the devices by which we make our measurements.[5] Of course such natural or general facts (including facts about balances, yardsticks, and the like) are *what* they are, are called by certain names, are used in certain ways, and so forth, owing to conventions and rules that we have formulated and for the most part follow. But *that* nature includes materials that have or can be assigned these characteristics—so far from being a result of our ruling or rule making—is a condition of the latter.

It would be impossible—as impossible as it would be useless—to iterate all of the facts of nature on which our rules and rule following depend. It is worth underlining, however, that a great many such facts are about *us*, are part of our "natural history" as human beings.[6] Wittgenstein observes that his remark about lumps of cheese "will become clearer when we discuss such things as the relation of expression to feeling and similar topics" (1953, I, p. 142). He pays on this promissory note in arguing against the notion that pain, as well as intention and a wide array of other "mentalistic" concepts, refers to necessarily "private" sensations or experiences.[7] Such sensations and experiences, or at least their "primitive, natural expressions," are a necessary but not a sufficient condition of much of the public, rule-governed language that we in fact use. "What is the natural expression of an intention?—Look at a cat when it stalks a bird, or a beast when it wants to escape. ((Connexion with propositions about sensations))" (1953, I, p. 647).[8]

We now move (albeit by way of gradual and uneven transitions) from (1) the facts of nature presupposed by all rules and rule following to (2) conditions and circumstances, dependent on but not reducible to facts of nature, that accompany any practice or institution that "involves" rules, and to (3) respects in which our acting is and must go beyond rule following. Because these further conditions and characteristics are also often left unmentioned, indeed are often "excluded from view," attention to them is pertinent to the question of what rules and rule following can and cannot do for and to us.

In discussing abnormalities such as color blindness and "aspect-blindness" (e.g., people who simply don't see figures three-dimensionally; see especially 1953, II, p. xi; 1956, passim), Wittgenstein calls attention to kinds of rule following that are simply impossible for some people. These observations about natural defects or deficiencies dramatize the importance of affirmative characteristics that loom very large in all of his accounts of rule following and more generally of "knowing how to go on" with an activity or practice. The most basic of these characteristics is what might be called "educability," including the capacity to profit from instruction in rules and rule following; to grasp the meaning, see the point or purpose of a rule (1953, I, p. 564); to "master the techniques" (1953, I, p. 199) of applying this or that rule.[9] Educability in this sense is a fact of nature presupposed by rules and rule following. But it is only a *general* fact of nature. Just as many but not all dogs can be trained to retrieve, so most but not all human beings can "get the knack" of rule-governed activities and practices such as parsing sentences and doing simple arithmetic.

Various of the words that make up rule-governed languages refer to "things" and are defined or taught "ostensively," that is, by physically singling out the things that are their referents or objects. At once echoing and going beyond Hobbes, Wittgenstein insists that these definitions and teachings can "be variously interpreted in every case" (1953, I, p. 28). In pointing, the teacher or definer has necessarily selected among various "aspects" of the "things" in her perceptual field. In addition, her pointing or other gesturing is itself a communicative device no less equivocal than the word it seeks to teach or define. "The arrow points only in the application that a living being makes of it" (1953, I, p. 454). "One has already to know (or be able to do) something in order to be capable of asking a thing's name. But what does one have to know? When one shews someone the king in chess and says: 'This is the king,' this does not tell . . . [the learner] the use of this piece— unless he already knows the rules of the game up to this last point: the shape of the king" (1953, I, pp. 30–31).[10]

Yet more radically, if ostensive teaching establishes an association between word and thing, it can do so "only together with a particular training. With different training the same ostensive teaching . . . would have effected a quite different understanding. 'I set the brake up by connecting rod and lever.' Yes, given the whole of the rest of the mechanism. Only in conjunction with that is it a brake-lever, and separated from its support it is not even a lever; it may be anything, or nothing" (1953, I, p. 6).[11]

The idea of already prepared places, mechanisms, or systems necessary to the meaning of the set of words that forms a rule is generalized in Wittgenstein's notions of "language games" and "forms of life." These latter concepts stand for more or less integrated ensembles or gestalts the recurrent elements of which have come to be recognized as having "family resemblances" one to the other. As Montaigne emphasizes in a slightly different diction, what we might call famili-arity with these "families" is a condition of understanding stipulations or ostensive teachings of this or that word and therefore also of being able to understand and follow (or refuse to follow) rules made up of sets or sequences of words.

Of the numerous components that (variously) compose or constitute such families, Wittgenstein lays particular emphasis on what he calls "agreements in judgment."

It is what human beings *say* that is true and false [right and wrong, apt or inept]; and they agree in the *language* they use. This is not agreement in opinions but in form of life. If language is to be a means of communication there must be agreement not only in definitions [stipulations, promulgations] but also (queer as this may sound) in judgments. This seems to abolish logic [arithmetic, law, industrial management] but does not do so." (1953, I, pp. 241–42)

Rather, rule-governed practices and activities would be impossible in the absence of agreements in judgments."We do not learn the practice of making empirical judgments by learning rules: we are taught *judgments* and their connexion with other judgments. A *totality* of judgments is made plausible to us" (1969, p. 140).[12]

What if all of the foregoing conditions are satisfied, all of the non-rule-governed elements of rule-governed practice are in place? Several points need to be made here. The first is that these are the circumstances in which we most often have a sense of definiteness, fixity, and certitude concerning our affairs and interactions. It is under these conditions that we are most likely to use expressions such as "surely you can see," to think that going on in a particular way is "a matter of course," and to regard nonstandard behavior as abnormality. Accordingly, they are also the circumstances in which rules and rule following are most prominent in our self-characterizations, explanations, and evaluations of our own conduct and the conduct of others. Nor, to repeat, are these characterizations and estimations of the prominence of rules erroneous or unwarranted. Rules *do* have these features; rule following *does* consist of conduct that occurs under the foregoing conditions and has the foregoing characteristics; rules and rule following *are* prominent in our affairs.

The further points I have anticipated above are consistent with the first one but they have an importantly different tendency. As already discussed in part, *explicit attention to* item 3, the non-rule-governed elements presupposed by or usually present in our rules and rule following, is neither necessary to nor ordinarily a part of our rule-governed practices and activities. Rather, these practices and activities exclude numerous of their elements from our view, blind us to them. "It may be . . . that *enquiry on our part* is set so as to exempt certain propositions from doubt, if they are ever formulated" (1969, p. 88).[13] There are respects in which this must be the case. "If the true is what is grounded, then the ground is not *true*, nor yet false." "'How am I able to obey a rule?'—if this is not a question about causes, then it is about the justification for my following the rule in the way I do. If I have exhausted the justifications I have reached bedrock, and my spade is turned. Then I am inclined to say: 'This is simply what I do.'" "When I obey a rule, I do not choose. I obey the rule *blindly*" (1953, I, pp. 217, 219).

Taken at all literally, these further remarks sharply diminish the sense that rules and rule following are means by which we achieve control over and give deliberate direction to our activities. In these remarks Wittgenstein treats rules and rule following as having a mechanical, a mindless character. They produce regularity and predictability, but often without or at the expense of critical self- or mutual awareness.

If we shift to the key of miracle/misfortune, blessing/curse, these remarks remind us that, of those who would agree with the foregoing characterizations of rules and rule following, some estimate them favorably because they give assurance of continuity and stability, others condemn them for engendering unthinking and nonadaptive behavior. Wittgenstein does not declare himself in these evaluative terms. Rather, he calls attention to respects in which, even when all of the foregoing elements or features of rules and rule following are firmly in place, rules remain indeterminate as to what they require and forbid. Even the most conscientious rule following necessarily involves judgments, decisions, and choices that are (but is this a redundancy?) non-rule-governed.

The proposition that I obey the rule blindly is "symbolical"; it is a "mythological description of the use of a rule" (1953, I, pp. 220–21). This is not to say that the proposition is false. Rule following *is* "blind" in the sense that it ordinarily excludes from view presuppositions and accompaniments of the rule and the activity of following it. But the proposition perpetrates and perpetuates the mythology that rules—even taken to mean not only the rule formulations but all of their presuppositions and accompaniments—do or could determine all of the steps that I take in following them.

The first and (in the present perspective) arguably the most important point here is that the fact that something is an established rule may raise but cannot itself settle the question of whether the rule ought to be obeyed. As Hobbes, Hume, H. L. A. Hart, Oakeshott, and numerous other thinkers have emphasized, the obligation to obey a rule presupposes (in addition to the presuppositions that Wittgenstein foregrounds in passages discussed above) my acceptance, commitment, or subscription to the rule or to the system of rules of which this rule is a part. In respect to legal rules, Hart famously argues that the "primary" rules that require or forbid this or that form of conduct presuppose a "secondary" rule (the "rule of recognition") according to which this or that purported law actually has authority or standing. But even if such a secondary rule is established in the sense of being widely accepted in my society, it is a rule *for me*—and hence the primary rules it authorizes are legal rules *for me*—only if I accept or subscribe to it. I may accept or subscribe to the secondary rule as a "matter of course" or I may invoke general moral principles as reasons for doing so. But just as there neither are nor can be *moral* rules for accepting the foundational or constitutive principles of morality, so there neither are nor can be *legal* rules for accepting the "secondary" rule that lends legal authority to primary legal rules (Hart, 1962). However determinate or indeterminate rules may be in further respects, in this perspective they are and must remain underdetermined and underdetermining.[14]

Focusing on language generally, in remarks such as the following Wittgenstein makes a related but more widely applicable point:

> I said that the application of a word is not everywhere bounded by rules. But what does [e.g.] a game look like that is everywhere bounded by rules? whose rules never let a doubt creep in, but stop up all the cracks where it might?—Can't we imagine a rule determining the application of a rule, and a doubt which it removes—and so on?
> . . . [No!] A rule stands there like a sign-post.—Does the sign-post leave no doubt open about the way I have to go on? Does it shew which direction I am to take when I have passed it; whether along the road or the footpath or cross-country? But where is it said which way I am to follow it; whether in the direction of its finger or (e.g.) in the opposite one?— And if there were, not a single sign-post, but a chain of adjacent ones or of chalk marks on the ground—is there only *one* way of interpreting them? (1953, I, pp. 84–85)

The issue is not whether we usually or often respond in uniform and predictable ways to signposts, directives, and rules. Of established rules it will usually be redundant to say that most of us do so. Rather, the issue is the extent to which the existence of a signpost, directive, or rule sufficiently explains the regularities and predictabilities in our conduct and how, at the same time, that explanation can be made consistent not only with occasional irregularities and deviance but with the frequent fact of disagreement concerning what counts as obeying the rule.

It is important to remember that rules, rule following, and related practices themselves form families of cases that vary along differing dimensions. I may issue the directive,

> "Stand roughly here"—may not this explanation work perfectly? [Yes.] . . . But isn't it an inexact explanation? Yes; . . . Only let us understand . . . [that] "inexact" . . . does not mean "unusable." . . . "Inexact" is really a reproach, and "exact" is praise. . . . Am I inexact when I do not give our distance from the sun to the nearest foot, or tell a joiner the width of a table to the nearest thousandth of an inch? No *single* ideal of exactness has been laid down; we do not know what we should be supposed to imagine under this head. (1953, I, pp. 88)[15]

Postponing for the moment the question of whether there are cases that involve a more established and definite notion of exactness, as regards the innumerable cases to which the foregoing remarks readily apply it suffices to say that "the sign-post is in order—if, under normal circumstances, it fulfills its purpose"—that is, its purpose as more or less generally understood or agreed upon by those actually involved in the activity in question. The arrival of a demand for a more determinate account of how rules and rule following are and *must be* exacting, do and (if they are to deserve the standing of rules and rule following) *must* produce or yield "exact" results, is an indication that the demand is driven by an "engine" (most commonly the engine that is a certain conception of philosophy, of law, of computation, of musical composition, or the like) that is not usefully connected to practice, an engine that is no more than "idling" in respect to the activities in which rules and rule following play a practical part (1953, I, p. 88).

What if we the rule makers or enforcers are convinced that a rule *is* exact? Here is a case that we are likely to think of in this way. Teaching someone simple arithmetic, we train a pupil to add 2 + 2 and get 4, to add 2 to 566 and get 568, and so forth. Having learned the rule "X + 2" we expect that the rule itself will determine, for our pupil as for ourselves, an indefinitely large number of further calculations. If the rule did not do so, either we could not have arithmetic at all or the rule governing "+2" could not be a rule of or in it.

But now we ask the pupil to continue the same series "beyond 1000—and he writes 1000, 1004, 1008, 1012."

> We say to him: "Look what you've done!"—He doesn't understand. We say: "You were meant to add *two*: look how you began the series!"—He answers: "Yes, isn't it right? I thought that was how I was *meant* to do it."—Or suppose he pointed to the series and said: "But I went on in the same way."—It would now be no use to say: "But can't you see . . . ?"—and repeat the old examples and explanations.—In such a case we might say, perhaps: It comes natural to this person to understand our order with our explanations as *we* should understand the order: "Add 2 up to 1000, 4 up to 2000, 6 up to 3000 and so on." (1953, I, p. 185)

Wittgenstein then imagines his interlocutor to object: "What you are saying . . . comes to this: a new insight—intuition—is needed at every step to carry out the order +n correctly." This response fails to appreciate, or begs the question raised by, the example.

> To carry it out correctly! How is it decided what is the right step to take at any particular stage? . . . that is just what is in question: what, at any stage, are we to call "being in accord" with that proposition (and with the *mean*-ing you then put into the proposition—whatever that may have consisted in)? It would almost be more correct to say, not that an intuition was needed at every stage, but a new decision was needed at every stage. (1953, I, p. 186)

This response is not wrong. In another place Wittgenstein notes that whereas he often speaks of "being compelled by a rule," it is "equally important" "that I can *choose* to follow it" (1956, V, p. 46). Insofar as we can align this "choosing" with deciding how rather than whether to go on following the rule, we get an intricate combination of characteristics of rule following. On the one hand, rules dictate to us, determine our conduct. But at the same time, rule following not only allows but requires and enables decisions and choices on our part.

This same combination of characteristics is present in one of the most widely discussed passages in Wittgenstein's numerous remarks about rules and rule following:

> This was our paradox: no course of action could be determined by a rule, because every course of action can be made out to accord with

the rule. The answer was: if everything can be made out to accord with the rule, then it can also be made out to conflict with it. And so there could be neither accord nor conflict here. (1953, I, p. 200)

It seems to follow that rules and rule following are indeed mirages. Although we write, speak, and otherwise act as if we guide and are guided (see 1953, I, pp. 172–73), determine and are strictly determined by rules, in fact our "rules" are, at best, never more than after-the-fact redescriptions of actions that we took for other reasons or for none. Our most clearly formulated rules "leave loopholes open, and the practice has to speak for itself" (1969, p. 139).

This is correct and important. What is correct and important about it is that "'obeying a rule' is a practice" (1953, I, pp. 200–201), a practice or continuing activity that includes the various elements discussed above. In this sense, rules do not and cannot speak for themselves, do not and cannot fully determine conduct. Yet "it can be seen that there is a misunderstanding here." This can be seen

> from the mere fact that in the course of our argument [that is, in attempting to give an account (perhaps especially a philosophical or jurisprudential account) of rules and rule following] we give one interpretation after another; as if each one contented us at least for a moment, until we thought of yet another standing behind it. What this shews is that there is a way of grasping a rule [i.e., the way we often "grasp" a rule that we are actually following] which is *not* an *interpretation*, but which is exhibited in what we call "obeying a rule" and "going against it" in actual cases. (p. 201)

What in ordinary language we *call* obeying and going against a rule is conduct that has the features—some number of the features characteristic of this family of related activities—of the practice of rule following.

The immediate lessons are threefold. The first, which has two closely connected parts, is that we must not "sublime" rules. As participants in the practices of ruling and rule following we ought not (though we often do) delude ourselves into thinking that rules form "strict calculi," calculi that, by themselves or of their own accord as it were, do, could, or should fully determine our actions. And as theorists or philosophers of ruling and rule following, we must not delude ourselves into thinking that we have or could identify the "essence" of these practices, have or could hope to discover (or to stipulate success-fully) the necessary and sufficient conditions of any and all instances of such practices. The second lesson teaches us to avoid those dogmatic forms of practical and theoretical skepticism that, reacting inappro-priately to the first lesson, deny the reality or possibility of what we ordinarily call rules and rule following.[16] The third lesson is not to confuse the ensemble of ruling and rule-governed practices with the numerous activities that include, *if at all*, the characteristics of such practices only in that they involve the partly rule-governed phenome-non of language.[17]

III

I remarked above that we ought not but often do (and are often urged to) sublime rules, ought not but often do overestimate the range and decisiveness of rules and rule following in our affairs and activities. These remarks are faithful to Wittgenstein's texts. In teaching the les-sons of his investigations and reflections, he is (and Montaigne and Hobbes are) intensely aware that his pedagogy is countercyclical, that it goes against the grain of what is widely (and not unreasonably or at least not absurdly) believed and certainly against the grain of what is (e.g., by Descartes) fervently hoped. We might speculate that, se-lectively read and appropriated, Wittgenstein's (and Montaigne's and Hobbes's) remarks will give a certain comfort to those for whom it is of the utmost importance that human affairs be stable if not static, reliably calculable and perhaps readily and routinely predictable.[18] After all, no one of these three thinkers denies or deplores the fact that there is substantial regularity and continuity in human affairs. And if they are correct that these characteristics are due primarily or importantly to rote, habitual, and even mindless conformity with the received and the established, this may be reason for rejoicing rather than regret, reason to expect greater stability and reliability than could be expected from self-conscious and self-critical rule making and rule following. Plato was not the first and certainly not the last to believe that reflection and deliberation, unless confined to the reliable few, are disruptive and unsettling.

From a social, moral, and especially a political and legal perspective, the foregoing remarks suggest the following question-cum-hope or aspiration. If the members of a social, moral, political-legal system *believe*—can be induced to believe—that they "have no choice" but to act in this or that particular way in these or those circumstances, that belief might itself bring about the order and predictability that regularian theorists and practitioners crave. In this perspective what matters is not the logic or truth of the arguments but the contents and effects of the beliefs. And whereas Wittgenstein not only insists on but is untroubled by the "prodigious diversity" and "open texture," the flux, indeterminacy, and opacity, of our language games,[19] these are the very features that many of those whom I have styled regularians are keen to diminish if not to eradicate. In attempting to eradicate the diverse and difficult to classify elements of our affairs by promoting firm and uniform beliefs that in turn produce and sustain order and predictability, they dramatize the ideological character of their thinking.[20]

I do not mean to deny that there are proponents of "well-ordered" societies, of constitutionalism and the rule of law, of principled and rule-governed moral, political, and economic practices, who genuinely believe that these desiderata can and ought to be sustained by considered, deliberative, and self-critical rationality (Hayek, Rawls, and Habermas are prominent among numerous recent advocates of such views). Thinkers and practitioners of this persuasion are likely either to dissent from or to regret sharply any concessions they feel obliged to make to the views I have been canvassing. From such perspectives, Montaigne, Hobbes, and Wittgenstein lend or attribute to ruling and being ruled a large and objectionable element of arbitrariness. Arbitrariness being, from a regularian perspective, the antithesis of ruling and rule-governedness, any regularities or predictabilities that may result from it compromise the possibilities that regularian thinking cherishes and promotes.

In order to assess the regularian project further, I appropriate elements of a view that is analogous to Wittgenstein's, Montaigne's, and Hobbes's, but that has a yet sharper critical edge.

In a lively engagement with Kafka's stunning miniature *Before the Law*, Jacques Derrida plays out by repeatedly playing on Kafka's maddening image of the rustic who is summoned before the law but who is prevented by the law's guardian from actually "reaching" it, prevented from closing the juridical and normative, the conceptual and psychological, distance between himself and the law itself.

Derrida gives a twofold account of the "inaccessibility" of the law. One part of this account is strongly continuous with Wittgenstein's discussions of rules and rule following. From the moment that the law "begins to speak and to question the moral subject," that is, from the moment that legislators, judges, and police officers, CEOs and union officials, colonels and sergeants, provosts, deans, and teachers attempt to promote the authority and bindingness of rules, "historicity," "narrativity," and hence "imagination" and "fiction" are introduced "into the very core of legal thought" (1992, p. 190). With these features inevitably come those uncertainties and indeterminacies that Wittgenstein foregrounds. In part for this reason, the subjects, try as they might, can never achieve "a rapport of respect" with the law (p. 203).

The guardians of the law further complicate matters by deliberately as well as unwittingly "interrupting" the relation between the subject and the law or other rules. Why? Because, Derrida suggests, they realize—however dimly—that full access to the rules would profane them, would deprive the law of what Kant called its "categorical authority." In order for laws and other rules to have such authority there must be a "law of laws," one that is "without history, genesis, or any possible derivation." If "historicity and empirical narrativity" would permit the subjects of this law of laws to achieve rapport with it, these same qualities would jeopardize the majesty or sanctity that the law must have in order to govern conduct effectively. Representatives of the law (Kafka's doorkeeper) are "interrupters as well as messengers"; by preventing the subjects from gaining access to the law of laws and hence to the law they combat the effects of the historicity and narrativity that they themselves—sometimes inadvertently, sometimes knowingly—have introduced into both (p. 204).

It is of course no part of Derrida's (or Kafka's) view that there is or could be such a thing as a purely or entirely ahistorical concept or idea—of the law of laws, of law, or of anything else. But what if subjects can be gotten to *believe* that there is a law of laws with these characteristics, a Law that authorizes, sanctifies, makes binding each of the particular laws or rules that gather under the "genre" that the law of laws regulates or constitutes? What if they believe—can be gotten to want desperately to believe—that somewhere in the forbidden recesses guarded by the uncountable doorkeepers there is a pure and perfect LAW, a LAW unsullied by the contingencies and indeterminacies that come along with historicity, narrativity, and imagination. If, as appears to be the case with Kafka's doorkeeper, the guardians believe that they are the keepers of such a LAW, they might be more unyielding and otherwise resourceful in sustaining their belief in its purity and the rigor appropriate to conformity to it. If the subjects of the law believe that there is such a LAW, as appears to be the case with Kafka's man from the country, they might be more likely to submit "blindly" to the directives and punishments of the guardians. As a matter of conduct, "blind" acceptance of the deep convention that is the law of laws might make up the deficits left and created by the laws themselves and by the less determinate and more fluctuating conventions intermediate between the law of laws and the law.

Faithful to Kafka's tale, Derrida thinks that, in reality, the subjects of law (and also, if with less self-awareness, the guardians?) are always and inescapably in "the terrifying double-bind" of Kafka's man from the country. They at once must and cannot know what the law is. They desperately want the assurances of a legal or otherwise rule-governed order and the respect that comes with recognized fidelity to it. What they get is doubt, guilt, and shame. They are "both . . . subject[s] of the law and . . . outlaw[s]" (p. 204). The upshot seems to be that subjects of law are fated to the despair and humiliating shrinkage of self that befalls Kafka's rustic.

Derrida does not draw the anarchist or the powerfully antinomian inference that his story might appear to mandate. Like Montaigne, Hobbes, and Wittgenstein, he knows perfectly well that there are effective laws and working legal, moral, and other normalizing and disciplinary systems; that in fact we often "go on" successfully with activities that bring us "before" such systems. And it seems to be his view that a law of laws, and messengers/interrupters who at once enforce and restrict access to that law, are always or at least typically elements of such ruled and rule-governed activities and practices. In this and numerous other volumes, Derrida is concerned with the "law of the genre" that purports and is widely believed to stand to "Acts of Literature" as the law of laws is alleged to stand to the acts of adopting, enforcing, and obeying the laws that governments make. By engaging texts that are uncontroversially within the genre of literature and are therefore "before" the purported Law of that genre, he exposes the dissonances and paradoxes of that relationship, displays their effects on the activities that produce and surround Acts of Literature. The anarchist and antinomian counsel, we might say, is a counsel of despair. Alternatively, if it is our own beliefs, at once force-fed to us and desperately maintained by us, that sustain the law of laws, it is so disturbing a counsel that we will all but certainly reject it.

In these respects, Derrida's and Wittgenstein's view of regularian thinking departs from those of advocates of such thinking and practicing. The former depart from the latter primarily in their refusal to make exaggerated claims concerning the certitude and predictability that rules and rule-governedness, as such, do or can afford. Insofar as certitude and predictability obtain, they are produced not by rules and rule following "themselves," but by the inculcation and acceptance of beliefs and attitudes that surround and inform the practices of ruling and rule following. Even if we grant the claim of Hume and Kant, Hayek, and any number of other thinkers that regularian thinking and acting sometimes yield estimable results, we should be aware of how and why they do and do not do so and we should be alert to the ways in which such thinking and acting diminish our agency as well as produce patterns of conduct that are objectionable by instrumentalist standards. In a larger sense than I have employed above, this is the lesson taught by the several thinkers considered in the foregoing sections.

IV

By way of concluding, I examine a theory, or rather an imagining, of kinds of rules and a kind of rule following that, could they be realized, would recommend a less chastened or distancing stance toward these notions and practices.

"Taken precisely," Michael Oakeshott avers, "the expression 'the rule of law'. . . stands for a mode of moral association [consisting of *personae* indistinguishably and] exclusively [related in respect of] . . . the recognition of the authority of known, non-instrumental rules . . . which impose obligations to subscribe to adverbial conditions in the performance of self-chosen actions of all who fall within their jurisdiction" (1983, p. 136).[21]

Dense if not turgid, this passage demands considerable unpacking. The idea that is finally most important in the vision it enunciates is that of a mode of human association that would be characterized and distinguished from all others not by its collective purposes or its institutionalized, rule-constituted and rule-governed structures, but by the "personae" of its subscribers and the qualities that their thinking and acting do and do not manifest. It is the vision of an association all of the members of which have their own ends and purposes that they pursue through their self-chosen actions. Members as such (*"cives"*) are associated with one another not by agreement in objective or purpose but exclusively by their subscription to "adverbial" considerations, considerations that do not require them to do this or that but rather that they do whatever they do in certain (civil) ways or manners, obligate them to avoid doing whatever they do in an uncivil fashion.

As is evident from Oakeshott's willingness to denominate his vision as association in terms of the "rule of law,"[22] institutionalized rules and rule following are integral to it. The distinguishing features of this vision, however, are not its institutions or practices in what we might call their material, rule-governed form but rather the understandings its *personae* have of themselves, of their relationships with one another, and of the arrangements to which they mutually subscribe. They think of themselves, in part, in the instrumental terms of agents disclosing and enacting themselves by "imagining" and pursuing various and fluctuating "substantive satisfactions." More important for present purposes, they also understand themselves as agents who pursue their purposes with consideration for adverbial requirements enunciated in law and in various other principles and rules.

These features of Oakeshott's vision of political associations governed by the rule of law inform my thought that subscribers to such associations would adopt an affirmative stance toward its rules and the requirements those rules place on them. To pursue this thought, I consider respects in which Oakeshott's construal of the rule of law is continuous with and departs from reflections about rules and rule following already discussed.

A pronounced feature of Oakeshott's account, one that at once accentuates and deepens views discussed above, is his insistence on the nonpurposive, noninstrumental, purely adverbial character of the rules and relationships that compose a rule of law association. In this respect his view of the rule of law participates in the refusal, common among the thinkers previously discussed, to make exaggerated claims concerning the certitude and predictability that rules afford. Laws "are unavoidably indeterminate" and the judicial procedures through which they are applied to particular cases are not only "an exercise in retrospective casuistry" but something of a "devious engagement," one that has no concern with the intentions of legislators, knows of no absolute rights, and looks to previous cases not for binding precedents but for "the analogical force of the distinctions they invoke" (1983, p. 147). Although largely operating with and through its own internal rules of procedure and evidence, and in part because the latter are also "un-

avoidably indeterminate," judicial deliberations "float upon the acknowledgement that the considerations in terms of which the *jus* of
lex may be discerned are neither arbitrary, nor unchanging, nor uncontentious, and that they are the product of moral experience which is
never without tensions and internal discrepancies" (pp. 143–44).

By contrast with the view that rules and rule following require resolutely held beliefs concerning what the rules require and forbid, association in terms of the rule of law has "no place for enthusiasm."
It postulates, rather, "a severe and incurious kind of faithfulness or
ceremoniousness which modifies without emasculating the self-chosen
character of human conduct" (1983, pp. 148–49). The freedom or agency
subserved by the rule of law is a presupposition, not a consequence, of
the mode of association it names (p. 161); the rule of law "bakes no
bread, . . . is unable to distribute loaves or fishes, . . . and [what in the
violent history of the modern European state has proved to be its most
serious deficiency] it cannot protect itself against external assault."
Nevertheless, "it remains the most civilized and least burdensome conception of a state yet to be devised" (p. 164).

In the "Rule of Law" Oakeshott is decidedly sparing of examples
of rules that are purely adverbial in character; he leaves—perhaps
deliberately—that notion in a somewhat obscure or elusive condition.
In the more extensive discussion in *On Human Conduct*, in the course
of arguing that the norms and rules of moral and all other human
"practices" are of this character, he elaborates on the notion in the following terms: "A practice may be identified as a set of considerations,
manners, uses, observances, customs, standards, canons, maxims, principles, rules and offices specifying useful procedures or denoting obligations or duties which relate to human actions and utterances. It is . . . an
adverbial qualification of choices and performances . . . in which conduct is understood in terms of a procedure." The emblems of such
considerations are concepts "such as punctually, considerately, civilly,
scientifically, legally, candidly, judicially, poetically, morally, etc." These
concepts "do not specify performances; they postulate performances
and specify procedural conditions to be taken into account when
choosing and acting" (1975, pp. 55–56). (The conditions they postulate,
however, are very different from those supposed or promoted by regularian thinking and practice.)

All human action involves both substance and procedure. The former enters through the agent's choice of an "imagined and wished-

for" outcome or satisfaction, the latter are given by, become available to and obligatory for agents by virtue of practices that specify conditions in which choices are made and acted upon. Returning more explicitly to our present concern with language, we can say that language is a practice or set of practices (a collection of loosely related language games, in Wittgensteinian parlance) the grammatical and other rules of which specify conditions in or under which these or those linguistic performances can/should be enacted. But a "practice [e.g. the practice of musical composition and performance] is an instrument to be played upon, not a tune to be played."[23] By the same reasoning, all languages and their rules are devices or tools that allow us to say this and that but do not and cannot determine *what* we can or should say.[24] "A rule (and *a fortiori* something less exacting, like a maxim) can never tell a performer what choice he shall make; . . . The appearance procedures and rules may have of excluding (forbidding), or more rarely enjoining, substantive choices and actions is illusive. Practices identify actions adverbially; they exclude (forbid) or enjoin them in terms of prescribed conditions."

Turning to the practice in respect to which the illusions he is dispelling are perhaps most widely promoted (because most avidly desired), Oakeshott declares that "a criminal law . . . does not forbid killing or lighting a fire, it forbids killing 'murderously' or lighting a fire 'arsonically'" (1975, pp. 58, 58n.). Of course, because one can, for example, light a fire arsonically only by lighting a fire, laws can forbid arson only by prohibiting certain classes of action.[25] *Cives* who subscribe to such laws will therefore be under obligations to desist from actions they might otherwise take with impunity. Oakeshott is hardly unaware of this. In observed fact, proposals for new laws commonly take their origins from the purposes of their proponents; "there is, indeed, no want which may not set going a project" to change the laws. In actuality, laws commonly yield substantive "benefits or advantages to . . . assignable interests"; for example, "every piece of legislation has an outcome of advantage to a legal profession" (pp. 169–70).

The *personae* of a rule of law association do not (would not) deny these realities. But neither do they make them the primary focus of their thinking and acting. In deliberating proposed changes in *lex*, their question—rather than *Cui bono?*—is how the proposed law would affect the adverbial conditions under which all associates would thereafter be obligated to act. In choosing courses of conduct in the domain of *lex*, they ask (ought to ask) whether the actions they are considering could be performed in a manner consistent with their own civil characters and of the civility of associational life.

Accordingly, life in a rule of law association requires no less than a "disciplined imagination" (1975, p. 165). *Cives* must cultivate their human capacities to imagine desirable outcomes and to devise ways of pursuing them. At the same time, they must subject that imagination and those pursuits to the discipline of the considerations signaled by words such as *politely, temperately,* and *fastidiously; resolutely, candidly,* and *forthrightly; morally, legally,* and *civilly.* If they fail in the first of these endeavors they deteriorate into the dull, ressentiment-laden characters that Oakeshott calls the "individual manqué" and the "anti-individual" (1975, third essay). If they fail in the second task, practices and the rule of law society are gone, the latter in all likelihood replaced by a teleocratic enterprise association the ugly insignia of which are "Purpose, Plan, Policy and Power" (1983, p. 125).

Agreeing with Derrida, Oakeshott insists that attempts at creating and sustaining rule of law association have never succeeded entirely and have rarely succeeded at all for very long. There are deep reasons for this dispiriting fact. In addition to the intricate and never fully harmonious or harmonizable combination of characteristics it demands of its *personae*, the deliberations that such association requires have to be sustained despite the certainty that "there always must be more than one opinion" concerning the questions that arise and hence that the engagement to deliberate them will most often be "vexatious." It "calls for so exact a focus of attention and so uncommon a self-restraint" that we cannot be "astonished to find this mode of human relationship to be as rare as it is excellent" (1975, p. 180).

V

Oakeshott rightly insists that, so understood, "the rule of law cannot" be taken entirely or adequately to characterize any "modern European state" (1975, p. 155). As he articulates and idealizes it, the "expression . . . 'the rule of law' stands for a mode of human relationship that has been glimpsed, sketched in practice, unreflectively and intermittently enjoyed, half understood, left indistinct" (1983, p. 120). If we agree, as we should, with this judgment, we cannot take his accounts of rules and rule following to be entirely accurate descriptions of the goings-on that are usually so denominated and classified. In the teleocratic, rule-fetishizing associations that predominate in our experience, the wary, skeptical stances or attitudes considered above are appropriate. But this conclusion leaves open the possibility that Oakeshott is also correct that the conception of civil or rule of law association that he has glimpsed represents, to repeat, "the most civilized and least burdensome conception of a state yet to be devised." It is civilized in postulating individuality, plurality, and freedom; it is civilized and potentially civilizing in looking to qualities of character, understanding, and spirit rather than power-driven political mechanics to abate the difficulties inherent in political association. The demands it makes, severe as they are, would be as little burdensome for the human beings it postulates and promotes as life in a politically organized and ruled association can be.

If we also agree that the possibility of associations with these characteristics has been and remains elusive, then Oakeshott's reflections concerning the rule of law and related rule-governed practices reinforce results reached through consideration of more widely influential thinking about these institutional devices and the ideologies that surround and inform them. If known politically organized associations (including those said by less discriminating theorists to approximate satisfaction of the requirements of the rule of law) are predominantly teleocracies, then human beings who treasure individuality, plurality, and freedom will (perhaps informed and emboldened by awareness of the contrasting ideal offered by Oakeshott) stand in a vigilant, defensive, even antagonistic posture toward their laws and other institutions and institutionalisms. Oakeshott's idealized conception of rule of law association and of rule-governed practice more generally carries further the Montaignian-Hobbesian-Bakhtinian, the Wittgensteinian-Derridian exposure of the practices and institutions, and more particularly the beliefs and ideologies that most commonly inform and pervade them, that bear the names of ruling, rules, and rule following. Indeed, it stands as a rebuke to prevalent understandings of the latter.

VI

It would be a misunderstanding to think that the theorists I have been discussing aim to abolish ruling, rules, and rule-governed institutions and practices. Moreover, there is little reason to expect that their exposures and rebukes will eradicate the beliefs or void the influences of the ideologies that they critique. To the extent that the beliefs and ideologies in question rest on or are derived from unwitting but corrigible misdescriptions or misestimations of rules and rule following, attention to investigations and reflections such as here considered might diminish somewhat the sway of the dogmas and doctrines in question. As Oakeshott in particular makes clear, however, it is much more plausible to regard regularian thinking as an expression of anxieties and aspirations that are too pervasive and deep-seated to yield readily to such "therapy."

Nor are either the apprehensions or the yearnings that inform regularian thinking difficult to appreciate. The disorder and arbitrariness with which regularians characteristically contrast rule-governed institutions and practices are salient and understandably distressing features of human affairs. If this contrast is well drawn, and if rules and rule following are a mirage, there is ample reason to think that we will go, but not easily, into a dark night of discord and mutual destruction.[26] More affirmatively, ideals such as "Perfect service is perfect freedom" and of a life devoted unqualifiedly to the law of God or the law of a people, nation, state, or other supremely, transcendentally meaningful being or entity, have had and continue to have an irresistible attraction for numerous human beings.

The anti- or reticently nomian thinkers considered here, then, are not mere scolds; they aim at more and better than reproving us for our misunderstandings and admonishing us for our diminishing conceptions of ourselves and our possibilities. On the first count, they help us to understand both how and why exaggerated conceptions of the determinateness of rules and rule following have arisen and have remained influential among us. On the second, they promote a distinctive stance toward rules and rule following, one that, in the often religious terms just invoked, insists that the spirit—as figured in the passage Hobbes quotes from Paul or, better, in the remarks I earlier quoted from Nietzsche—must give life to the letter of the law. They honor the ideals that animate others, but they raise their voices against all attempts to impose, through a system of rules or in any other way, a single ideal on all of us. They agree with Hume and Kant that there is indeed something miraculous about the human capacity to devise and follow rules, to make such devisings and accommodatings mainstays of a wide variety of our activities. The truly miraculous, the blessing of all blessings, is that human beings are sometimes able to harmonize this capacity with a robust and resourceful individuality that goes beyond the spirit as well as the letter of their rules, an individuality that might take any one of us to places where no rule could go.

5 / Liberalism and the Suspect Enterprise of Political Institutionalization: The Case of the Rule of Law

Liberals who promote the ideals of individuality, plurality, and freedom have sometimes been and ought always to be skeptical concerning institutionalism and wary of established political institutions. As with "institutionalizing" a person, to institute an organization, arrangement, or procedure is to attempt to fix and to settle, to structure and to secure, to order and to control, larger or smaller aspects of the thinking and acting of some number of human beings. It is to attempt to render uniform, constant, and predictable that which would otherwise be diverse, fluctuating, and uncertain. By adopting and enforcing the norms and rules, offices and procedures of which institutions primarily consist, successful processes of institutionalization confine and direct the conduct of those who are subject to the arrangements that those processes establish (MacIver, 1914, pp. 109–10). As antinomians and individualist anarchists—whose thoughts haunt the best liberal thinking—constantly insist, these processes stand in a troubling and often troubled relationship with the ideals of individuality, plurality, and freedom.

Of course, liberalism as a specifically political tendency of thought cannot altogether do without institutions or entirely avoid commitment to the values forwarded by institutionalism. As an outlook that accepts (however ruefully) the all-things-considered desirability of some rule by government, liberalism is also obliged to accept the on-balance benefit of the institutionalization of some aspects of human affairs. Lacking the resolve or courage, perhaps reckless, of the antinomian and the anarchist, liberals perforce accommodate themselves to authority, power, and the fixity, structure, and control that those who possess them incessantly seek to establish.

As exemplified by prominent liberal treatments of the rule of law, influential liberal thinkers and much liberal practice have gone far beyond accommodating to institutionalization and institutions, have lost or suppressed awareness of the tensions between liberal ideals and the array of values and procedures that collect under the ideological rubric of institutionalism.

The minimal and least objectionable manifestation of institutionalist thinking is the view that institutionalized government can *contribute* to the realization of the ideals of individuality, plurality, and freedom. I have argued elsewhere that this is the view of that "protoliberal" Hobbes (Flathman, 1993), and I maintain here that a stance akin to Hobbes's skepticism concerning institutionalism is the appropriate one for liberalism to take.

A substantially stronger manifestation of the tendency is the view, argued by Locke and Kant and dominant in liberal theory from Kant to Rawls, that institutionalized government is a *causally necessary* condition of the realization of liberal ideals. This view allows rejection of particular forms of government and sometimes includes skepticism concerning forms of institutionalization such as corporatism. But it excludes the possibility, held open by Hobbes's view, of circumstances in which commitment to liberal ideals requires opposition to the institution of government as such. More serious, it loads the liberal argumentational and rhetorical dice against positions that seek to engender a nervous combination of grudging acceptance and pervasive suspicion of government and politics.

There are many further variations on these themes and instances of yet stronger connections between liberalism and institutionalism. Particular institutional forms—for example representative or direct democracy, the separation of powers or cabinet government—are often viewed as strongly contributive to and even as necessary conditions of achieving liberal values and objectives. Such views inform bastard expressions such as "liberal democracy" that conflate liberalism with a particular institutional form, and they are at the heart of theories of liberalism that consist in articulations of preferred institutional structures.

We have also been treated to delineations of liberal ideals—for example Montesquieu's definition of liberty as the "right of doing whatsoever the laws permit"—that link those ideals *conceptually* and hence necessarily to particular institutional forms or arrangements.[1] On such views—for example the *Rechtsstaat*-cum-Hayekian view that virtually reduces "liberal society" to fidelity to the rule of law and liberalism to advocacy of such a society—there can be no conflict or tension between the ideal and the institution, not so much as the possibility of pursuing the ideal by weakening the institution. Liberalism melds into institutionalism such that the former cannot be understood or supported without reference to and support of the latter.

With the exception of the position I have attributed to Hobbes, these views are hasty and otherwise ill considered. Theorists who proclaim a causally necessary or otherwise invariant relationship between an institutional form and the flourishing of liberal projects exceed the evidence on which they depend and introduce rigidity and overdetermination into liberal thinking and practice. All institutionalization necessarily disserves liberal ideals to some extent; empirically, the institutions that these positions privilege have sometimes worked largely for, have not infrequently worked importantly against, realization of those ideals.[2]

Liberal proponents of the views to which I have alluded aim to use less dangerous forms of institutionalism to contain what they regard as at once the most necessary and most dangerous of all institutions. Convinced that government is essential to a liberal society, they seek to control what they fully expect to be persistent attempts to put its authority and power to unnecessary and otherwise unwarranted uses. They recognize that government's institutionalized standing, together with wide acceptance of the doctrine that established institutions ought to be supported, is the source of much of the danger that government poses. Accordingly, they look to institutionalization and institutionalism themselves as means of keeping government under restraint. They fight the dangerously spreading fire of institutionalized government with the fires of institutionalization. Those who, like Hobbes, depend primarily on non- or little-institutionalized means to keep government within proper bounds are regarded as favoring oppressive government, as naive, or both.

Abstractly considered, there are undeniable merits to the view that institutions and institutionalism can be potent weapons in the struggle to confine and control governmental authority and power. As intersecting and interwoven arrays of beliefs and ideas, principles and rules, offices and procedures, established institutions are concentrations of that which is regarded as authoritative, of formal authority itself, and often of expertise that gives individual persons the standing of authorities concerning certain subject matters and issues.[3] When buttressed by acceptance of the institutionalist view that the rules, procedures, and decisions of established institutions ought to be honored and obeyed, they also become formidable concentrations of power. Successful creation of a variety of institutions, within and without government, may enhance the resources of those who are disposed to restrict and control the activities of government. On the widely received assumption that authority and power can only or can best be controlled by authority and power themselves, institutionalization and institutionalism are necessary or valuable means of achieving this objective. The former propositions, and the latter plausible if risky assumption, inform the view that prudence if not the science of government requires intragovernmental institutional devices such as elections, federalism, and the separation of powers, as well as the proliferation of organized and well-provided extragovernmental institutions such as political parties and interest groups, corporations and unions, churches and professional associations.

Skepticism concerning this view, however, should not be confined to those whose objective is to maximize the range and the efficacy of governmental activity. The authority and power of all such institutions are exercised over those who are in their jurisdictions as well as against the activities of other institutions. If those in positions of institutional authority identify or agree with one another rather than with those who are subject to their jurisdictions—hardly a rare phenomenon—the proliferation of institutions is likely to weaken rather than advantage the positions of the latter. Whatever the merits, for our time, of Hobbes's view that it is less costly to sate the lusts of one than of many rulers, the day of optimistic eighteenth-century political mechanics has passed. We know too much about collusion and co-optation, about the oligarchic tendencies of bureaucratic and other forms of organizational behavior, about the proclivity of institutional elites to generate and effectuate hegemony over those subject to their rule.[4]

In the perspective I have outlined, the institution and form of institutionalism known as the rule of law offends several times over. Its very name doubles both the nominal and the verbal notions of imperative control. The desirability of some number of rules of the distinctively impositional type called laws is presupposed, and a chief thrust of the theories that privilege the rule of law is that promulgated rules and laws ought strictly to govern the conduct of those to whom they apply. It is true that, taken abstractly or formally, the idea of the rule of law speaks primarily to the question of fidelity to law and leaves largely unresolved the issue of the proper scope and content of legal regulation.[5] Perhaps, however, because the significance of the institution they cherish would diminish to the extent that law became a negligible feature of social and political life, more likely because they prize the values of order, control, and predictability that they associate first and foremost with law, numerous proponents of the rule of law have favored extensive use of lawmaking and law-implementing authority. And those of its advocates who have partly dissented from this recommendation have nevertheless held that "free" activities (for example, those that occur in "the market") are successful only or primarily to the extent that they occur in the regularian setting established by perspicuous, general, and prospective legislation and sustained by an impartial and meticulously rule-governed bureaucracy and judiciary. Thus versions of institutionalism that strongly promote the rule of law typically accord high if not principal value to imperatival control and mandatory obedience.

It is less than obvious that this stance is favorable to individuality, plurality, and freedom. If in practice it has sometimes proven to be more favorable to those ideals than competing points of view, we have to consider whether this circumstance is itself an artifact of the too ready, the insufficiently skeptical and cautious, acceptance of the institution of government itself.[6]

I

From Plato and Aristotle through the Roman jurists, the medieval natural law thinkers, the neo-Stoics and modern natural law theorists, Montesquieu and the American founders, the nineteenth-century advocates of the *Rechtsstaat*, and up to contemporary enthusiasts such as Friedrich Hayek and John Rawls, Lon Fuller and Theodore Lowi, champions of the rule of law have assumed the desirability or at least the ineliminable reality of extensive political rule of human conduct. For the thinkers in this long and otherwise varied tradition, anarchism and antinomianism are not attractive but regrettably unrealizable ideals; they are ideas to be disdained and conditions to be feared. The dominant concern of these thinkers, accordingly, has not been whether or how much governance there should be, but rather how to prevent arbitrariness and other misuses of political authority and power.

These general remarks obscure an imperfect but important distinction within rule of law thinking. In the *Laws*, Plato treats a proper system of law as a poor but in all likelihood unsurpassable approximation of the ideal source of constraint, namely, fully philosophical knowledge of the good on the part of rulers. In the *Politics*, Aristotle defines law as "reason without passion." Law suffers the limitations inherent in all practical reasoning and judging, but the laws of a well-conducted "polity" consolidate the best reasonings of its citizenry, while the requirement that rule be by law diminishes the influence of the irrational passions of those "men" whose turn to rule happens to be now. In these views, as in various Roman, traditional, and modern natural law theories, and in theories of the common law as an accretion of the wisdom of experience, the idea of the rule of law includes requirements concerning the content that laws must or must not have in order that rule by them be justified. In some of these views, rules that do not satisfy such requirements are not laws at all, and rule by them is not rule by law. In others, such as those of Hobbes and his legal positivist followers, the question of whether a rule is a law is decided based on its source, not its content, but laws that do not satisfy further criteria may not deserve obedience and rule by them may be unjustifiable.[7]

By contrast, the nineteenth- and twentieth-century thinkers who have given the idea of the rule of law its currently most influential formulations have labored to distinguish between the content of this or that law and the form or formal characteristics of law as such. Many of these thinkers are legal positivists who treat the source of law as its defining property. They argue, however, that the rule of law demands more than that all laws emanate from a jurally authoritative source. Rule by laws that lack characteristics such as clarity, generality, and prospectivity may be rule *by* law or "legality," but it does not meet the requirements of the rule *of* law. Similar requirements are imposed by antipositivist theorists of the rule of law. The theory of the rule of law leaves the content and particular purpose of this and that law to the lawmaking authorities. But it is part of the task of that theory to identify the qualities of law necessary to achieve the purposes of the institution that is the rule of law.

There is, moreover, substantial agreement among recent proponents of the rule of law that the chief such purpose is to subject human conduct to rules, thereby affording predictability in legal relationships and in the interactions that occur within the frame of law. It is also widely agreed that "arbitrariness," primarily defined as particularity and retroactivity but also as uncertainty and unpredictability (little if at all in terms of the intentions or purposes of particular lawmakers), is the single greatest antagonist of these objectives. Assessing these views, which now constitute the version of institutionalism that is the idea of the rule of law, is the present task.

II

As is clear from the distinction between mere legality and the rule of law, the latter is a set of ideas that stands apart from law itself. The ideology provides criteria for determining the extent to which the requirements of the rule of law are satisfied by actual legal systems. Most proponents of the rule of law allow, moreover, that it is an ideal that legal systems may approach but can never entirely realize. This is true concerning those elements of the ideology that are themselves matters of more or less rather than either/or, such as stability, readiness of lay comprehension of the laws, and avoidance of conflicts among the laws.[8]

It is also true of requirements that are frequently taken to allow of complete satisfaction, such as the categorical prohibition of retroactivity and bills of attainder in criminal law. In actuality, *all* general and prospective laws, regardless of the clarity of their formulations, require interpretation in order to be applied to actions and events. For this reason, and because the ideology itself requires that criminal convictions be for actions already taken, those subject to laws can never be entirely certain, when they act, whether their actions will later be adjudged legal or illegal.

The widest and deepest difficulties here reside in the two requirements most frequently associated with the rule of law, generality and prospectivity. In canvassing these difficulties, I begin by attending to the often fulsome formulations of Friedrich Hayek.

Commonly explained by contrasting laws with commands, the generality proper to law concerns the subject of laws in two senses:

their addressees, that is, the persons who are subject to them; and their subject matters, that is, the actions they require or forbid. (I leave aside laws that permit or license rather than require or forbid.) The clearest case of a law that violates the requirement of generality in the first respect is a bill of attainder, a law addressed exclusively to an unambiguously identified person or number of persons. Equally, the clearest case of a law that violates this requirement in the second respect is one that requires or forbids a particular action at a specified time and place (frequently identified as a command, as distinct from a law). Thus in both respects generality is defined by opposition to particularity.

As every reader of Rousseau will attest, it is far more difficult to give an affirmative account of generality. In respect to the addressees of laws, this is the vexed question of classification and of equality before the law. As Hayek concedes, classification is inevitable in law, but "it must be admitted that, in spite of many ingenious attempts . . . no entirely satisfactory criterion has been found that would always tell us what kind of classification is compatible with equality before the law. To say . . . that the law must not make irrelevant distinctions or that it must not discriminate between persons for reasons which have no connection with the purpose of the law is little more than evading the issue" (1960, p. 209).

Matters are no easier in respect to generality in the second sense. To quote Hayek again, "Law in its ideal form might be described as a . . . command that is directed to unknown people and that is abstracted from all particular circumstances of time and place and refers only to such conditions as may occur anywhere and at any time." The notion of obedience to laws that meet these criteria of abstraction is at best elusive; subjects will have no easy time determining what conformity requires. And however perspicuous our *criteria* of generality might become, in all known legal systems the "degree of . . . abstractness ranges continuously from the order that tells a man to do a particular thing here and now to the instruction that, in such and such conditions, whatever he does will have to satisfy certain requirements." Thus "it is advisable . . . not to confuse laws and commands, . . . [but] we must recognize that laws shade gradually into commands as their content becomes more specific" (pp. 149–50).

The utility of conceptions related to Hayek's notion that all actions "will have to satisfy certain requirements" will concern us as we proceed. At this juncture, my interest is in the discordant relation be-

tween the requirement of generality and the objective of predictability. Hayek contrasts predictability with being subject to the "whims" of
those who are in positions of authority. "Arbitrary" rule makes it impossible for subjects to know what rules are in place or forthcoming
and hence makes it impossible for them to plan their activities so as to
avoid punishments. By contrast, in a regime that respects the rule of
law, I as a subject can "know beforehand that if I place myself in a particular position, I shall be coerced." Hence I can "avoid putting myself
in such a position." In this circumstance, "insofar as the rules . . . are not
aimed at me personally . . . they are no different from any of the natural
obstacles that affect my plans. In that they tell me what will happen *if* I
do this or that, the laws of the state have the same significance for me
as the laws of nature" (1960, p. 142).[9] Again:

> In observing such rules, we do not serve another person's end, nor
> can we properly be said to be subject to his will. My action can
> hardly be regarded as subject to the will of another . . . if I use his
> rules for my own purposes . . . and if that person does not know of
> my existence or of the particular circumstances in which the rules
> will apply to me. . . . The law merely alters the means at my disposal
> and does not determine the ends I have to pursue. (pp. 152–53)

These passages are at war with one another. I can avoid being "coerced" and can otherwise confidently predict and plan because the law
gives definite descriptions of the "this's and that's" the doing of which
is required or forbidden. Calculability in this sense requires that I can
know what I may, must, and must not do. Laws have the obtrusive particularity of "natural obstacles." Pursuing this side of his ideal, Hayek
favorably quotes Aristotle's prescription that "it is of great moment
that well drawn laws should themselves define all the points they possibly can, and leave as few as possible to the decision of the judges." Laws
that satisfy this requirement leave "the judge . . . no choice in drawing
the conclusions that follow from the existing body of rules and the
particular facts of the case" (pp. 153–54).[10]

On the other hand, laws avoid being "whims" of the lawgivers only
if, by "abstracting" from the particulars of persons and circumstances,
they leave "many kinds of action permissible as satisfying the conditions the law prescribes." The giver of "true laws" "cannot foresee
what will be their effects on particular people or for what purposes
they will use them. . . . specific ends of action, being always particulars,

should not enter into general rules" (Hayek, 1960, p. 152). "In fact, that *we* do not know their concrete effect, that *we* do not know what particular ends these rules will further . . . is the most important criterion of formal rules." "It is in this sense alone that it is at all possible for the legislator to be impartial. To be impartial means to have no answer to certain questions—to the kinds of question which, if we have to decide them, we decide by tossing a coin. In a world where everything was precisely foreseen, the state could hardly do anything and remain impartial" (Hayek, 1960, pp. 74–76; emphasis added).[11]

There are numerous possibilities intermediate between entire predictability and tossing coins. Hayek's lurch from the one to the other, and his identification of rationality with the first and impartiality with the second, dramatize the Janus-faced, one might say the schizoid, character of his rule of law thinking.

But there is nothing distinctively Hayekian about the generic problem before us. Gains in the kind of predictability that rule of law theorists contrast with arbitrary rule can be achieved only through an increase in the detail and specificity of laws and regulations. Gains in this respect necessarily entail losses regarding the range of actions all of which will satisfy "the conditions the law prescribes" and hence also the extent to which subjects can put laws "to their own purposes."

In this conspicuous respect it is seriously misleading to say that the rule of law is an ideal that can be approximated albeit not fully achieved. A legal system that embraces this ideal can pursue (through law and lawlike devices such as administrative regulations) particularity and predictability in this or these domains, generality and diversity of legally permissible action in that or those domains; it cannot pursue (by use of these devices) both objectives on one and the same terrain. If we make individuality, plurality, and freedom depend on specificity in law, laws that are general will disserve these values. If we associate individuality, plurality, and freedom with generality in law, laws that are definite in reference and hence afford predictability necessarily disserve the same values.[12]

III

There have been a number of responses to these complications. Consideration of a few of the more influential proposals will underscore the discrepancies and will suffice to show that none among them does more than ameliorate the difficulties to which they are addressed.

Late-nineteenth- and twentieth-century proponents of the *Rechts-staat* gestured to the ideal of generality in statute law but bent their efforts to achieving definiteness, particularity, and hence predictability through the more supple means of administrative regulation. Legislatures were to adopt general policies or set broad objectives. Administrative agencies were accorded wide discretion in formulating the rules that would actually govern the conduct of citizens. The problem of arbitrariness in administrative law or regulation was addressed less by leaving subjects with numerous legally sanctioned options than by creating a cadre of officials expert concerning particular domains of social and economic life and instilled with a strong sense of discipline. Consistency and equality were to be achieved and responsibility enforced through a strictly defined hierarchy of administrative authority and power. Administrative action was to be subject to court review, but by administrative tribunals whose primary task was to ensure that officials faithfully implement the directives issued by their superiors.

Rule of law thinkers who oppose the tendencies just sketched often concede that the *Rechtsstaat* established effective state control over large parts of economic and social life. Some favor and some oppose such control, but from Weber and Dicey through McIlwain and Neumann and up to Oakeshott and Hayek, Fuller and Lowi, they have objected that such efforts produce the antithesis of the rule of law (see Dicey, 1992; McIlwain, 1939; Lowi, 1979; Oakeshott, 1983). The administrative states they have empowered, whether or not they have consolidated and fortified the freedom-, plurality-, and individuality-destroying "iron cage" that Weber thought modernity was becoming, are pervaded by arbitrariness, are destroying the independence of the judiciary, and are in blatant conflict with the norm of equality before the law.

What, then, to do? If statutes that are general and prospective leave their addressees in debilitating uncertainty, and if the administrative state that remedies this defect substitutes the arbitrary rule of caste-serving bureaucrats (the rule of banal but often deeply evil "nobodies," as Hannah Arendt, 1963, acutely characterized them), how can governance that deserves the honored name of the rule of law be achieved and sustained?

Articulating his Humean views concerning the vital role of custom and convention in human affairs, Hayek seeks to diminish the incompatibility between the ideas of generality and predictability by invoking tacit but widely shared understandings that constitute the background of any effective rule-governed activity or practice. Attempting to explain how judges (and subjects or their lawyers) can have "no choice" but to draw "the conclusions that follow from the existing body" of abstract "rules and the particular facts of the case" before them, he argues that the determined and determinate character of judicial decisions rarely results from the "explicit, written down beforehand in so many words" formulations of the rules they are following.

> There are "rules" which can never be put into explicit form. Many of these will be recognizable only because they lead to consistent . . . decisions and will be known to those whom they guide as, at most, manifestations of a "sense of justice." Psychologically, legal reasoning does not . . . consist of explicit syllogisms, and the major premises will often not be explicit. Many of the general principles on which the conclusions depend will be only implicit in the body of formulated law and will have to be discovered by the courts. This, however, is not a peculiarity of legal reasoning. Probably all generalizations that we can formulate depend on still higher generalizations which we do not explicitly know but which nevertheless govern the working of our minds. Though we will always try to discover those more general principles on which our decisions rest, this is probably by nature an unending process that can never be completed. (1960, pp. 208–9)

Hayek's inconsistencies aside, there is much to agree with in these remarks and with the wider view that *all* rule following, regardless of the clarity and consistency of the rules in question, presupposes a setting of widely shared and seldom-examined concepts, beliefs, and dispositions, of capacities and skills acquired early in one's involvement in an activity and thereafter taken for granted, and the like. Wittgenstein (among numerous others) has surely taught us this much.

But there are major components of the Wittgensteinian curriculum from which Hayek has averted his glance or that he rejects without defense (he relies on Hume and Michael Polanyi in these regards). As discussed in Chapter 4, Wittgenstein advances a variant of the view that we often do "know how to go on" with our language games, do succeed in conducting our practices and in sustaining our institutions. He also promotes a version of the view that often we think of ourselves as having "no choice" but to go on in a particular manner, that our conventions, rules, training, and the like allow us one and only one action, judgment, or conclusion. Regularity, certainty, and predictability are indeed salient features of many of our practices and activities.

Contrary to Hayek, however, this steadiness and certitude are not due to the logical or rational necessities somehow resident in the "calculations" strictly if inexplicably mandated by our norms and rules. As with all ostensive definitions and all uses of language, rules can "be variously interpreted in every case." When we are most likely to think of ourselves as deducing or inferring rather than interpreting, we are, instead, "acting blindly." In the circumstances in which we have the strongest sense of certitude or necessity these result from the less gratifying fact that we "cannot see" the beliefs and assumptions, the "agreements in judgment" rather than in "opinion," that subtend our thinking and that enable and inform our conclusions. Moreover, Wittgenstein insists on the innumerable respects in which we are enigmas to one another, in which, despite sharing a language and hence a "form of life," we cannot "find our feet" with one another.[13]

In these views, the regularity and predictability in our activities stem importantly from what Hayek's (but not Wittgenstein's) criteria would oblige us to regard as "arbitrariness" in our affairs. In the same views, the considerations Hayek summons to explain the possibility of the orderliness and calculability for which he yearns are necessary but never sufficient to produce them and are often radically inadequate to doing so. Hayek (and Fuller, Ronald Dworkin, John Finnis [1980], et al., who make importantly comparable moves) is right to introduce these considerations into his rule of law thinking; his treatments of them are naive and his confidence in them excessive.

My larger purposes in this essay suggest a quite different characterization of and response to appeals to custom, convention, principles, laws of nature, and so on to close the "gaps" left by the letter of the law. If the subjects of a legal system *believe* that they and their judges "have no choice" but to act in a particular way, that belief might itself bring about the order and predictability that rule of law theorists ardently desire. It is the effect of the beliefs, not the logic or truth of the arguments for them, that matters. And whereas Wittgenstein is untroubled by the "prodigious diversity" and "open texture," the flux, indeterminacy, and opacity, of our language games, these are the very features that rule of law theorists want to lessen if not eradicate. In attempting to eradicate them by promoting firm and uniform beliefs that will produce the order and regularity they desire, they dramatize the ideological character of rule of law thinking.

To assess this anything but entirely agreeable project, I appropriate to my purposes elements of a view that is analogous to Wittgenstein's but that has a sharper critical edge. (Although addressed to more particular issues, the following paragraphs, and to a lesser extent the subsequent discussion of Oakeshott, substantially repeat some of the discussion in Chapter 4. Those who have read that chapter may want either to pass quickly over them or to ask themselves whether they read differently in this context.)

In a lively engagement with Kafka's stunning miniature *Before the Law*, Jacques Derrida plays out by repeatedly playing on Kafka's maddening image of the countryman who is summoned before the law but who is prevented by the law's guardian from actually "reaching" it, prevented from closing the conceptual, normative, and psychological distance between himself and the law itself.

Derrida gives a twofold account of the "inaccessibility" of the law itself. One part of this account is strongly continuous with Wittgenstein's discussions of rules and rule following. From the moment that the law "begins to speak and to question the moral subject," that is, from the moment that legislators, judges, and their subjects attempt to theorize and promote the authority and bindingness of laws, "historicity," "narrativity," and hence "imagination" and "fiction" are introduced "into the very core of legal thought" (1992, p. 190). And with these features inevitably come those uncertainties and indeterminacies that Wittgenstein foregrounds. In part for this reason, the subjects can never achieve "a rapport of respect" with the law (p. 203).

The guardians of the law, however, "interrupt" the relation between the subject and the law deliberately as well as unwittingly. Why? They do so, Derrida suggests, out of realization that full access to the law would profane it, would deprive it of what Kant called its "categorical authority." In order for laws to have such authority there must be a "law of laws" that is "without history, genesis, or any possible derivation." If "historicity and empirical narrativity" would permit subjects of the law of laws to achieve a measure of rapport with it, they would thereby jeopardize the majesty or sanctity that it must have. Representatives of the law (Kafka's doorkeeper) are "interrupters as well as messengers"; by preventing the subjects from gaining access to the law, they combat the effects of the historicity and narrativity that they themselves—sometimes inadvertently, sometimes knowingly—have introduced into it (p. 204).

There is no such thing as an ahistorical concept or idea—of law or anything else. But, again, what if subjects can be gotten to *believe* that there is a law of laws, a law that authorizes, sanctifies, makes binding each of the particular laws that gather under the "genre" that the law of laws regulates or constitutes? What if they believe—can be gotten to want desperately to believe—that somewhere in the forbidden recesses guarded by the uncountable doorkeepers there is a pure and perfect LAW, a LAW unsullied by the contingencies and indeterminacies that come along with historicity, narrativity, and imagination. If, as appears to be the case with Kafka's doorkeeper, the guardians believe that they are the keepers of such a LAW, they might be more unyielding and otherwise resourceful in protecting its purity. If the subjects of the law believe that there is such a LAW, as appears to be the case with Kafka's man from the country, they might be more likely to submit to the directives and punishments of the guardians—indeed to do so "blindly." As a matter of conduct, "blind" acceptance of the *deep* convention that is the law of laws might make up the deficits left or rather created by the laws themselves and by the less determinate and more fluctuating conventions intermediate between the law of laws and the law.

Faithful to Kafka's disturbing tale, Derrida thinks that the subjects of law (and also, if with less self-awareness, the guardians?) are always and inescapably in "the terrifying double-bind" of Kafka's man from the country. They at once must and cannot know what the law is. They desperately want the assurances of a legal order and the esteem that comes with recognized fidelity to it; what they get is doubt, guilt, and shame. They are "both ... subject[s] of the law and ... outlaw[s]" (p. 204). The upshot seems to be that subjects of law are fated to the despair and humiliating shrinkage of self that befalls Kafka's man from the country.

Derrida does not draw the anarchist or antinomian inference that his story would seem to mandate. Like Wittgenstein, he knows perfectly well that there are effective laws and working legal, moral, and other disciplinary systems; that in fact we often "go on" successfully with activities that bring us "before" such systems. And it seems to be his view that a law of laws, and messengers/interrupters who at once enforce and prevent access to it, is always or at least typically a feature of such institutionalized activities and practices. In this and numerous other volumes he is concerned with the "law of the genre" that purports and is widely believed to stand to "Acts of Literature" as the law of laws stands to the acts of adopting, enforcing, and obeying the laws that governments make. By engaging texts that are uncontroversially within the genre of literature and therefore taken to be "before" the purported Law of that genre, he exposes the dissonances and paradoxes of that relationship, displays their potent effects on the activities that produce and surround Acts of Literature. The anarchist and antinomian counsel, we might say, is a counsel of despair. Alternatively, if it is our own beliefs, at once force-fed to us and desperately maintained by us, that sustain the law of laws, it is so disturbing a counsel that we will all but certainly reject it.

Let us treat the metalegal doctrine of the rule of law as the LAW of that genre that consists in the law of the state, that is, as a delineation or prescription of the criteria that do or ought to govern what law is. If we must be "before" this Law, cannot simply deny or otherwise dispose of it, how should we think about it and our relationship to it?

At a minimum, we should follow Derrida'a example and expose and contest the highest pretensions of that law of laws that is the rule of law. We, especially we liberal theorists, should expose the historicity and contingency of the rule of law and thereby contest the claim that fidelity to it will banish arbitrariness and indeterminacy from the law. Doing so will not eliminate, may well deepen, the difficulties inherent in being before the law. As Wittgenstein and Stanley Cavell say about all of our "criteria," we cannot do without standards by which to identify and assess laws, and in much of our thinking and acting we do and must accept them "blindly." But if we recognize, at least in our more self-critical moments, that they inevitably "disappoint" us,[14] we may loosen their hold on our thinking, may prepare ourselves to think and act against as well as with the law and its messengers/interrupters. If so, taking this stance may help us to stave off the diminution and despair that overtake those who, like the man from the country, persist in the naive faith that the law is or "should surely be accessible at all times and to everyone."

"But is it not necessary for all literature [all law and acts before the law] to exceed literature? . . . The work, the opus [the thought and the act within, around, against the law] does not belong to the field, it is the transformer of the field" (Derrida, 1992, p. 215).

IV

By way of concluding, I consider a number of views concerning the rule of law that are at least partly in the spirit of these last remarks. But first I examine a theory, or rather an imagining, of the rule of law that, were it fully and durably realizable, would recommend a less suspicious or antagonistic stance toward this institution and institutionalism.

"Taken precisely," Michael Oakeshott avers, "the expression 'the rule of law'. . . stands for a mode of moral association [consisting 'of *personae* indistinguishably and'] exclusively ['related in respect of'] . . . the recognition of the authority of known, non-instrumental rules . . . which impose obligations to subscribe to adverbial conditions in the performance of self-chosen actions of all who fall within their jurisdiction" (1983, p. 136).[15]

In the largest perspectives of this chapter, the idea that is finally most important in Oakeshott's vision is that of a mode of human association that would be characterized and distinguished from all others not by its collective purposes or institutional structures but by the "personae" of its subscribers and the qualities that their thinking and acting do and do not have. It is a vision of an association each of the members of which have their own ends and purposes that they pursue through their self-chosen actions. Members as such ("*cives*") are associated with one another not by agreement in objective or purpose but exclusively by their subscription to "adverbial" rules, rules that do not require them to do this or that but rather to do whatever they do in certain (civil) ways or manners, obligate them to avoid doing whatever they do in uncivil ways.

As is evident from Oakeshott's willingness to denominate his vision as association in terms of the "Rule of Law,"[16] a version of institutionalism is integral to it. The constitutive and distinguishing features of this vision, however, are not its institutions in what we might call their material form, but rather the understandings its *personae* have of themselves, of their relationships with one another, and of the institutions to which they jointly subscribe. They think of themselves as disclosing and enacting themselves by "imagining" and pursuing various and fluctuating "substantive satisfactions" and as doing this with consideration for the adverbial requirements enunciated in law and in various other principles and rules. In short, the institutions of such an association, including the rule of law in at least some of the more familiar senses that I have been exploring, are fashioned to be consonant with the demands of that understanding or conception, not the other way around.

These features of Oakeshott's vision of the rule of law inform my thought that subscribers to such an association would adopt an affirmative stance toward it and the requirements it places on them. Quite rightly, however, Oakeshott states unequivocally that, so understood, "the rule of law cannot" be taken to characterize any "modern European state" (1975, p. 155). As he articulates and idealizes it, the "expression . . . 'the rule of law' stands for a mode of human relationship that has been glimpsed, sketched in practice, unreflectively and intermittently enjoyed, half understood, left indistinct" (1983, p. 120). Agreeing with this judgment, I postpone further discussion of the apparently more encouraging possibility to consider respects in which Oakeshott's construal of the rule of law is continuous with and departs from formulations already discussed.

Viewed as a version of institutionalism, the distinctive feature of Oakeshott's account is his insistence on the nonpurposive, noninstrumental, purely adverbial character of the rules and relationships that compose a rule of law association. But let us note respects in which the core idea in this distinction is akin to Hayek's notion that subjects put the laws to their own, not the lawmaker's, purposes and to his closely related prescription that laws specify not particular actions but "conditions" that all actions must satisfy. We should also note that Oakeshott incorporates into his conception of the rule of law a number of the requirements common to virtually all current rule of law thinking and endorses Fuller's view that these "formal" characteristics are "inherent in the notion . . . of law itself . . . and [that] in default of [them] . . . whatever purports to be a legal order" does not deserve that designation.[17]

In these respects Oakeshott's view of the rule of law departs from those considered earlier primarily in his refusal to make exaggerated claims concerning the certitude and predictability that the rule of law might afford. The reader will have noticed the somewhat casual quality of his remarks about the features inherent in the notion of the law (the sentences quoted in note 17 are the entirety of his remarks on this topic). Yet more striking is his repeated insistence that laws "are unavoidably indeterminate," that the judicial procedures through which they are applied to particular cases are not only "an exercise in retrospective casuistry" but something of a "devious engagement," one that has no concern with the intentions of legislators, knows of no absolute rights, and looks to previous cases not for binding precedents but for "the analogical force of the distinctions they invoked" (1983, pp. 146–47). Although operating with and through its own internal rules of procedure and evidence, and in part because these too are "unavoidably indeterminate," judicial deliberations "float upon the acknowledgement that the considerations in terms of which the *jus* of *lex* may be discerned are neither arbitrary, nor unchanging, nor uncontentious, and that they are the product of moral experience which is never without tensions and internal discrepancies" (pp. 143–44). (Thus Oakeshott is neither a legal positivist nor a natural law thinker.)

Association in terms of the rule of law has "no place for enthusiasm." It requires "a severe and incurious kind of faithfulness or ceremoniousness which modifies without emasculating the self-chosen character of human conduct" (Oakeshott, 1983, pp. 148–49). The freedom subserved by the rule of law is a presupposition not a consequence of the mode of association it names (see Neumann, 1957; Shklar, 1964; Unger, 1986; Kelman, 1987); the rule of law "bakes no bread, . . . is unable to distribute loaves or fishes, . . . and [what in the violent history of the modern European state has proved to be its truly fatal defect] it cannot protect itself against external assault." Nevertheless, "it remains the most civilized and least burdensome conception of a state yet to be devised" (p. 161).

In the essay to which I have been responding, Oakeshott is decidedly sparing of examples of rules that are purely adverbial in character, and leaves that notion—perhaps deliberately—in a somewhat obscure or elusive condition. In the more extensive (and hence vulnerable?) discussion in *On Human Conduct*, in the course of arguing that the norms and rules of all human "practices" are of this character, he elaborates on the notion in the following terms: "A practice may be identified as a set of considerations, manners, uses, observances, customs, standards, canons, maxims, principles, rules and offices specifying useful procedures or denoting obligations or duties which relate to human actions and utterances. It is . . . an adverbial qualification of choices and performances . . . in which conduct is understood in terms of a procedure." The emblems of such considerations are concepts "such as punctually, considerately, civilly, scientifically, legally, candidly, judicially, poetically, morally, etc." These concepts "do not specify performances; they postulate performances and specify procedural conditions to be taken into account when choosing and acting" (1975, pp. 55–56).

All human actions involve both substance and procedure. The former enter through the agent's choice of an "imagined and wished-for" outcome or satisfaction, the latter are given by, become available to and obligatory for agents by virtue of, practices that specify conditions in which choices are made and acted upon. A "practice is an instrument to be played upon, not a tune to be played." This is a matter of the distinctive logic and categorical character of practices, not of the preferences of their practitioners. "A rule (and *a fortiori* something less exacting, like a maxim) can never tell a performer what choice he shall make; . . . The appearance procedures and rules may have of excluding (forbidding), or more rarely enjoining, substantive choices and actions is illusive. Practices identify actions adverbially; they exclude (forbid) or enjoin them in terms of prescribed conditions." Turning to the practice in respect to which the illusion he is dispelling is most widely promoted (because most avidly desired?), Oakeshott declares, "A criminal law . . . does not forbid killing or lighting a fire, it forbids killing 'murderously' or lighting a fire 'arsonically'" (1975, pp. 58, 59n.).

Because one can light a fire arsonically only by lighting a fire, laws can forbid arson only by prohibiting certain classes of action. *Cives* who subscribe to such laws will therefore be under obligations to desist from actions they might otherwise take with legal impunity. Oakeshott is hardly unaware of this. In observed fact, proposals for new laws commonly take their origins from the purposes of their proponents; "there is, indeed, no want which may not set going a project" to change the laws. In fact, laws commonly yield substantive "benefits or advantages to . . . assignable interests"; for example, "every piece of legislation has an outcome of advantage to a legal profession" (pp. 169–70).

The *personae* of a rule of law association do not deny these realities. But neither do they make them the focus of their thinking and acting. In deliberating proposed changes in *lex* their question—rather than *Cui bono?*—is how the proposed law would affect the conditions under which all associates would thereafter be obligated to act. In choosing courses of conduct in the domain of *lex* they ask whether the actions they are considering could be performed in a manner consistent with their own civil characters and of the civility of associational life.

Accordingly, life in a rule of law association, particularly participation in the "politics" in which the *lex* of such an association is deliberated, requires no less than a "disciplined imagination" (Oakeshott, 1975, p. 165). *Cives* must cultivate their human capacities to imagine desirable outcomes and to devise ways of pursuing them. At the same time, they must subject that imagination and those pursuits to the discipline of the considerations signaled by words such as *politely, temperately,* and *fastidiously; resolutely, candidly,* and *forthrightly; morally, legally,* and *civilly.* If they fail in the first of these endeavors they deteriorate into the dull, torpid, and ressentiment-laden characters that Oakeshott calls the "individual manqué" and the "anti-individual" (third essay). If they fail in the second task rule of law society is gone, in all likelihood replaced by a teleocratic enterprise association the ugly insignia of which are "Purpose, Plan, Policy and Power" (1983, p. 125).

As we have seen, attempts at creating and sustaining rule of law association have never succeeded entirely and have rarely succeeded at all for very long. There are deep reasons for this perhaps dispiriting fact. In addition to the intricate and never fully harmonious combination of characteristics it demands of its *personae,* the deliberations such associations require have to be sustained despite certain knowledge that "there always must be more than one opinion" concerning the questions that arise and hence that the engagement to deliberate them will most often be "vexatious." It "calls for so exact a focus of attention and so uncommon a self-restraint" that we cannot be "astonished to find this mode of human relationship to be as rare as it is excellent" (1975, p. 180).

V

Oakeshott is correct that the conception of civil or rule of law association that he has glimpsed in the theory and practice of the modern European state represents "the most civilized and least burdensome conception of *a state* yet to be devised" (1983, p. 164; emphasis added). It is civilized in postulating individuality, plurality, and freedom; it is civilized and potentially civilizing in looking to qualities of character, understanding, and spirit rather than power-driven political mechanics to abate the difficulties inherent in political association. The (Hobbesian) demands it makes, severe as they are, would be as little burdensome for the human beings it postulates and promotes as life in politically organized association can be.

If we also agree that the possibility of associations with these characteristics has been and remains elusive, then Oakeshott's reflections concerning the rule of law reinforce results reached through consideration of more widely influential thinking about this ideology-cum-institutional device. If known politically organized associations (including those said by less discriminating theorists to approximate satisfaction of the requirements of the rule of law) are predominantly teleocracies, then human beings who treasure individuality, plurality, and freedom will stand in a wary, defensive, even antagonistic posture toward their laws and other institutions and institutionalisms. Oakeshott's idealized rule of law association carries further the Wittgensteinian/Derridian exposure of the institutions that, empirically, bear this name; indeed, it stands as a rebuke to those institutions.

It is therefore no difficult matter to join the company of theorists who, while respecting the rule of law as a sometimes valuable institutional idea and device, nevertheless take a less-than-celebratory stance toward it. It is especially easy to agree with the view of H. L. A. Hart and of proponents of civil disobedience that the fact that a rule is a law is anything but a conclusive reason for obeying it. The fundaments of this view were persuasively argued by Hobbes in respect to a state that (as Hobbes conceived it) had many of the attributes of an Oakeshottian civil association and in any case was intended to be far less active and powerful than the juggernaut enterprise associations under the thrall of which we now live. Given the emergence and consolidation of the latter, the presence of citizens ready and willing to disobey law, however good its credentials by rule of law standards, is a necessary condition of realizing the liberal ideals.

It must be emphasized that this is a decidedly political stance. Of course it is not a "participationist" or "civic republican" position, does not urge us to sacrifice our other concerns to political involvement or to look to political activity as the chief source of gratification or self-realization, of virtue, of fraternity or communal solidarity. Rather, it warns against enhancing the power of the state by adding the force of one's own thinking and acting to the politics that energizes it. From Hobbes forward, however, proponents of this point of view have insisted that subjects of the state must give close attention to the activities of government, must watch it warily and be prepared to contest and resist laws and commands that threaten their interests and their well-being as they severally conceive of them.

From the point of view in question, life in the states we in fact have makes demands akin to but arguably yet more difficult to meet than Oakeshott's "exact focus of attention" and "uncommon self-restraint."

Insofar as these states do act by authority not power, insofar as they do rule by laws not commands, the understandings and sensibilities that Oakeshott promotes are appropriate if not essential. In particular, subjects must sustain the distinction between the authority and the substantive merits of laws. Because, as Hobbes says, a body politic makes policy rather than policy making a body politic, if this distinction is lost "government" is supplanted by action more or less in concert—typically the concerted action of some against and over some number of others.

But whereas these states have some of the elements of a civil society, they are predominantly enterprise associations that use their authority to pursue ends or goods purported to be common to all their members. This being the case, it seems that their subjects are faced with a choice between actively involving themselves in the politics through which highly purposive laws are adopted or resigning the care of numerous of *their* ends and purposes to some number of other people. In short, if the understandings and attitudes characteristic of the *cives* of a civil association were transferred, wholesale as it were, to states as we know them, those understandings—particularly the understanding that they should practice a "severe and incurious faithfulness"—might have the same unwelcome implications and consequences as do the preachments of conventional rule of law thinkers.

Oakeshott agrees with the last of these judgments. For subjects of an enterprise association state to choose resignation or political withdrawal is tantamount to abdicating, throughout whatever domain of life the state elects to regulate, the activities of self-disclosure and self-enactment. Those who make this choice thereby become "individuals manqués" and very likely "anti-individuals." He attempts, however, to identify a third option that is political in a sense close to the one that emerged in the discussion of Hobbes, Hart, and civil disobedience. But let us first consider views of critics of the rule of law who work primarily with the two options identified above.

If those are the options, avid participationists are not the only theorists who have disdained withdrawal and argued for forms of political involvement and activity that include but go well beyond wary attentiveness and ready disobedience. For otherwise diverse thinkers such as Franz Neumann, Judith Shklar, and members of the Critical Legal Studies movement, the withdrawal option, and the doctrines of strict obedience to law that often go with it ("legal absolutism"), is so grossly imprudent as to be beneath consideration. Highly effective in displaying tensions and pretensions within the theory and practice of the rule of law, they go on to expose the deeply ideological character of rule of law mentalities, particularly the ways in which their underdefended but vigorously promoted assumptions concerning order and predictability serve class, caste, and other sectarian interests. Most important here, they argue that these assumptions are enforced by political authority and power. For this very reason, for the reason that the rule of law is a system of organized and institutionalized political authority and power, it must be contested and resisted by organized and institutionalized political means.

It is impossible to reject this position altogether. There have been, are, and will continue to be circumstances in which continuous, organized, and vigorously affirmative political activity is indispensable. Once contemporary and recent regimes such as those in China, Iraq, Syria, Nazi Germany, and the Stalinist Soviet Union have consolidated their massive resources of power and violence, the political attitude and stance I discussed earlier, even if—as seems to have been the case in the Soviet Union—they have their effects, are often suicidal. There are also extended periods in the histories of virtually all modern states in which organized and quite possibly violent action has been and is the only effective way to counter organized violence and cruelty. The evils of state-enforced racial segregation in the United States and South Africa were and continue to be diminished by those self-enacting and magnanimous free spirits who achieved and who sustain a distancing and resistant stance toward them. More than this was and is necessary to end these evils. If more Americans had steadily taken or would now take a skeptical and contestational stance toward government and law, atrocities such as the Vietnam "war" might not have been committed and would be less likely to recur. Once such brutal uses of state power have gained momentum, more than this has been and will be necessary to end them.

The achievements of rule of law thinking and practice notwithstanding, the fires of state power burn hot and destructively among us. If it is therefore sometimes necessary to fight them with flames of equal heat and intensity, we should not forget that all combustions reconstitute—rarely for the better when the "materials" are human beings—the matter they consume.

In configuring his "ideal characters" civil and enterprise association, Oakeshott treats them as categorically distinct. But every actual political association that can claim to include the rule of law is an unstable amalgam of the characteristics of these two ideal types. More important, no human association can be tolerable without the qualities of human character and spirit that he, along with Hobbes and Constant, Emerson and Nietzsche, Mill, William James, and other lovers of individuality, plurality, and freedom, treasure and promote. All forms of collective and hence institutionalized conduct, particularly those that add the force of our thinking and acting to the power of the state, diminish those qualities. Oakeshott's third option, never entirely unavailable to those with the willfulness to choose it, is the option of maintaining a "pathos of distance" vis-à-vis such conduct and the institutions and institutionalisms—including the rule of law—that it sustains.

6 / The Ideas, Ideals, and Practices of Liberalism and the Institutions and Institutionalisms of Police and Policing

The operative terms of the swollen title of this chapter are *liberalism* and *the police*. But saying this does not effect much by way of an economy. We have repeatedly seen in the foregoing chapters that there are numerous and variously conflicting theories of liberalism and that practices called liberal are highly diverse. As idea(s), as an array of practices, and especially as a multiplicitous set of ideals, liberalism is a many-splendored thing. As noted earlier, some say that it is not a "thing" at all, that (in Wittgensteinian terms) it is an anything and therefore a nothing. But this view of liberalism, in addition to being false—as indicated by its prevalence in our affairs, liberalism is a family resemblance but not a vacuous term—has the disadvantage of making it impossible to say that estimable formulations of liberal ideas and ideals have been betrayed or disfigured not only by political and moral actualities but by liberalism's self-identified proponents. If there is a central question I want now to address, it is whether the notions of police and policing have been among the main instruments or carriers of such betrayals and disfigurations. To anticipate, my answer to this question is, Yes, they have.

Focusing this question is made difficult by the fact that my second set of terms, police and policing, is also if not equally multiplicitous. Potent purchase on the concept and various conceptions of the police can probably be gained only by looking at various institutionalizations of police and the police power and at what, again following Judith Shklar (1964), I continue to call the institutionalisms (or ideologies) that inform and surround those institutions, that is, the suppositions, ideas, and beliefs that give life and direction to various police and policing institutions.[1] Despite the pretensions of criminology, "police science," and penology, the idea of an encompassing general theory of police, policing, and the police power flies in the face of this multiplicity.

Given this doubled complexity, there is no prospect of delineating *the* theory of liberalism, of police, or of the actual, best, or most appropriate relationship between "the two." There are nevertheless available strategies that encourage the expectation that a degree of general critical assessment might be attainable. The strategy here adopted consists of two (complexly related) parts. From the standpoint of the first term of the present discourse, it consists in privileging the construal of liberal ideals that I have been invoking throughout this and previous writings, that is, that liberalism as an idealism (in the normative but not the epistemological sense) treasures and promotes individuality and plurality as formal but not substantive ends and individual freedom as a substantive means essential to an indefinitely large and diverse array of manifestations or partial realizations of the formal end. From the standpoint of my second set of terms, the strategy consists fundamentally in giving pride of place (but not exclusive place) to the Weberian understanding that the police power is and the police who exercise it are jurally and by pervasive legitimating institutionalisms authorized to impose their decisions by coercive threats backed by the use, as they judge necessary and possible, of physical violence against those who are subject to their jurisdiction.[2] It is significant as well as true that the public police frequently relate to citizens or subjects in noncoercive, nonviolent ways. It is yet more significant that much that deserves to be called policing is done by agents and agencies other than what I will call the public police. Most important, as thinkers from Bentham, Tocqueville, and Mill to Foucault have tried to teach us, understanding and assessing the relationship between liberalism and the police requires appreciation of the many respects in which physical violence and the threat thereof are deliberately veiled in what these thinkers regard as the socially and politically most consequential of institutionalized police practices. But out of sight is not, is decidedly not intended to be, out of mind. Agents of the FBI, the CIA, the U.S. Immigration and Naturalization Service, and the Bureau of Alcohol, Tobacco and Firearms

Control (usually!) conceal their weapons. Officer Friendly wears her uniform but may leave her pistol and nightstick in the patrol car or at the station house. Judges wear robes but (so far as we know!) themselves leave weapon carrying to their bailiffs. Anticipating later discussions, if we enlarge our conception of the police to the extent of including under its rubric operatives of surveillance such as those of the IRS, of local housing authorities, of the FCC, of school principals and teachers, deans and professors, social workers, and others (later it will be appropriate to add parents and neighbors, priests and ministers, doctors and psychiatrists), these agents neither carry weapons nor wear uniforms or badges and are authorized to use coercion and violence primarily in self-defense. But weapons are within reach or on call. We will not fully understand police and the police power if we restrict ourselves to power as legitimated coercion and violence, but we will not understand them at all if we lose sight of their fundamental Weberian characteristics.

If police and the police power are thus understood or construed, what stance should individuality- and freedom-oriented liberals take toward these institutions and the institutionalisms that inform, legitimate, and otherwise support them?

I

A prominent feature of the astonishingly large literature concerning police and the police power (a literature that intermittently concerns itself with liberalism) is a distinction between "Anglophone" and "Continental" thinking and practicing. With malice aforethought, I abridge this learned discussion by borrowing the logo of the police departments of a number of major cities in the United States: "To serve and protect." In the view to which I have referred, in the United States, in Great Britain, and in the predominantly Anglophone countries of the former British Empire and Commonwealth, this slogan should be reversed and perhaps halved. According to the distinction in question, in these places the police are regarded as agents and agencies whose primary task is to protect against threats posed and (in alliance with the system of criminal justice more generally) to punish harms inflicted by delinquent individuals and groups. Of course, police in Anglophone countries also "serve" in that they assist the public in coping with misfortunes and disasters, by providing various informational and administrative services, performing symbolic functions, and the like. But in the understanding to which I refer, many of these latter activities are or should be carried out by fire departments and medics, by social service, disaster relief, and related agencies. To the extent that the public police are requested to provide them, either the services they render can be connected to protection against actual or expected criminality (by far the usual case) or such services are strictly subordinated to the tasks of preventing crime and apprehending criminals. Most important here, the societies in question do not look to the police and the police power, as do countries such as Germany and France (the examples most frequently mentioned in the literature), to "serve" in the encompassing sense of taking authoritative concern for and with the happiness, the "health, morals and well-being" as well as the "safety," of—as Foucault is wont to put it—the "population."

In what follows I question, conceptually and to a lesser extent empirically, the viability of this distinction. But let us provisionally accept the distinction and consider its bearing on the relationship between liberalism and the institutions and institutionalisms of the police power and the public police.

In the empirical/historical/genealogical studies presented in *Discipline and Punish* (1979) and various related works, Michel Foucault argues that, beginning in the seventeenth century and gathering intellectual and practical momentum in the eighteenth and nineteenth centuries, there emerged and was consolidated a conception of the police power and the more general notion of a disciplinary society, a conception that greatly extended the range and deepened the penetration of various forms or expressions of the "policing" of the "populations" of European countries. (Most of Foucault's examples come from France and Germany, but his texts suggest that the lessons taught by those examples could be generalized to much of Western Europe.) Emboldened by the conviction (akin to but going well beyond a conviction of John Stuart Mill's that I discuss below) that the burgeoning human sciences had achieved or were in the way of achieving reliable knowledge concerning the actualities and desirabilities of human conduct and relationships, those theorists and practitioners who believed that they had acquired such knowledge sought to develop "technologies of power" (of "micro" or "capillary" or "pastoral" power as Foucault famously liked to call them) by or through which they could inform, construct, and control legal and political, social and moral relationships and activities.

These efforts produced a "carceral archipelago" consisting of four intricately interwoven elements. As before and elsewhere, there were (1) laws and edicts, policies and teachings, that defined criminal or otherwise unacceptable conduct; (2) individuals (criminals or "delinquents") who were adjudged to have violated or to be in the way of violating those laws and norms; (3) police who watched for, identified, and apprehended criminals and delinquents; and (4) prisons and other institutions that incarcerated and otherwise punished the latter. But whereas previously the law, the police, and the prisons were primarily concerned with apprehending and punishing those guilty of some form of lèse-majesté, out of the emerging understanding there developed "state apparatuses [generically, 'the police'] whose major function . . . [was and] is to assure that discipline reigns over society as a whole" (Foucault, 1979, pp. 214–15).

> Athough the police as an institution was certainly organized in the form of a state apparatus, and although this was certainly linked directly to the center of political sovereignty, the type of power that it exercises, the mechanisms it operates and the elements to which it applies them . . . must be coextensive with the entire social body and not only by the extreme limits that it embraces, but by the minuteness of the detail it is concerned with. Police power must bear "over everything": it is not however the totality of the state nor of the kingdom as visible and invisible body of the monarch; it is the dust of events, actions, behaviors, opinions—"everything that happens"; the police are concerned with "those things of every moment," those "unimportant things" of which Catherine II spoke in her Great Instruction. . . . With the police, one is in the indefinite world of a supervision that seeks ideally to reach the most elementary particle, the most passing phenomenon of the social body . . . the infinitely small of political power. (pp. 213–14)

Quoting Vattel, Foucault says that on this understanding "by means of a wise police, the sovereign accustoms the people to order and obedience" (pp. 214–15). Quoting Bonneville, he says: "The organization of an isolated illegality, enclosed in delinquency, would not have been possible without the development of police supervision. General surveillance of the population 'silent, mysterious, unperceived vigilance . . . it is the eye of the government ceaselessly open and watching without distinction over all citizens'" (p. 280). Invoking N. Delamare's *Traite de la Police* of 1705, Foucault says that "life is the object of the police. The indispensable, the useful and the superfluous: These are the three types of things that we need, or that we can use in our lives. . . . That is exactly what the police have to insure." Enlarging further in a related essay, he says that "Delamare makes a political object of human happiness. . . . Happiness of individuals is a requirement for the survival and development of the state. . . . People's happiness becomes an element of state strength. And . . . Delamare says that the state has to deal not only with men, or with a lot of men living together, but with society. Society and men as social beings . . . are now the true object of the police" (1988, pp. 157–58).[3]

Later in this chapter I return to these Foucauldian themes and relate them to the thinking of recent Anglophone students of the police such as James Q. Wilson, to Wilson's conservative and neoconservative bedmates, and to the *soi-disant* liberal formulations of (as I continue to call them) virtue-oriented liberals such as Rawls and Raz, Gutmann and Galston. Before I do so, it will be useful to develop somewhat further (and to note briefly some non-Anglophone objections to) the "Continental" conception of the police that is so vividly presented in Foucault's work.

In Foucault's accounting, at the level of articulate theorizing the development of this conception reached a kind of culmination in von Justi's book *Elements of Police*. In particular, von Justi melded the notion of a society pervasively disciplined by the police with the conception of a discipline in the sense of a body of reliable knowledge, called *Polizeiwissenschaft*, that informs and gives epistemic justification for the activities of the police. As a part of doing so, he drew a distinction that is pertinent to present concerns.

Here is Foucault on von Justi:

[In *Elements of Police*] the purpose of police is . . . defined, as in Delamare, as taking care of individuals living in society. . . . [But] von Justi . . . draws an important distinction between what he calls police (*die polizei*) and what he calls politics (*die politik*). *Die politik* is basically for him the negative task of the state. It consists in the state's fighting against its internal and external enemies, using the law against the internal enemies and the army against the external ones. Von Justi explains that the police (*Polizei*), on the contrary, have a positive task. Their instruments are neither [exclusively, primarily?] weapons nor laws, defense nor interdiction. The aim of the police is the permanently increasing production of something new, which is supposed to foster the citizen's life and the state's strength. The police govern not by the law but by a specific, a permanent, and a positive intervention in the behavior of individuals. [See the discussion of the *Rechtsstaat* in Chapter 5.] Even if the semantic distinction between *Politik* endorsing negative tasks and *Polizei* insuring positive tasks soon disappeared from political discourse and from the political vocabulary, the problem of a permanent intervention of the state in social processes, even without the form of the law, is . . . characteristic of our modern politics and of political problematics. (1988, p. 153)

Earlier in this same essay, Foucault had noted that the problem of developing technologies of power that would permit the "insuring of positive tasks" had been recognized and given a name, "*police* in French and *Polizei* in German." He then observed, parenthetically, that "I think the meaning of the English word, police, is something very different" (p. 153). And the passage I have quoted just above concludes as follows: "The discussion from the end of the 18th century till now about liberalism, *Polizeistaat*, *Rechtsstaat* . . . and so on originates in this problem of the positive and negative tasks of the state, in the possibility that the state may have only negative tasks and not positive ones and may have no power of intervention in the behavior of people" (p. 159).

Whether or not Foucault sustains this distinction between French and German dictions and rhetorics on the one hand and English ones on the other, the passages just quoted appear to credit the very distinction I am addressing. To that extent my argument here, while obviously much indebted to Foucault, is also against him.[4]

Foucault relies heavily on Delamare, von Justi, and a few other authors for theorizations of the developing practices the day-to-day workings of which his work is primarily concerned with uncovering and critiquing. But it will repay us to pause briefly to note that something very close to those practices was theorized, at a much higher level of abstraction, by a far more famous thinker.

Hegel participates in, extends, but also significantly circumscribes and supplements the cognitive or epistemic confidence that Foucault thinks fueled and justified the *Polizeistaat*. He is of course disdainful of the merely empirical medical and psychological ("clinical"), social and economic, criminological and penological sciences to the birth of which Foucault attributes so much significance. (Which is not to say that Hegel did or would have disagreed with Foucault's estimations of the de facto social and political consequentiality of these "sciences.") In Hegel's view, these studies are at the level of contingent and subjective particularities and can never exceed or escape from the "infinity of the Understanding." He had no doubt, however, that his philosophical investigations (as, with a certain irony, we might call them) had yielded truths that are, in Reason, incontrovertible. In particular, there is, in Reason, in Truth, and hence in Reality an objective Ethical Order that consists of "absolutely valid laws and institutions," an order that forms or constitutes "a circle of [Rational] necessity whose moments . . . regulate the life of individuals" (Hegel, 1942, para. 145, p. 105). When, where, or to the extent that these Truths of Reason had been grasped and instantiated in actually existing states, every subject is "directly linked to the ethical order by a relation which is more like an identity than even the relation of faith or trust" (add. to para. 147, p. 106). Accordingly, in his duty to the state the subject "finds his liberation; first, liberation from dependence on mere natural impulse and from the depression which as a particular subject he cannot escape in his moral reflections on what ought to be and what might be; secondly, liberation from the indeterminate subjectivity which, never reaching reality or the objective determinacy of action, remains self-enclosed and devoid of actuality. In duty the individual acquires his substantive freedom" (para. 149, p. 107).

We might say that philosophical Reason and Truth justify the existence and activity of the state and its public police (the "public authority" as Hegel frequently calls the police). But with Freedom as well as Reason, Truth as well as Reality on its side, it is better to say that at this, its most "Concrete" level, the question of justification cannot so much as arise. As regards the objective ethical order, the police not only should but must substitute, for the "extravagent" subjective particularities of individuals and groups, "the pursuit of the [True] ends of society and the individuals concerned." True, the ethical order accords subjects various objective rights, including "the right to demand subsistence" and even "welfare"; but for Hegel it follows from this very fact that those authorities who are responsible for that order and its ends "must protect . . . [the subject] from himself" (add. to para. 148, p. 277). "The public authority takes the place of the family where the poor are concerned [but also as regards those in whose hands "disproportionate wealth" has become concentrated (para. 244, p. 150)] in respect not only of their immediate wants but also of laziness of disposition, malignity, and the other vices which arise out of their plight and their sense of wrong" (para. 241, p. 149).

Insofar, then, as Reason has unfolded and manifested its Truths, everything is for, nothing stands against, the use of the police power to direct and control subjective particularity. By comparison with Vattel, Bonneville, Delamare, and von Justi as Foucault construes them, Hegel elevates this conclusion to the standing of a Truth of Reason, a Truth that, because it is beyond the reach of merely empirical studies, cannot be annulled or qualified by inquiries of the latter kind.

As already noted, however, there is another and epistemologically— but not legally or politically—qualified side or dimension to Hegel's argument for the *Polizeistaat*.

Reason (or *Geist*) consists of necessary Truths, but "the relations between It and external existents [subjective particularities] fall into the infinite of the Understanding," that is, into that lesser cognitive domain from which cogent disagreement can rarely if ever be eliminated.

> There is, therefore, no inherent line of distinction between what is and what is not injurious, even where crime is concerned, or between what is and what is not suspicious, or between what is to be forbidden, or subjected to supervision and what is to be exempt from prohibition, from surveillance and suspicion, from inquiry and the demand to render an account of itself. These details are determined by custom, the spirit of the rest of the constitution, contemporary conditions, the crisis of the hour, and so forth. (para. 234, p. 146)

Hegel concedes, moreover, that "when reflective thinking [that is, the active, self-conscious operations of the Understanding] is very highly developed [e.g., on the part of the police] public authority may extend its reach into all aspects of social life . . . [and] may set to work very pedantically and embarrass the day-to-day life of the people." But here too, he adds, "However great this annoyance, no objective line can be drawn" (add. 144, p. 276).

We have, then, an incorrigible, an allegedly apodictic, argument for some laws and institutions. And although that argument does not and cannot carry through to the resolution of all of the particular questions that present themselves to the public authorities, it does authorize the latter to settle those questions as they see fit. Buttressed by the view that "the absolutely valid laws and institutions . . . are the substance or universal essence of individuals"—that is, by the view that "whether the individual exists or not is all one to the ethical order" and that "the empty business of individuals is only a game of see-saw" (para. 145, p. 105; add. 144, p. 259)—this philosophically absurd conception is indeed a recipe for what liberalism as I conceive it must regard as a truly terrifying *Polizeistaat*.

II

If the ideas and developments that Foucault studied, as philosophically extended and embellished by Hegel and his followers, represent the "Continental" conception of policing and the police power at their most fully developed, we should note that various "Continental" thinkers, in particular Francophone and Germanophone liberals such as Constant and von Humboldt, stood resolutely against it. And if Hegel represents the culmination or apotheosis of this understanding, the powerfully anti-Hegelian elements in the "Continental" thinking of Kierkegaard and Nietzsche present (as do the critical aspects of Foucault's work) potent challenges to it. But Foucault and numerous other students of the institutions and institutionalisms of the police tell us that, minority Continental voices aside, the significant alternative to the "service" or "positive tasks" conception of policing and the police power has been provided, rather, by the Anglophone conception that the police do and should operate primarily in the domain that von Justi calls *Die Politik*, that their task is to protect the law-abiding members of society against those who are criminal or otherwise delinquent. More particularly, the significant alternative to the encompassing Continental conceptions that Foucault has studied is provided by those (mainly) Anglophone thinkers and practitioners who, as Foucault himself says, rejected *Die Polizei* and the *Polizeistaat* and promoted liberalisms that, whatever other differences there may be among them, agree in holding that the state and its police "have only negative tasks and not positive ones and may have no power of intervention in the [noncriminal, nondelinquent] behavior of the people" (1988, p. 159).

Whatever may be the case regarding institutionalized legal, political, and moral practice, at the level of ideas, ideologies, or institutionalisms this is a familiar and an at least partly creditable distinction or differentiation. Leaving aside the complicated case of that protoliberal Hobbes and the contentious cases of Bentham, James Mill, and the theological utilitarians, if the formulations of Anglophone liberals (from, say, Locke to Green, Mill and Hobhouse and up to Rawls, Hayek, and Dworkin) are compared with those of Delamare, von Justi and Hegel, or with the *Raison d'Etat* and *Etatiste* conservative and communitarian thinkers to their ideological Left and Right, the former evidence a suspicion of or at least an ambivalence concerning the state and the police power that is entirely absent from the works of, say, De Maistre and De Bonald, Robespierre and Lenin, that on Foucault's account rarely appears in the texts and text analogues that he studied, and that is suppressed or sublimated in communitarian writings from Rousseau, Hegel, and Burke to Charles Taylor, Alasdair MacIntyre, and Robert Bellah.[5]

Of course, a different picture emerges if we compare the canonical Anglophone liberals with anarchists such as Paine and Godwin, Proudhon, Bakunin, and Kropotkin (perhaps also if we compare them with the likes of Nietzsche and William James or the more consistent of recent libertarian thinkers such as Rothbard). Virtually all of these liberals acknowledge (as do Nietzsche, James, and Rothbard) the enduring reality of criminality and the need for protections against it. They not only recognize but insist that such protections can be effectively afforded only if there are police who are authorized and empowered to discipline and punish those who engage or threaten to engage in criminal activities. The ambivalence mentioned above arises from the fact that the protection is widely desired, indeed is judged essential to the realization of liberal values, while the authority and power to discipline and punish bring with them the danger that the police power will be used to restrict, unnecessarily, freedom of action and to enforce or cultivate conformity and homogeneity rather than plurality and individuality.

My argument is that these latter eventualities, rather than being mere "dangers" that might be avoided or diminished to insignificant proportions (e.g., through democratization, constitutionalism, the separation of powers, the rule of law, or other institutionalizations and institutionalisms) are consequences not only invariably but inevitably attendant upon the institution of the police power and the authorization of some number of assignable individuals to exercise it. My further argument is that influential liberal thinkers and practitioners, increasingly obsessed as are their fellow citizens by the reality or the perceived threat of crime, have overcome their ambivalence concerning the police and policing and have adopted views strongly analogous to those of the Continental thinkers and practitioners discussed above. I argue that this development is at once understandable and regrettable.

Even assuming some version of the distinction between protection and service, it is obvious that the police cannot protect you against me without restricting my freedom of action. If I have no intention of harming you, show no active disposition to do so, the question of protection does not arise at all or arises only to be dismissed because you are evidently paranoic or otherwise unjustifiably fearful. If I make it plain that I have such a purpose and am prepared to act on it, the police can protect you against me only by restricting what would otherwise be my freedom to do what I intend to do. As to demanding or inculcating conformity and homogeneity, the minimal point (to be enlarged upon below) is that the police power cannot effectively protect you against me if its agents restrict themselves to intervening after I have commenced to act on my criminal or otherwise harmful intentions. In conceptual/juridical rather than psychological or sociological terms, the police power must establish, more or less generally and prospectively, the forms, kinds, or types of conduct that are prohibited. And whereas enthusiasts for the rule of law such as Hayek regard these general and prospective rules as enabling individual freedom of action, simply by virtue of having these characteristics such rules demand uniformity, that is, demand that each and every member of the jurisdiction submit to the rules or to their enforcement should the police and other public authorities judge that they have violated them or are in the way of doing so.

Even if we restrict our attention to the foregoing minimal or elemental features of police and policing, it is easy to see why individuality- and freedom-oriented liberals and liberalisms are—or ought to be—suspicious of them. Bentham, hardly an exemplar of liberalism of this kind, rightly insisted (following the excellent example of Hobbes in at least this one respect) that every law and more particularly every enforcement of law restricts liberties and hence requires justification. But he and (in this respect) followers of his such as Green, Mill, and Hobhouse, Rawls, Hayek, and Dworkin found or find it easy to provide the required justifications. A certain suspiciousness or at least ambivalence concerning the police power remains a feature of virtually all liberalisms (manifested primarily by emphasis on the rule of law and constitutional guarantees thought—or hoped—to constrain actual police conduct). But the arguments that criminality is the most (or, after threats from abroad, the second-most) serious threat to liberal values, and that an effective police is a if not the primary deterrent to it, have dominated liberal thinking from Locke, Kant, and Bentham to the present.[6]

And why not? Why should liberals be suspicious of or resistant to police and policing if, to quote John Stuart Mill, the "only things . . . [policing seeks to] prevent are things which have been tried and condemned from the beginning of the world until now"? More particularly, why should individuality- and freedom-oriented liberals balk at or shrink from the police and energetic policing if the latter do no more than prevent or reduce the occurrence of "things which experience has shown not to be useful or suitable to any person's individuality" (1951, p. 184)?

Of course, Mill attributes the more epistemically self-confident of such views to others ("it is said," "it will be said"; 1951, p. 184). His intermittent skepticism cautions him against such assurance and this and other elements in his eclectic thinking prompt him to issue warnings against enthusiasm for or insouciance concerning legal as well as moral policing. But the passages I have quoted are strategic to Mill's unwavering conviction that policing, in both the juridical and the wider social and moral senses, is necessary not only to security but to pleasure, happiness, or well-being. If he is at his most unequivocal regarding the necessity and desirability of the stringent policing of barbarian peoples and of the as yet uncivilized members of comparatively advanced or enlightened societies, he is convinced that no amount of socialization and education will eliminate the need for it.

In various expressions and articulations, Mill's views resonate in much liberal as well as in illiberal and antiliberal discourse. If the already discussed views of Michel Foucault are to be believed, the development of increasingly disciplinary societies, societies characterized by elaborate and pervasive mechanisms of surveillance, intrusion, and punishment, was fueled by growing epistemic or cognitive certitude concerning the ends appropriate to human conduct as well as or more particularly concerning the means of assuring that those ends will be pursued and achieved. (Indeed, viewed from the perspective of Foucault's studies, Mill's is a cautious, at intervals a hesitant, voice.) If we know, have no doubt, as to what is good or at least what is bad for human beings, and if we are certain as to the modes of behavior that will serve or disserve human well-being, on what ground should, could, we hesitate to use the police power to assure good or at least prevent bad behaviors? True, various liberals have opted for more circumscribed versions of these certitudes. The later Rawls, for example, eschews universalist and transcendental claims and restricts himself to the argument that *this* (i.e., *his*) culture has or has the wherewithal to achieve assurance concerning forms of conduct (those that affect the "basic structure" and "constitutional essentials" of politically organized society) that must be forbidden and punished, even some forms of conduct that must be required. Again, it is arguable that the "right answers" that Ronald Dworkin thinks judges can provide in even the hardest of cases will vary from society to society or polity to polity. But with few and qualified exceptions (for example, Interpol), the police are a municipal institution and policing a municipal practice. If or to the extent that these institutions and practices are informed and emboldened by these and comparable certitudes, liberal ambivalence concerning them is either annulled or reduced to the narrowly circumstantial.

This constitutes a betrayal of liberalism.

III

I come back to Mill's and comparable warnings below. As preparation for doing so, and by way of deepening the concerns just expressed, it will be useful to give further attention to the differentiation between *Die Politik* and *Die Polizei* and its relation to competing tendencies within liberal theory and practice. I do so, first, by reference to Mill's thinking.

Mill's standing (notwithstanding the attacks of Rawls and others on his utilitarianism) as a paradigmatic Anglophone liberal is importantly based on his argument that the state and the society more generally are justified in interfering, violently or coercively, with the actions of sane and civilized adults only if or to the extent that those actions harm or directly threaten harm to assignable others. This argument has generated a considerable cottage industry devoted to distinguishing "harms" that justify coercive or violent interventions from other consequences (annoyances, irritations, competitions, and so on) that either ought to be tolerated by those on whom they are visited or at least responded to by the latter without recourse to the public or even the "moral" police. As important as this discussion is, we should not neglect the prior assumptions that locate and inform it. Recall the famous passage in *On Liberty*: "It is hardly necessary to say that this doctrine is meant to apply only to human beings in the maturity of their faculties. We are not speaking of children, or of young persons . . . [or of any others who] are still in a state to require being taken care of by others." All of these latter "must be protected against their own actions as well as against external injury." In relating to persons who remain in these immature or debilitated conditions, "a ruler full of the spirit of improvement is warranted in the use of any expedients that will attain an end, perhaps otherwise unattainable. . . . Liberty, as a principle, has no application to any state of things anterior to the time when mankind [or this or that, these or those members of humankind] have become capable of being improved by free and equal discussion" (p. 96).

I do not share the view, argued by Maurice Cowling (1963), that this and related passages contradict, annul, or betray the hypocrisy of Mill's commitment to freedom and individuality. There is no doubt that Mill found the preponderance of those with whom he was obliged to live uncongenial, unpalatable, and indeed vulgar. But he struggled to sustain the conviction that they had absorbed enough of civilization to make them "capable of being improved by free and equal discussion" as distinct from imposed training and coercive or violent constraints. To the considerable extent that he succeeded in this struggle, he urges liberal education rather than training,[7] the celebration of diversity and especially individuality, and a confined, primarily protective police power and policing.

The passage nevertheless resonates with those remarks, quoted above, in which Mill evidences his conviction that there are clear and readily implemented distinctions between actions that should be permitted and those that are unacceptably harmful to society, to other individuals, even to those whose actions they are. And the passage makes clear that when or to the extent that those distinctions are not respected, Mill is as ready as Bonneville or Delamare, von Justi or Hegel, to employ or to license the employment of police and policing to enforce them. It would be wrong simply to assimilate Mill and Millian liberalism to the thoughts and practices that Foucault associates with the latter thinkers, but it would be equally mistaken to deny the continuities or affinities between them.

My purpose, then, in discussing Mill is less to criticize him than to expose assumptions that are (as I briefly document below) widely accepted in liberal as well as antiliberal thinking and practice, assumptions that, as Mill's texts reveal, sharply qualify the distinction between Anglophone and Continental, protective and service-oriented, *Politik* and *Polizei* conceptions of police and the police power. In the "Anglophone" as well as the "Continental" view, the police "educate" and otherwise induce conformity concerning not only those actions that from time immemorial have been condemned as harmful to others, but concerning a wide array of beliefs and dispositions that the police and their constituents think might possibly do harm or of which they, for any number of other reasons, disapprove.

IV

We might say that the notion of police and policing as exclusively protective encompasses and to that extent accounts for the activities of juridically authorized bodyguards and private protectors. In various jurisdictions, bodyguards and other private security forces—that is, agents and agencies privately hired to protect particular persons, properties, and the like—are jurally authorized (variously in differing jurisdictions) to carry and use certain weapons of coercion and violence. But their activities are doubly constrained. First, as is officially the case with the public police whose official duty is to protect all members of the population, they can use force only to protect their clients against actions or threatened actions that do or might violate prohibitions already legally established. My bodyguard or our hired neighborhood security force cannot use force to protect me or us against actions or threatened actions, however unwelcome, that are legally permissible.

More important, jurally speaking, policing agents and agencies that are private in this sense are restricted to reactive as distinct from anticipatory or proactive measures. They watch for and respond to actions that are or are in the way of becoming criminally harmful to me or us. If they *suspect* the intentions or dispositions of these or those persons they may heighten their vigilance but they cannot respond (other than by alerting the public police) unless and until a criminal action is actually under way. By contrast, the public police are authorized to take various deterrent, precautionary, and prophylactic measures. The most obvious of such authorizations are provided by anticonspiracy statutes and by laws (e.g., curfew, antivagrancy, and antiloitering ordinances) that authorize the public police to use coercion and force against conduct that is harmless (to others) in itself but that has been officially adjudged to be predictive of criminally harmful conduct. (So-called preventive detentions are a yet clearer case.) But as Mill's discussion forcefully reminds us, the public police are not only authorized but expected to do much more than this. Indeed, the widely and increasingly received view is that the police cannot hope to protect "us" from criminality unless they engage in far more widely ranging forms of preventative activity. The most salient of these further activities consist of nothing more than the threatening "presence" of the police—cops on the beat, cruising patrol cars, the 911 systems that promise, in response to reported actual or imminent criminalities, the rapid and focused dispatch of protective and detaining, investigative, retaining and punishing officers. Unlike the private security agencies and services that also attempt to maintain this deterrent presence, however, the public police and more especially the public police power is/are expected to influence, to intervene authoritatively in, earlier moments or stages in believings, thinkings, and actings that might otherwise eventuate in criminal conduct.

The clearest but at least apparently most circumscribed respect in which this is the case is that the public police represent, we might say instantiate or exemplify, the prohibitions and requirements of the criminal law. In strict or narrow versions of the "Anglophone" view, this body of law provides the minimal or elemental distinctions between acceptable and unacceptable conduct. By enforcing and by themselves scrupulously respecting the prohibitions of the law, the public police educate the populace against criminal conduct, thereby augmenting protections against such conduct. Accordingly, criminal conduct by police officers is subject not only to legal sanctions but to more general condemnation. This is because police criminality teaches, dramatically, ordinary citizens to disrespect and violate the law. By contrast, unlawful conduct on the part of bodyguards and private security agencies, who are not assigned this educative or proactive as distinct from responsive and narrowly protective function, is regarded as *mere* criminality.[8] (It is perhaps for a related reason that "cop killers" are viewed—not only by the police—with a special horror and treated with distinctive severity. Because police officers represent the law, criminality on their part teaches others to violate the law. Killing a police officer as opposed to an "ordinary citizen" teaches the yet more dangerous lesson that, contrary to the representations that police officers instantiate, there is no effective monopoly and hence no hope for an effective circumscription on killing.)

Even if narrowly conceived as protecting against criminality, then, the exercise of the police power involves, integrally, a variety of interventions in the lives and activities of citizens, interventions that go well beyond vigilance concerning and coercive or violent responses to immediately threatened, actually occurring, or already consummated criminal activity. In order to protect, the police must *surveiller,* must attend to, interest themselves in, and attempt to influence and ideally to limit, direct, and control what philosophers sometimes call the "antecedents" of behaviors or actions that might, in the absence of policing influences or interventions, take a criminal or otherwise objectionable turn.

If we say protections against criminal activity, in respect to practice as distinct from theory, the least problematic among the foregoing assertions are the claims that the police power must identify, generally and prospectively, what will count as criminal actions or behaviors and that by doing so it demands and seeks to inculcate conformity to the laws and rules that forbid various classes of action. As indicated by the time-honored slogan *Sine lege, nulla poena,* in the absence of an antecedently promulgated law or command forbidding a class of actions, no action of that class can be criminal. In practice, of course, there are and must be numerous exceptions to this dictum. Leaving aside Hegel's and numerous other skeptical views (for example those views discussed in Chapters 4 and 5) concerning the relationship between general rule and particular application, and bracketing issues concerning Lockean prerogative, Schmittian decisionism, and the like, the police intervene in activities because they *suspect* them of being criminal or likely to cause harms or disturbances that it is their responsibility to prevent.[9] But as police are well aware, arrest and detention (not to mention the violence and other abuses that the police routinely employ even when there is no serious prospect of their making an arrest), whatever the ultimate juridical outcome, are themselves harms that, even if not formally punishments, are punishing to those subjected to them.

What about my remarks about the yet further proactive, prophylactic, and conformity-inducing activities of the allegedly protection-oriented Anglophone police? Foucault's detailed studies have dramatized the pervasive and pervasively intrusive "positive" objectives of "Continental" policing; investigations comparable to his would be necessary in order to establish or disestablish analogous conclusions concerning policing in the Anglophone world. A less patient, certainly a less energetic man than he, I have made no such investigations. But I am helped by the fact that numerous others, usually without evidencing sympathy for or even awareness of Foucault's work, have closely studied conceptions and practices of policing in the United States, Great Britain, and other Anglophone countries. Given my objective of assessing relationships between liberalism and the institutions and institutionalisms of policing, it is particularly instructive to consider the studies and reflections of one of the most prominent of such students, James Q. Wilson.

V

Wilson shares the objective of the great preponderance of criminologists, penologists, and—we can presume—most ordinary citizens, namely, to find effective ways to reduce the incidence of crime. From the perspective of my discussions thus far, an initially striking feature of his work is his animus against the view that the best way to pursue this objective is first to identify the "root causes" of crime, the social and economic conditions that breed criminality, and then, armed with this knowledge, to adopt policies and forge mechanisms that will eliminate or alter those conditions and hence the behaviors they produce. As Wilson sees it, the theoretical reach of this strategy always exceeds its practical grasp. Social science may or may not be able to discern the root causes of criminality.[10] What it cannot do is supply a plausible basis for the advocacy of positive or productive public policy. "By directing attention toward the . . . states that preceded or accompanied criminal behavior, the sociological (or more accurately, social psychological) theories directed attention toward conditions that cannot be easily and deliberately altered." "Society, of course, shapes attitudes and values by its example, its institutions, and its practices, but slowly and imprecisely, and with great difficulty" (1985, p. 45). "If it is hard by plan to make the good better, it may be impossible to make the bad tolerable so long as one seeks to influence attitudes and values directly" (p. 45). "The one thing we cannot easily do, if we can do it at all, is change, by plan and systematically, the minds of men" (p. 47). Accordingly, as regards public policies aimed at reducing crime, Wilson primarily adopts what he sometimes calls the Hobbesian, Benthamite, or Beccarian view (see 1985, pp. 241–45; Wilson and Hernstein, 1985, chap. 20 and passim) (in present circumstances it is tempting to call it the Posnerian or, better, the Beckerian view) that we most effectively deter crime by treating actual or potential criminals as rational calculators and by attempting to give them incentives to avoid criminal acts.

Reading these words at this time, it is hard to resist construing them as part of the neoconservative effort to discredit welfare state policies. Given the pervasive fear of crime, many who might otherwise oppose antipoverty, antiunemployment, affirmative action, and related programs will support such policies if they are convinced that doing so will contribute to the fight against crime. By arguing that such government programs have little or no documentable effect on crime rates, Wilson and those of his persuasion may hope to eliminate or diminish a major source of support for policies that he and they oppose on other grounds. However this may be,[11] in the present context the more striking (albeit not unrelated) feature of Wilson's argument is that it, in company with his arguments for "deterrence" and "incapacitation" as the most effective ways of combating crime, is that it appears to align him with Anglophone, *Die Politik*, or protection views of the police and policing. Whether or not it would be desirable or justifiable for government and its police to intervene in the "minds of men," to "subject" them to what Foucault calls its pervasive and docility-inducing "discipline," they have few and narrowly limited prospects of doing so effectively. Accordingly, government and the police must accept "men" as they are and combat crime, rather, by providing those disposed to criminality with what they themselves are most likely to regard as sufficient incentives to avoid engaging in it.

As I have thus far sketched Wilson's argument, I have more than a little sympathy for it. It appears that, rather than promoting the reshaping or remaking of the members of society according to some privileged *episteme*-cum-morality, he thinks that, *faute de mieux* and perhaps on the axiologically stronger grounds that he sometimes entertains, we should accept them as they are but present them with incentives that, given their own self-understandings and purposes, might influence them to avoid actions that are criminally harmful to others. If they persist in harmful conduct, they so to speak take upon themselves the responsibility for whatever punishments "we" are able to inflict upon them. This understanding is not one that an individuality- and freedom-oriented liberalism can readily reject.[12]

But this is, or these are, instrumental and in that sense derivative tendencies in Wilson's thinking. He is persistent in his rejection, as adequate explanations for rates of crime, of what he takes to be the most influential views concerning social causation. He is only slightly more qualified in his rejection of welfare liberal and rehabilitationist remedies for the problem of crime. But he is by no means averse to "causal" analyses of his own. Wilson is neither his own nor anyone else's liberal. But he is relevant here because his assessments of the deepest sources of crime, and of the proper role of the police in responding to it, resonate, eerily, with those of influential liberals.

In language prevalent in political and social theory, Wilson's most general analysis of large-scale changes in rates of crime is in terms of "community" and its maintenance or breakdown. In his fundamentally Rousseauian-Durkheimian understanding, "community" exists and is strong to the extent that there are widely agreed-upon and observed standards "of right and seemly conduct" (p. 28), "a sense of mutual regard and the obligations of civility" (p. 38), and a readiness to impose "informal sanctions" (p. 30) against those who violate these norms. He claims that Jeffersonian America was comparatively crime free and, in company with the original Anti-Federalists, other recent communitarians, and Straussian republicans, argues that this was because that America was characterized by local communities that "controlled behavior by a combination of moral tutelage, reciprocal obligations, and public humiliations" (p. 225). These communities were weakened by immigration and other demographic developments, industrialization, the Civil War, and so on, predicting (in this view) increased rates of crime. Powerfully abetted by "intellectuals" (yet another *trahison des clercs!*) who repudiated (then and now) not only community but the whole notion of "moral uplift" and who promoted "self-expression" rather than self-control, "happiness" rather than "success" (pp. 234–35, 231), these changes eventually produced the lamentably crime-ridden society that now exists in the United States.

This outcome was postponed by the emergence, at the national level, of a "civilizing process" (Elias) that produced a "Victorian" culture that exercised a "moral hegemony" over those who resisted its moral and political demands (pp. 226–32). The institutionalization of local police forces assisted in controlling latent or incipient criminality (p. 226), but this was primarily because the role of the police and the criminal law was then (as it ought to be now) to "shape conduct" to accord with accepted moral standards and thereby to help to "sustain communities" (p. 238). Where community norms have broken down, where informal sanctions no longer produce "stigmatization" and "sentiments of shame" (pp. 252–53), the police can do relatively little to control crime (pp. 37–38). "It is because of the *absence* of community (that is, of shared, spontaneously enforced values) that crime control and police-citizen relationships are so difficult" (p. 110).

A truly effective response to increasing rates of crime, then, would require (in the American case, with which Wilson is primarily concerned) that we turn back the clock, that we return, if not to the "Jeffersonian" America of local communities, at least to the "Great Awakening" and its Sunday schools, temperance movements, and religiously informed collective moral rigor.

For reasons already discussed, Wilson thinks that the prospects for such a reversal-cum-rejuvenation are dim. As we have seen, and in keeping with the generically "conservative" stance that pervades his thinking,[13] he holds that attitudes and beliefs, as distinct from "choices" (p. 9) made from within or on the basis of an already established set of attitudes and beliefs, are extraordinarily difficult to change. The reality is that the United States has deteriorated into a largely "atomistic" society the several governments of which are therefore reduced to attempting to influence, by rather crude means, choices rather than attitudes, beliefs, and values. Accordingly, the best known of Wilson's policy recommendations, frequently advanced in a spirit or mood of "so be it" (p. 249), concern improved tactics of deterrence and incapacitation. In these respects, Wilson's thinking appears to manifest a *Die Politik* or narrowly protectionist conception of policing and the police power. Or rather it seems to argue that this is the only conception effectively available to the United States and similar societies.

Insofar as he endorses these views, however, Wilson does so—and this is the important point for present purposes—against the grain of his deepest convictions. We have seen his view that the fundamental task of the police and the criminal law is not to deter, arrest, and punish but to "shape conduct and sustain communities," to reinforce the informal control mechanisms of community (p. 83). It is for this reason that he strongly supports the creation of private security forces, but forces modeled on the older notion of "community watchmen" and even vigilantism (p. 87) as well as public police practices that keep police officers in intimate contact with the law-abiding as well as the criminal elements of neighborhoods. More generally, he argues that there is no clear distinction between positive and negative sanctions, between providing or offering benefits and threatening harms and punishments.[14] The law enforcement and order-maintaining functions of the police are or should be inextricably intermixed and interwoven with their provision of community-cultivation and -maintenance activities and responsibilities (pp. 111–12). Shaping and directing thinking and acting is the most important of the "services" that the police can provide. Policing and related activities and policies, broadly construed, cannot change attitudes and beliefs swiftly or surely, but over time they can help to do so (p. 51). If we give up on this possibility, if by preference or because we have become convinced that our atomized society reduces us to this Hobson's choice, we resign ourselves to an "Anglophone" conception of police and policing, we delude ourselves concerning the realities of policing and we abandon to the police themselves valuable possibilities of social construction and control. The predictable outcome is a society ridden by crime and very likely by both police misconduct and pervasive antagonism between citizens and the police.

VI

The materials I have assembled do not demonstrate that the United Kingdom or the United States, Canada or New Zealand are full-blown Hegelian states and they do not show that Foucault's analyses of France, Germany, and the other cultures and nations that he studied, to the extent that he was correct concerning them (which I do not attempt to judge), are equally perspicuous concerning the Anglophone societies with which he occasionally contrasted them. Taken together, however, the foregoing evidences, considerations, and reflections, diverse as they are or rather because of their diversity, show that the related distinctions between negative and positive police tasks, between protection and service, are much less than clear and distinct. Conceptually or theoretically as well as empirically, protection cannot be effectively afforded apart from "services" that aspire to, and that claim epistemic and axiological supports and justifications for, "policing" that goes well beyond the forbidding and requiring, the juridical or less formally authorized punishing or rewarding of particular forms of individual and group conduct. Protection- or anticriminality-oriented conceptions and practices presume upon and promote beliefs concerning what is right or wrong, tolerable or intolerable, constructive or destructive, even palatable or repugnant. In these views, there is no such thing as a police power or a policing practice that does or could operate apart from beliefs and convictions of these kinds. Hegel's philosophical extremism notwithstanding, he is representative of much liberal as well as antiliberal thinking. To say this is to answer, in the affirmative, the question of whether liberal thinking about the police has betrayed the most estimable formulations of liberalism.

Members of the extended family that is liberalism may be more or less beguiled by or uncomfortable in the presence of anarchisms, antinomianisms, and even nihilisms, but they do not embrace these views. Diverse as liberalisms are, every liberalism is a something not an anything, and among the "things" that every liberalism includes is the recognition or acknowledgment of crime, the recognition or acknowledgment that human beings injure, wrong, and harm one another. But this recognition or acknowledgment raises rather than answers the question of the stance that liberalism ought to take toward crime.

For a liberalism of the kind I sketched at the outset, a liberalism committed first and foremost to individuality and individual freedom, the answer to this question must turn primarily on how to combat crime while putting the fewest possible restrictions on freedom and individuality. It is perhaps true that there is no such thing as a liberalism that does not have somewhere in its mind, heart, or soul a commitment to these values. But in virtue liberalisms this commitment is subordinated to other values and objectives, to justice and other virtues, to we-feelings, solidarities, and various related qualities of human character and relationships. Because crime and criminality threaten, weaken, or destroy these relationships and the virtues judged necessary to them, virtue liberals look to various forms of policing to cultivate and protect them against crime. Being liberals, they can hardly avoid a certain hesitation before or ambivalence concerning the idea of a public police authorized to use coercion and violence. Accordingly, their preference is for other forms of policing—training, suasion, mutual surveillance, education—that, because they affect the believing and thinking from which human conduct proceeds, are less (or less manifestly) violent. But virtue liberals look to the public police as well as to the family and the neighborhood, the church and the school to provide these more pervasive and hopefully more efficacious influences and constraints.

Various as they are in their particulars, all of these understandings and proposals depend on assumptions or possibilities that, I have in effect been arguing, are conceptually or theoretically dubious and empirically ill-supported or undersupported. The more skeptical aspects of Mill's thinking cast serious doubt on the possibility of a secure distinction between the harmful and the merely irritating or annoying (to say nothing of the harmful versus the beneficial), and his own historical examples (Socrates, Jesus, the Mormons, Thomas Poole) are hardly encouraging as regards the probabilities of agreement in either opinion or judgment concerning these matters. We could but do not need to invoke more potent skepticisms to appreciate the difficulties confronting the other virtue liberal conceptions and proposals thus far discussed. Late-Rawlsian "avoidancism" assumes—in the face of an abundance of contrary evidence—an emergent if not already established consensus that there is and will remain a rationally ineliminable plurality of "reasonable" conceptions of the good that should be tolerated if not welcomed. But it also assumes that there is or easily could be a consensus as to what is "unreasonable" and hence deserves to be rejected and as necessary policed and suppressed. Similarly, neutralist and "private versus public" liberalisms amount to not much more than the evidently false claim that there is little disagreement concerning what is or (readily correctable errors and confusions eliminated) could and should be regarded as public and private.

These several and variously doubtful epistemic-cum-cultural-cum-moral/political/juridical assumptions underwrite or subtend the several related distinctions on which I have focused: between the positive and negative tasks of the police; between the police as protectors of values already widely accepted against those who, "unreasonably" or fanatically, refuse to plight their troths to them; and between the police as enforcers of beliefs and values and the police as cultivators/producers of beliefs and values.

It is not difficult to understand the attraction, to liberals, of these distinctions. The "Continental" conception is offensive to them because it implies that it is for the police and those wider public authorities vested with the police power to determine, with or without regard to recognizably liberal beliefs and values, which forms of conduct ought to be prohibited and required and which forms of believing and thinking should be cultivated. The distinctions sustain the comforting thought that the public police, despite being authorized to employ coercion and violence, could and should employ those instrumentalities exclusively to protect liberal beliefs and values.

To return to Mill's warnings, all of the liberal theorists I have mentioned recognize, regret and sometimes try their hands at devising restraints upon the actualities of police misconduct: they lament the prevalence of corruption, brutality, and related abuses of police power and authority. What they do not do, what their epistemic, historical-cultural, or axiological assumptions make it impossible for them to do, is question the deeper notion, the agreement in judgment that lies beneath both agreements and disagreements in opinion, that there are beliefs, values, and corresponding modes of conduct that anyone of a recognizably liberal persuasion must accept and reject, celebrate and contemn. Of course they hope to *persuade* their fellow citizens of or to their convictions. By assembling evidence, by conducting thought experiments, by giving arguments, by employing various rhetorical strategies, and by providing education and training that make use of these devices, they promote agreement concerning those beliefs and values and concerning the prohibitions and requirements that they take them to justify. In this understanding, the public police power is necessary only to the extent that there are some among us whose "nature is their misfortune" (Rawls), who, irrationally, unreasonably, or out of a perhaps congenital incapacity for "solidarity," refuse the "we-feelings" and "obligations" (Rorty) that are presupposed by or required for a liberal society. It then falls, à la Mill, to the rational, the reasonable, and the dutiful members of liberal societies to see to it that the police use the power and authority with which they are vested exclusively to serve certifiably liberal objectives. In the United States their heros are Earl Warren and Orlando Wilson.

VII

There is a familiar Anglophone liberal rhetoric according to which this understanding of the disciplinary-cum-carcereal society is attributed primarily to radical-Right, radical-Left, communitarian, and other hard-nosed illiberal and antiliberal theorists, publicists, and practioners (for example, James Q. Wilson). A strong association of this kind is of course fully justified. Thinkers and actors properly so classified, such as de Maistre, Hegel and Schmitt, Metternich and de Gaulle, Bradley, Bosanquet and Thatcher, Marx, Lenin and Stalin, Strauss, Bloom and William Bennett, Rousseau, MacIntyre and Pat Robertson, have promoted the view that, at the level of theory or principle, legal and moral policing are warranted because there are truths concerning human affairs that must be accepted and respected. They have also embraced the view that such policing is practically justified because there are many who cannot comprehend or will not act upon those truths.

But illiberal and antiliberal thinkers and practitioners have no monopoly on these convictions and dispositions. The liberal thinkers I have mainly discussed, Mill, Rawls, Rorty, and Habermas, neutralists such as Ackerman and Larmore, make commendable if not notably convincing efforts to delimit the domain (hence the proper dominion) of conceptions of the harmful, the just or reasonable, the essential, or the properly shared, agreed or public. By doing so, they seek to circumscribe the realm in and over which public policing and perhaps less organized forms of surveillance and disciplining are cognitively warranted and axiologically justified. Within that realm, however, they are adamant in their insistence on policing that is not only protective but as productive as may be.

From Locke, Kant, and Bentham through Green and Hobhouse and up to contemporary thinkers such as Raz and Galston, Gutmann and Macedo, numerous yet more pronouncedly virtue-oriented liberals (to do no more than mention welfare-liberal practitioners such as Humphrey, Johnson, Clinton, and their analogues in other "liberal-democratic" countries) have argued for a more pervasive, a less confined or diffident policing. Of course they are reticent about assigning, explicitly, "productive" tasks to the uniformed, weapons-carrying public police, agencies to which and to whom they officially or professedly assign a primarily "protective" role. But if my overall argument is correct, in their view the public police cannot effectively perform its protective tasks without engaging in productive activities.

No liberalism can entirely avoid something like this view. As I said above, every liberalism is a something, not an anything. All liberalisms are idealisms; they all stand for certain beliefs and values and they therefore must stand against forms of thinking and acting that they believe to be destructive of the beliefs and values they stand for. For both but especially for the second of these reasons, all liberalisms (as distinct from anarchisms, antinomianisms, nihilisms, and perhaps radical libertarianisms) support institutions of police and policing, and all of them proffer some institutionalism that is intended to inform and direct the workings of the institutions and practices of police and policing.

But these commonalities among liberalisms conceal or repress more than they reveal or illuminate. At the level of ideals, the great difference between virtue- and individuality- and freedom-oriented liberalisms concerns what we can call the teleologies that they respectively advance. Virtue liberalisms (numerous protestations to the contrary notwithstanding) feature more or less encompassing and substantive conceptions of what is good for human beings generally or good for the members of this or that culture or society. Confident that anyone who rejects these conceptions can be shown to be in error (philosophical or rational) or in the grip of some form of misapprehension (cultural or historical), virtue liberalisms assert that if policing is an effective way to correct mistaken thinking and acting, there is no reason to hold back from it. And if policing is the only way to make those corrections, then it becomes wrong not to police.

Because it too is an idealism, "agency-oriented," "willful," or "strong-voluntarist" liberalism also advances conceptions of good and harm. The human goods are individuality, distinctiveness, and singularity, and the freedom to pursue and enact them. Human beings are diminished by homogeneity, harmed by conformity and unnecessary restrictions on freedom. But as the pro-words in these formulations themselves begin to indicate, these ideals or these ends are more formal than substantive. We distinguish individuality from numerous other things— from conformism, slavish imitation or submission, herd and mob behavior, and so on—but there are as many forms of individuality as there are individuals who bring off some degree of self-enactment. We make judgments and assessments of the characters and personalities, styles and sensibilities, ends and purposes that individuals enact, develop, and adopt, but the notion that there is one or a small number of right and wrong ways to be an individual is a contradiction in terms. Again, we distinguish freedom from being compelled, coerced, restrained, and the like, and we may assign special importance to certain freedoms in the sense of the assured liberty to engage in various classes of action such as political speech and religious worship. But there are as many forms of political speech as there are political speakers, innumerable forms of religious worship, and the idea of a fixed inventory of free actions is absurd on its face.

For these and related reasons, a liberalism that privileges individuality and freedom implies a stance or general attitude toward policing very different from that which I have attributed to virtue-oriented liberalisms. As a "practical" matter, many virtue-oriented liberals are suspicious of or apprehensive concerning the police and policing, particularly the public police. They are of course aware of the frequency of discriminatory and excessive uses of force, of corruption, and so on. Hence they promote, with Mill, vigilance concerning police conduct, they may favor various restrictions on police authority, and they prefer to pursue, as far as practicable, their cultural, moral, and political objectives through education, persuasion, provision of positive incentives, and like means and methods. But they have no principled reasons, no reasons grounded in the fundaments of their theories, to oppose policing.

By contrast, for a liberalism that gives pride of place to individuality and freedom the very idea of police and policing is objectionable, offensive. To police is to order, to make alike, to restrict and require, to subject thinking and acting to rules and commands. Liberalisms of this type accept the necessity of police and policing, but they do so ruefully and with regret.

Do these general observations have any bearing on the issues that arise in the day-to-day conduct of policing? Clearly they yield no very definite answers to questions such as how police patrolling should be organized and conducted, whether and how the police should be armed, whether there should be civilian review boards, what sentencing policies should be followed, how prisons should be organized and administered. If a theorist claims that her theory answers these questions she becomes, in Oakeshott's derisive sense, a "theoretician," an "impudent mountebank."

I want to claim, however, that liberalism of the kind I favor does have important implications concerning some of the most general but also sharply contested issues concerning police and policing. In order to make this argument I have to execute something of an about-face—a maneuver always difficult in itself and that in this instance will put me in what many of my fellow liberals will think is pretty bad company.

I have argued that the distinction between protection and service, between the negative and the positive tasks of policing, does not withstand examination, that protection invariably involves attempts to re-shape, re-form, rehabilitate. Or, more precisely, I have argued that all attempts known to me to articulate and deploy (and take comfort from) this distinction not only recognize the need for "positive" policing but betray an enthusiasm for it. But now I want to argue *for* this distinction, want to argue that it articulates an ideal that we ought to pursue as best we can. We should think of the police, in particular the armed public police but also that myriad of policing agents and agencies of which we have so many, as protecting you against me, me against you. For the most part, each of us has to protect herself, has to take precautions against and maintain defenses against the incursions of others. But there are limitations on and dangers involved in self-help. (I favor, for example, gun control legislation, not because it does much to keep weapons out of the hands of criminals but because it might restrict somewhat the distribution of weapons among folks like you and me.) We should think of the police not as obviating self-help but as supplementing it and diminishing its most obvious dangers.

In more inflammatory terms, I want to argue for a "law and order" conception of policing. I agree with *a lot* of what James Q. Wilson says. Or rather I agree with a lot of the recommendations he makes. I think we should regard the law and the police as providing disincentives to criminal and other forms of action that we regard as harmful to us. I favor swift arrest, certain punishment, and incapacitation. I find convincing Wilson's evidence and arguments that these policies and these measures are the most effective ways of reducing rates of crime, that is, of affording such protections as we may hope for against it.

Less speculative and much more important, I think that this is the least objectionable conception of the police. The notions of reshaping and rehabilitating are arrogant in their assumption that there is some true or right answer to the question of how one should or should not live one's life. I don't like murder or (very many!) murderers, and I don't like rape or rapists, child abuse and child abusers. And I candidly admit to taking solace from the fact that there are those (specialists, as it were) who are prepared to make their livings by contending with those who are disposed to actions of these kinds (just as I take solace from the fact that there are those prepared to specialize in fighting wars, in "serving" in Congress, as deans, chairs, and other, to me distasteful, policing offices). But those who commit crimes, including "hardened criminals," are people for all of that and there is no justification for thinking of them as animals to be trained or objects to be molded according to my or our—invariably disputable—"ethic" or conception of the good.

There are human beings who are disposed to actions that, to the extent that my paths cross theirs and that they are not deterred or prevented from enacting their dispositions, thereby make it difficult or impossible for me to live my life as I see fit. Because *I am* (now) the person who (now) wants to live that life, *I* must do what I can to deter or prevent these others from taking those actions. If I do not do so, I resign my life and my*self* to them and to their lives.[15] Because in deterring or resisting them I am acting *for or on behalf of myself* (which can of course include acting for or on behalf of others with whom I strongly identify), I have reason (most particularly not to make myself dependent on and to that extent resigned to others) to do as much as I can *by myself*. But I also have a variety of general reasons to think that I will frequently be unable, out of my own personal resources, to deter or resist the actions of others. These reasons convince me not only to enlist the circumstantial support of various others, but to assure myself of the better-organized, provided, and hence (perhaps? hopefully?) more reliable assistance of various forms of police and policing.[16]

It is fundamentally on these grounds that I support the Wilsonian recommendations discussed above. Because others sometimes threaten me as I (now) want to be, my life as I (now) want to live it, and because there are predictable limits on my capacity to protect my*self* against them, self-concern, concern for my individuality and freedom, justifies or warrants my support for various modes of police and policing, for mechanisms of deterrence, resistance, and incapacitation that I am unable, alone, to generate, sustain or effectively employ. When or to the extent that I support coercive and violent police interference in the lives and activities of criminals and others whom I regard as threats to me, I do so on the ground that it is the intent or at least the predictable consequence of the actions of the latter that I be prevented from being and enacting the self I now want to be or become. And you, all of those among you who have the same concern for self that I do, have the same justification for supporting police and policing.

Haunted (as all genuine liberals are) by anarchist, antinomian, and nihilist/skeptical objections, I advance this line of thought, adopt this justification (or sketch of a justification) with numerous misgivings. The empirically most obvious objection to it is that I cannot hope to control the police. By agreeing to the creation and legitimation of a force designed (in part by me!) to be greater than my own, I inevitably make myself vulnerable to it. The far deeper difficulty resides in the claim, explicit in the justification, that I am warranted in interfering in, or supporting interferences in, the lives of those others (call them, for purposes of abbreviation, the criminals) in ways that they are not justified in interfering in mine. I said above that hardened criminals are people for all of that, are indistinguishable from me in that they too have conceptions of self and desired self-enactment and -becomings. And in arguing that the police should provide them with what they themselves will regard as negative incentives, I have accorded them the status of agents, of persons who hold beliefs, frame intentions, make judgments, and engage in actions that are, as Oakeshott puts it, "exhibitions of intelligence."[17] Inadequate as it is, this the best I can do to accommodate liberalism as I have tried to understand and promote it with thinking about criminality and the police.

7 / Liberal versus Civic, Republican, Democratic, and Other Vocational Educations: Liberalism and Institutionalized Education

Certainly, it is beneficial when the roles of man and citizen coincide as far as possible; but this only occurs when the role of citizen presupposes so few special qualities that the man may be himself without any sacrifice. . . .

Education is only to develop a man's faculties, without regard to giving human nature any special civic character.

Wilhelm von Humboldt, 1993, pp. 49, 50

In this chapter I consider education for civic and democratic citizenship in the context of a family of notions marked by terms such as *liberal* and *liberalism*, terms that are commonly but by no means innocently conjoined with them (e.g., *liberal democracy, liberal education*). More specifically, I assess education for democratic and other forms of citizenship as one institutionalized means of pursuing the ideals of political and moral liberalism. Continuing to presume on the construction of liberal ideals developed in the preceding chapters, I inquire concerning the understandings of education appropriate and ill suited to those ideals.

The distinction I draw between liberal education and vocational training is foreshadowed in the widely received view that nursery schools, kindergartens, and the elementary schools should convey bodies of information, nurture abilities, and impart skills that are "basic" in the sense that they can be expected to be essential or at least valuable regardless of the walks of life or pursuits that pupils may later choose.[1] This distinction is more frequently and insistently drawn as educational institutions diversify according to the extent to which they do or do not aim to prepare students for particular careers or professions. In ways that vary among and within contemporary societies, adolescents elect or are directed into a "high" or grammar as distinct from a vocational school. Those who matriculate to the former may later choose a college preparatory rather than a technical course of studies and may go on to a liberal arts program rather than attend a trade school or polytechnic or undertake predominantly preprofessional studies in a college or university. The distinction is rehearsed at the level of adult education, where some programs are designed to enhance prospects in particular vocations and others aim to enlarge understandings and appreciations that, even if contributive to various careers, may be specifically required by none.

As is evident from the title and epigraph opening this chapter, I value and attempt to sustain a version of the distinction between liberal and vocational education. Difficulties with the distinction—particularly with its seeming implication that liberal education entirely eschews definite or even identifiable ends or objectives—will have to be considered, but my primary purpose is to assess the bearing of the distinction on questions concerning "political" education. If or to the extent that "education" is qualified as "political," does it thereby become vocational as opposed to liberal?

There is one respect in which the answer to this question is, or once was, clearly in the negative. To the extent that political education involves the study of political history and ideas, institutions, and processes, it was traditionally and in most quarters still is regarded as part of the liberal as distinct from technical or professional curricula. The emergence of the idea that there could be a science or a scientific study of politics qualified and in a few places displaced this understanding. Nevertheless, studying the political dimensions of human experience continues to be regarded as appropriate regardless of the vocational intentions of students. Instruction concerning these subject matters becomes professional or preprofessional, if at all, only at late stages of formal or institutionalized education. These observations concerning educational history and practice, however, deflect from ambiguities—which not infrequently turn out to be equivocations—in conceptions and practices of political education. If education concerning politics has traditionally and rightly been regarded as liberal in the foregoing sense, institutionalized forms of political education have commonly been and are now widely intended to prepare students, if not for the technical or efficiency-seeking performances of which Michael Oakeshott famously and justly complained (1991, "Political Education"), at least for conduct judged to be appropriate to this or that politically organized society. These forms of education are "political" in the more formidable respect that they aim to convey particular political beliefs and install distinctive attitudes, values, and patterns of conduct. (A potent indicator of the prevalence of this tendency is the extent to which the contents of the political educations given, the ideas presented and the interpretations proffered, vary substantially from one regime to another.) Frequently described as *civic education, education for citizenship, for liberal democracy,* or *for democratic life,* this pronounced tendency raises two issues. The first but less important is whether education thus conceived merits the *educational* insignia "liberal." The second is whether educational conceptions and practices with this character can comport with a regime that merits the *ideological-political* insignia (here treated as honorific) "liberal."

I

We need first to consider some of the complications in the general concept of liberal education. The remarks above construe this concept negatively or privatively: liberal education is *not* vocational, *not* professional or preprofessional. Because my concern is with relationships between notions of liberal education and liberalism as a moral and political ideology, I note that this conception of liberal education is reminiscent of those versions of political and moral liberalism that promote its neutrality toward or among alternative conceptions of the good.[2] In this rendering of liberal thinking, a liberal regime is one that professes not to affirm, certainly not authoritatively to impose, any particular conception of the good (of the good or the worthy life). The aim of a liberal regime, rather, is to create and sustain conditions necessary or strongly contributive to the pursuit of a wide—albeit not unlimited[3]—variety of such conceptions. Analogously, liberal education seeks to nurture abilities and understandings regarded as valuable to a generous—albeit, again, not limitless[4]—array of careers or callings.

Both of these importantly complementary views are improvements on prominent alternatives. Sympathetically construed, proponents of liberal education and of neutralist political liberalism (occasionally the same writers) are reacting against doctrines that promote a single or unified conception of the moral, political, or educational good, creeds of the latter kind being associated with fanatical and impositional practices. In standing against such practices, we might say, thinkers of this generically liberal persuasion sustain that element in *liberal* and *liberalism* that is expressed when dictionaries define these terms as meaning "generous." But both of these views are deeply problematic.

There is abundant reason to doubt the possibility of antiseptically neutralist educational or political positions. Education and politics being purposive pursuits and practices, it is difficult to see how they could be conducted—or theorized—apart from judgments concerning ends or goals.[5] Momentarily gratifying as unmasking operations may be, however, the more important objection to neutralism is that its professed impartiality among conceptions of the good diminishes or erodes the respects in which liberalism at its most appealing is insistently a form of idealism, perfectionism, or even utopianism.[6] It is an enlivening or inspiriting rather than a merely tolerant or accommodating ideology. From this perspective, the issue here is whether moral and political liberalism can be idealist and inspiriting without becoming intolerant, intrusive, and dictatorial: whether it can support and promote vigorous end- or goal-seeking conduct and yet avoid a monistic or unified substantive teleology.

The same question arises concerning liberal education, but in this case we cannot postpone the question of substantive ends. According to Richard Peters (1967) among numerous others, all education, certainly all education in what Peters calls the "achievement" sense, supposes aims or outcomes that are valued and sought by the teacher, the student, or some agent or agency that authorizes the teaching and learning activities. In this persuasive view, although it is important that the aims and purposes of liberal education are *less* specific, *less* determinative of educational practice and its anticipated sequels than those of vocational training programs, it is illusory to think that liberal education could be entirely neutral among or indifferent to outcomes.[7]

This feature of the concept of education is inseparable from a characteristic of institutionalized educational practice that is troublesome from the standpoint of political and moral liberalism as here conceived. All institutionalized education necessarily involves a hierarchical relationship between teacher and student. Setting aside the compromised exception of Platonic views according to which the educatee already "knows" that which she is taught by the educator, the student either cannot have advance appreciation of or can appreciate only very generally or formally the value of what the educator teaches her.[8] If the educatee already knows what the educator has to teach, the educator is redundant if not otiose. Numerous other less clearly pedagogic factors affect the teacher–student relationship (see the disturbing remarks quoted from Durkheim below), but all save the most radically autodidactic forms of learning involve hierarchical relationships between educators and educatees. At least in this respect education, however liberal, is unavoidably in tension with the ideal of self-making central to moral and political liberalism as here conceived.

These considerations are not reason for abandoning the distinction between liberal and vocational education. The distinction is not and cannot be categorial, but liberal education typically—it might be better to say definitionally—involves *less* specific ends and correspondingly less impositional programs of instruction. Major proponents of liberal education have argued for it primarily on this ground. But if all institutionalized education is "achievement oriented," liberals who stand for individual self-enactment and freedom ought to take a wary and cautious, perhaps a skeptical, stance toward it.[9]

II

Some liberal thinkers and publicists have recognized the antipathy between their political and moral ideals and institutionalized education. Unwilling to give up either, they have contrived a variety of strategies to diminish the illiberal characteristics of the forms and styles of education that they favor.

One of these strategies is represented by a notion already introduced, that is, of education in "basic" knowledges and skills such as speaking and reading, writing, and arithmetic. Although often advanced by educationists with a declared antagonism toward liberal ideals, liberal proponents of basic education argue that schooling should contribute to the largest possible number of forms and styles of life and should be adapted, progressively, to the dispositions and preferences of its educatees.

If applied to education, neutralist moral and political liberalism would seem to support this educational outlook or orientation. Formal education should be devoted to providing skills and bodies of knowledge that are "primary" in the Rawlsian sense of valuable to lives with a wide diversity of styles and purposes. If education has a general or overarching end, it is to enhance the prospect that individuals will formulate and will be enabled effectively to pursue ends of their own. It follows that, as students form definite conceptions of their objectives, educators should adapt their teaching to serve student conceptions.

At its best—with celebration of difference and diversity replacing the dubious notion of neutrality toward or among them—this idea of education in basics has affinities with the Nietzschean notion of "preparations" necessary to a life of "self-overcoming"and "free-spiritedness" and to the analogous Oakeshottian ideal of learning that furnishes students not with a single and fixed body of knowledge or a settled identity but with the wherewithal for self-enactment.[10] "Liberal arts" education is sometimes understood in this way, but it is increasingly viewed as prevocational or in the service of a collectively defined good (for example, "social reproduction").[11] I argue that theorists of democratic and civic education pervert liberal education in this way.

Understood as described in the previous paragraph, the idea of education in basics is importantly consonant with liberal ideals. I say more about this conception and its considerable difficulties below. But let us first consider the more radical strategy represented by "liberationist" educational thinking. Views of this type challenge the assumption that young children and adolescents are incapable of forming and pursuing conceptions of themselves and their ends or goals. Liberationists regard schools—toward which they are often hostile (see Illich, 1970)—as settings in which students ought to have opportunities to articulate and explore, contest and reformulate their own conceptions of self, other, and world. *If* there is a distinction between "education" and later (i.e., adult) "life," we should reject the notion that the former is merely preparation for the latter.

Liberationist thinking appears to be more contributive to liberal moral and political ideals than are conceptions of basic education. If its proponents have sometimes betrayed their professions (Summerhill is often cited as an example), the more telling fact is the animus that their proposals have aroused among thinkers sometimes aligned with political and moral liberalism. From Rousseau to Durkheim, Dewey, and Arendt, liberationist thinking has been derided as a betrayal of the duties of educators generally, particularly of educators in democracies.[12]

These reflections, though preliminary, carry the following suggestions. In order to be as consonant with liberal principles as its inherently illiberal character permits, education should be private or personal in several connected senses. Teaching is first and foremost for the individual development of students. Educators should see themselves as in the service, even if they are not in the employ, of their students. Education ought to be adapted to the individuating characteristics of those it serves. As students form and reformulate conceptions of themselves and their purposes, they ought to take an increasing role in shaping the character of their educational experiences. Education can and perhaps must be tutorial, but ought to be as little paternalistic as possible.

Categorically rejected by Plato, and rejected all but nominally by Rousseau and the many educationists influenced by him, something close to this understanding is articulated in various works that are in the vicinity of liberal political theory. Because my concern here is with the intersection between educational and political theory, I briefly examine influential views concerning political education.

III

Surprisingly given the numerous illiberal elements in his thinking, a recognizably liberal view is available in John Locke's educational thinking. There are a few among us whose "natural constitutions" are so well formed that their education doesn't much matter either to them or to those affected by their conduct. But for "nine in ten" the quality of their own lives and hence also of those with whom they interact depend primarily on the education they receive (Locke, 1759, III, p. 1).[13] Locke's primary concern is with education to good character and disposition—as distinct, as we see below, from the transmission of bodies of knowledge and technical skills. He never doubts that education to good character presumes the authority of parents and teachers and their exercise of discipline over their charges. Regarding the manner of teaching as distinct from the content of what is taught, however, "imperiousness and severity is but an ill way of treating men ... who have reason of their own to guide them, unless," he warned, "you have a mind to make your children, when grown up, weary of you; and secretly say with themselves, 'When will you die, father'" (p. 14).

Issuing yet another caution, Locke argues that "we must not hope wholly to change their original tempers, nor make the gay pensive and grave; nor the melancholy sportive, without spoiling them. God has stamped certain characters upon men's minds, which, like their shapes, may perhaps be a little mended; but can hardly be totally altered and transformed into the contrary" (p. 20; see also pp. 42–43). More affirmatively, "The native and untaught suggestions of inquisitive children do often offer things that may set a considering man's thoughts on work. And I think there is frequently more to be learned from the unexpected questions of a child, than from the discourses of men, who talk in a road, according to the notions they have borrowed, and the prejudices of their education" (p. 54). Thus Locke has some good words for "pertness" (p. 54), for disagreement and controversy in conversation (pp. 64–65), and even for "raillery" (pp. 62–63). Tendencies toward a "misbecoming negligence and disrespect in . . . carriage" must be combatted, but a "sheepish bashfulness" is equally to be opposed. Both can be avoided if we are taught to observe "this one rule, 'Not to think meanly of ourselves, and not to think meanly of others'" (p. 61). In these respects, if Locke's puritanical moralism could somehow be excised from *Some Thoughts Concerning Education*, that work would be promote liberal education in strong senses of the term.[14]

There are two further and related dimensions of Locke's thinking that are directly pertinent here. The first, complementary to his concern for the development of character, is his sustained opposition to thinking of education as aiming to transmit particular bodies of knowledge or to cultivate these or those skills. "Latin and learning make all the noise: and the main stress is laid upon his proficiency in things, a great part whereof belong not to a gentleman's calling; which is, to have the knowledge of a man of business, a carriage suitable to his rank, and to be eminent and useful in his country, according to his station" (1759, p. 38; see also pp. 70–79). Education always has some content, some substance, but, Locke implies, there is no undeniably superior set of topics and texts. Each and every "gentleman" will eventually require expertise concerning various specialized matters, and Locke urges that general or basic education include the imparting of familiarity with "a trade or two or three," including some of the manual skills necessary to them (pp. 90–99). But "gentlemen" can and should acquire more particular knowledges and abilities as these become necessary to them.[15]

The second further dimension to which I just alluded concerns Locke's promotion of a virtue that he calls "civility." More particularly, it concerns what that virtue is and is not and how parents and teachers should and should not go about cultivating it in their children and students.

The happiness that all men so steadily pursue, consisting in pleasure, it is easy to see why the civil are more acceptable than the useful. The ability, sincerity, and good intention, of a man of weight and worth, or a real friend, seldom atones for that uneasiness that is produced by his grave and solid representations. Power and riches, nay virtue itself, are valued only as conducting to our happiness; and therefore he recommends himself ill to another, as aiming at his happiness, who, in the services he does him, makes him uneasy in the manner of doing them. He that knows how to make those he converses with easy, without debasing himself to low and servile flattery, has found the true art of living in the world, and being both welcome and valued everywhere. Civility, therefore, is what, in the first place, should with great care be made habitual to children and young people. (p. 63)

As with all true virtues, civility is taught "more by practice than rules" and Locke doubts whether a young student "should read any other discourses of morality, but what he finds in the bible; or have any system of ethics put into his hand" (p. 82).[16] As children mature, they should be asked to read Cicero and perhaps Pufendorf and Grotius. Also, "The general part of civil law and history, are studies which a gentleman should . . . constantly dwell upon" in order to acquire an "insight into the reason of our statutes . . . *and what weight they ought to have.*" For those, however, who do "not design" the law for their "calling," such studies should concern "not the chicane of private cases, but the affairs and intercourse of civilized nations in general, grounded upon the principles of reason" (p. 82; emphasis added).

Richard Battistoni observes, disapprovingly, that the

> idea of direct political education of citizens by public institutions is deprecated throughout the liberal tradition. Though Locke sees moral education as a fundamental part of a person's development, nowhere in any of his educational writings do we find a discussion of teaching a child to be a citizen or a participant in politics. All virtues to be learned are private or social, not political. In fact, since "direct virtue" [as Locke calls it] . . . "is the hard and valuable part to be aimed at in education," it is dangerous to entrust this "valuable part" of education to the schools or other political institutions. (1985, p. 33)

Badly mistaken as generalizations about *soi-disant* liberal thinking,[17] Battistoni's remarks are basically accurate concerning Locke's *Thoughts*. Rather than reason for disparaging Locke's reflections, they identify the most attractive features of his educational-political thinking. Strongly analogous features invite a turn to the less equivocal views of John Stuart Mill.

Mill reacted fiercely against Bentham's and his father's utilitarian educational thinking and particularly to the relentlessly end-driven education that the two of them imposed on him. Substituting the wider notions "liberal" and "humane" for what Locke calls "civility,"[18] in his *Autobiography*, in *On Liberty*, and most especially in his "Inaugural Address at the University of St. Andrews," Mill distanced himself from the mechanistic elements in the thinking of his mentors and developed views that are an enlargement of those of his empiricist predecessors. Attention to these views, and to more explicitly political arguments of Emile Durkheim and Hannah Arendt, will help us to answer the two major questions here posed: whether civic, democratic, and other specifically political conceptions of education are vocational rather than liberal and whether such conceptions are appropriate to a liberal regime.

Education in the sense of "the culture which each generation purposively gives to those who are to be its successors" should not be concerned "to teach the knowledge required to fit men for some special mode of gaining their livelihood. . . . [Its] object is not to make skilful lawyers or physicians or engineers [or citizens], but capable and cultivated human beings" (Mill, 1971, pp. 154–55). There is a place for schools of professional or vocational education, but what they teach is

> no part of what every generation owes to the next, as that on which its civilisation and worth will principally depend. . . . Whether those whose specialty they are will learn them as a branch of intelligence or as a mere trade, and whether, having learnt them, they will make a wise and conscientious use of them . . . depends upon what sort of minds they bring to it—what kind of intelligence and conscience the general system of education has developed in them. Men are men before they are lawyers or physicians . . . [or citizens?]; and if you make them capable and sensible men, they will make themselves capable and sensible lawyers or physicians [citizens?]. (p. 156)[19]

Mill is as keen as Locke to engender the sensibility called civility, but he also insists that education must impart a familiarity with the "general principles" that constitute the several arts and sciences. His emphasis on the cognitive objectives of education is in tension with his concern for personal style. But he is adamant that liberal instruction in these "general principles" is not for the specialist's purpose of applying or extending particular bodies of knowledge. Rather, it is to enable the members of society to appreciate and to assess critically the sciences, the professions, and other socially established institutions and practices. More particularly, it is to provide them with resources essential if they are to make and remake their conceptions of their own lives.[20]

Mill was aware that contemporary imperatives toward specialization threatened to make his view anachronistic. "But matters are not so bad with us; . . . It is not the utmost limit of human acquirement to know only one thing, but to combine a minute knowledge of one or a few things with a general knowledge of many things. . . . It is this combination which gives a . . . body of cultivated intellects . . . capable of guiding and improving public opinion on the great concerns of practical life" (pp. 165–66).

Despite retaining the confused notion of a "scientific politics," Mill insists that politics neither requires nor allows "having a set of conclusions ready made, to be applied everywhere indiscriminately." It calls for informed judgment concerning "the given case. And this, at present, scarcely any two persons do in the same way. What we require to be taught is to be our own teachers" (p. 204).

There is, however, a truth about politics. That truth is the inveterate tendency of politics and government (however democratic) to become "selfish, corrupt and tyrannical." Liberal education does not implant doctrines or promote institutional arrangements specific to particular regimes. Its task is to convey the "information" and to cultivate the dispositions and abilities essential to critical assessment of the "public transactions" and the institutionalized arrangements that produce and sustain this brutal and brutalizing tendency (p. 210).

IV

Sharing a concern prevalent among civic and democratic educationists, in *Moral Education* and elsehere Emile Durkheim insists that society and its educators abide no infractions of the moral discipline necessary to overcoming egoism and the anomie that results from it.[21] Every hint of disrespect for morality weakens the moral order on which civilized life depends (1961, pp. 170–73).

These features of Durkheim's thinking coexist with views contributive to liberal thinking about education and politics. He has a commitment to pluralism that—given his insistence on a single moral code that should discipline all members of society—is surprisingly robust. Because pluralism and individuality stand in an often antagonistic but sometimes complementary relationship, this commitment opens up engaging possibilities.

Although allowing that the family must begin the educational processes that make young children into human beings (pp. 18-19, 134), Durkheim rejects Rousseau's (and Locke's) preference for education by single tutors. The possibility of educating children is due chiefly to two of their "natural" characteristics. Along with their egoism and aggressiveness, children are susceptible to influence. Along with being impetuous and unruly, they form and adhere to habits and routines. "Thanks to his [the child's] marked propensity for habitual behavior, we can limit . . . his constitutional instabilities, and build in him a preference for an ordered life. . . . thanks to his extreme suggestibility, we can give him something like the first feeling for moral authority" (p. 144).

Durkheim sees perils as well as advantages in these human characteristics. He enlarges his scientistic concern for *what* is taught to include the manner in which teaching is conducted and the effects of institutionalized education on the character or spirit of the educatees. "Rather than there being no danger that the influence of teacher and parents is ever excessive, certain steps are indispensable to protect the freedom of the child." "One of the most effective [such] precautions . . . is to ensure that children are not trained exclusively under the influence of a single milieu, or still worse, by a single . . . person." Educating children in the internally diverse environment of schools helps to free them from "excessive dependency" and allows each of them to "develop his own personality" (pp. 144–45).

Durkheim agrees with Humboldt that schools have this liberating and empowering effect only if they are organized and conducted with the specific intention of producing it. With Emile's omnipresent tutor in mind, Durkheim asks, "[How could we] dream . . . of permitting the child to spend his entire life in the hands of a single instructor? Such an education would . . . easily lead to subservience. The child could not fail to reproduce passively the single model placed before him. . . . The only way of preventing this kind of servitude [the very servitude Rousseau avidly sought?] . . . is to multiply the teachers . . . so that the various influences prevent any one from becoming too exclusively preponderant" (p. 143). The "subjection of man to man" that Rousseau promoted, Durkheim intones, "is immoral" (p. 145).

What bearing does this dissonant set of views have on civic education? In its generic form, the morality indispensable to society "consists in the attachment to a social group," in accepting and conforming to norms that are "external" to all individual persons. The family being a social group, by this criterion the training that occurs in it is moral in character. But "all human societies are not of equal value. Indeed, there is one [level of] society that enjoys a real primacy over all others—the political society, the nation" (p. 79). Anxious concerning parochialism and egoism, Durkheim was concerned that the "state is far away." Because the French in particular are only rarely "directly involved in [the state's] . . . activities," they fail to internalize the higher norms that it represents (p. 233).

Along with his uncompromising anticlericalism, it was for this reason that Durkheim strongly favored state-funded and -supervised education. Nationally controlled education is the only antidote to the moral poisons of fragmentation and the alienation that results from it. The "school is the only moral agent through which the child is able systematically to learn to know and love his country. It is precisely this fact that lends pre-eminent significance to the part played by the school . . . in the shaping of national morality" (p. 79).

These passages will warm the hearts of civic and democratic educationists. They sound like, and in part are, a call for education that inculcates norms specific to the civic life of *this* nation-state. Happily, Durkheim is against as much as he is with educationists of this persuasion. He supports the family as a bulwark against egoism but in the next breath resists its narrowing influences; he promotes but then cautions against education for "love of country." A nation "can enjoy moral primacy only on the condition that it is not conceived of as an unscrupulously self-centered being." Nations are "but . . . one of many agencies that . . . collaborate for the progressive realization of the conception of mankind" (p. 79). Because nation-states are mostly conceived in the former, morally repugnant manner, education to "attachment to one's country" is dangerous business.

The school has a delicate combination of tasks to perform. It must provide students with knowledge and skills and it must instill moral discipline. But it must do both of these things without stifling the development of individual personalities. It must link the child to the state without engendering uncritical nationalism and without making the state and politics the exclusive focus of attention and activity.[22]

Although favoring state-sponsored schools, Durkheim shared Humboldt's worry that an educational system of this type would lead to centralization and uniformity. To counter this tendency he advocated intraschool plurality and also argued that principals and teachers should be accorded substantial independence from national educational authorities. But these devices carry great dangers. The very superiorities that allow principals and teachers to accomplish their educational tasks, the very authority and power that they must have if they are to protect the school from the state and maintain the necessary internal discipline, turn pedagogues into despots and schools into tyrannical regimes.[23]

There is no fully satisfactory solution to the difficulties Durkheim so vividly identifies. His remarks underscore respects in which educational processes are intrinsically or irremediably illiberal.[24] Given that liberalism should be wary of this and that educational practice but can hardly abandon education, what can be done to abate the difficulties?

In addressing this question, Durkheim looks outside of the schools themselves and beyond the governments that create and supervise them. "There is . . . a force that is . . . in a position to check this kind of [professional educational and statist] thinking; [namely] the prevailing climate of moral opinion. It is the force of moral opinion that is chiefly responsible for protecting the child, signalizing his nascent moral character and making him worthy of respect" (1961, pp. 195–96). "Moral opinion" must "ensure that the school does not shut itself up within itself . . . and does not have a too narrowly professional character" (pp. 196–97). Schools must be scrutinized by members of society who are neither professional educators nor officials of the state. The communal groups that constitute intermediate society must express an opinion more liberal than that which can be expected from educators and state officials (including persons who think of themselves first and foremost as that species of state official called a citizen).

Durkheim's own invocation of this liberalizing resource is compromised by his insistence on rigorously rational moral discipline and by his view that such discipline must be implanted by schools and the state. Would moral opinion in a society true to these among his principles protect the freedom and individuality of children? Would persons whose moral convictions were formed by the schools and the state of such a society contest the tendencies that he objects to in those institutions?

The first of the foregoing two questions is the one that matters most in respect to Durkheim. If we challenge his commitments to rationalist virtue, if we instead foreground the enthusiasm of Locke, Mill, and Durkheim for adverbial *virtùs* and individual freedom and individuality, and if we follow them in distinguishing between liberal and vocational education and Mill in promoting the former for all members of society, then we will have done the most important parts of what can be done to resist the propensities of professional educators and state bureaucrats—so often enemies in this or that intraeducational battle but allies in a war against freedom and liberal individuality.

V

Conceptions of civic and democratic education deepen the ineliminably illiberal character of all institutionalized education. Theories and practices of institutionalized education thus oriented and directed justify installing beliefs and attitudes and securing abilities and skills judged necessary to the end-states (the vocations or trades) denoted by concepts such as social and moral, civic and democratic. Conceptions of education for "social" life convert the adjective into a noun, one that signifies definite qualities and promotes specific attitudes; it also excludes or opposes perspectives and ways of acting that are isolating, privatizing, and alienating. More emphatically, conceptions of democratic and civic education engender regime-preferred characteristics (for example, Rawls's "reasonableness") as they combat what they regard as non- and antidemocratic or anticivic doctrines and orientations.

There are reasons to expect that education for civic or democratic ends will be impositional and indoctrinating. Proponents of these conceptions agree that it is no easy matter to instill the attitudes and install the beliefs they judge appropriate. Some among them think that human beings are "naturally" wayward and undependable if not aggressive and despotic. On these assumptions educators must devise means more powerful than the natural forces against which they contend. Others think that human beings are by nature sociable and cooperative, have a native tendency to participate actively and constructively in civic life. Yet others deny that there is a given human nature or reject the idea that the qualities necessary to democratic or civic life are incompatible with such native dispositions as there may be.

Irrespective of these differences, virtually all proponents of moral and social, democratic and civic education advance their ideals against what they take to be prevalent tendencies, whether "natural" or the effects of life in "commercial" or "liberal," "industrial-technocratic," "modern" or "postmodern" societies and cultures. They can hope to achieve their objectives only if they defeat the forces that produced and sustain these tendencies. Education is the chief battleground on which this war must be fought. Schools partially remove students from the family and the general cultural milieu, thereby affording educators leverage on student beliefs and attitudes. Because virtually all schooling is now either provided or supervised by government, the outcome of this struggle depends first and foremost on whose army controls the commanding heights that public education affords.

It follows that education for democratic or civic life could be said to be liberal (if at all)[25] only if civic or democratic beliefs and values are necessary to a liberal society. Numerous proponents of these forms of education have no interest in making such a case. If we align arguments for civic education with recent versions of classical republicanism, or democratic education with participatory or "strong" democracy, we find that the proponents of these ideologies are opponents of liberalism. It is not uncommon, however, for proponents of civic and democratic education to claim that republican or participatory democratic regimes are the only ones that allow freedom properly understood and the only ones that enable worthy forms of self-fashioning. "Liberal democrats," proponents of education for "liberal democracy," make related arguments and claim that their position represents liberalism at its most fully realized.[26]

Accordingly, at this juncture I look more directly at the notions of democratic and civic politics and the forms of education they are thought to require. There are three questions, one quite general and two somewhat more specific, to be addressed. The general question is whether "civic," "republican," "democratic," or any other specifically political conception of education is compatible with liberalism.[27] The first more particular question is whether there are specific beliefs and values, virtues and dispositions that are necessary to the various kinds of regimes—liberal or otherwise—with which we are acquainted. (If so, there might be an intraregime argument for educational arrangements and practices that install and instill those qualities and characteristics.) The second is whether civic, republican, or democratic regimes best serve what might be called whole-life freedom and individuality, or serve those objectives longer or better than the liberal regimes with which civic, republican, and democratic theorists contrast them. (If so, one or more of the latter conceptions of education might be justified, despite the illiberal character of its educational practices.)

I begin with a remark (distinctive in this book in that it might be styled polemical!) concerning the general question. In their most relentlessly teleological versions, arguments for education appropriate to civic, republican, and democratic regimes require a postponement of gratifications so severe as to portend the radical instrumentalization of childhood. Machiavelli, James Harrington, and Cato's Letters at their most republicanly insistent; Rousseau, Bentham, and James Mill at their "radical" worst; Durkheim at his most societal/moral; and contemporary civic, democratic, and participationist theorists such as Bruce Ackerman, Battistoni, Benjamin Barber, Gutmann, and Pangle in their most uncompromising moments. To the extent that these writers give consideration to the characteristics distinctive of childhood, they do so for the unswervingly forward-looking reason that doing so is the most effective means of producing and "reproducing" the adults necessary to the kinds of regimes they favor. Even if we agreed that some one among these regime types is optimal as regards adult liberty and individuality we might resist these political and educational conclusions on the ground that Jamesian zest, Nietzschean free-spiritedness, or Oakeshottian self-enactment are as valuable in childhood as later. To do so *might* be to degenerate into the most sentimental versions of liberationist thinking. It could equally express the view that abusing children is not only evil in itself but a reliable way of producing abusive adults.[28]

Having underlined, perhaps redundantly, my antipathies, I turn to the two less general questions mentioned above.

Politics and government are distinctive domains or dimensions of human affairs. However we identify their distinctive features, it seems to follow that (1) there are qualities of character, bodies of knowledge and belief, and sets of skills and abilities that are essential to each among them. More emphatically, if politics is viewed as a vocation and governing as a profession, it will readily be thought that good performance in them requires prevocational or preprofessional training. If we further agree that civic republican, participatory democratic, liberal democratic, and so on, government and politics are notably distinct from one another, it appears to follow that each of these regime types requires (2) more particular understandings and expertise and (3) a quite particular array of values and virtues.[29] Virtually all arguments for specifically civic and participatory democratic education assume propositions 1 through 3, and various liberal democrats have argued for 2 and, in the tradition of Rousseau, Tocqueville, and T. H. Green, especially for 3.[30]

We have seen that Mill is cautious about proposition 1 and actively resistant to propositions 2 and 3. Having followed him in advancing a circumscribed version of 1, I now concentrate on 2 and 3.

We can begin with a characteristically elegant formulation of Michael Oakeshott's:

> As a deliberative and argumentative engagement directed to reaching conclusions sustained by reasons designed to persuade others of their cogency, politics is identifiable not in terms of persons, places or occasions, but only in respect of a focus of attention and a subject of discourse. The conditions of a *respublica* . . . allow for the election or appointment of certain persons to devote themselves to political deliberation and negotiation; but, although some will be better equipped to do it than others, there is nothing in the engagement itself to suggest a profession and much eloquently to deny it. (1975, p. 165)[31]

Governance does involve specialized tasks that require "servants" who are "civil" (apt characterizations of how those in such positions *ought* to view their professional activities) but who also are expected to have various kinds of "expert knowledge." There are good reasons to think that most of this "expertise" should be acquired "on the job" rather than through prevocational training. There may be a place for training of the latter kind, but it can hardly substitute for a liberal education that prepares experts to make humane uses of such expertise as they may acquire.

Because politics consists importantly of assessing and controlling the activities of those in authority and power, it is desirable that there be others not thus professionally placed who are able effectively to critique the activities of officials. In the old but still good phrase, all of these experts should be "on tap, not on top." If politics consists in "attending to the general arrangements of a set of people whom chance or choice have brought together" (Oakeshott), more particularly in maintaining vigilance concerning the activities of those who are hired or otherwise make it their "business" to attend to those arrangements, the first requisite of a tolerable politics is a populace whose "general system of education" has been to the "kind of intelligence and conscience" that Mill promotes.

Because of the aversion of both political liberalism and liberal education to authoritatively determined ends, the previous paragraph is not much more, but also not much less, than a reiteration of the tenets shared between these cousin ideologies. But proponents of civic republicanism and participatory democracy evidence no such aversion. Rather, they indefatigably campaign to seduce us to a substantive and encompassing telos. For this reason, in respect to them the issues primarily concern the merits of their ideals. If we endorse those ideals it will be difficult to resist the notion that politics and governance are specialized vocations, institutionalized instruments to be used efficiently in pursuing the ends to which those vocations are dedicated. It will be equally difficult to resist the attendant notion that education should produce and service a politics and a governance thus conceived.

It is nevertheless worth pausing to consider thinking that subscribes to such ideals but strenuously opposes the conceptions of education commonly associated with them. Thoughts of Aristotle might well be invoked here, but the theorist who comes most forcefully to mind is Hannah Arendt.

The singularities of Arendt's theorizing defy classification under any of the familiar rubrics of political theory, but her thinking manifestly includes elements of the civic republican and participatory democratic ideologies. Yet while her political theory is certainly not liberal and her educational thinking anything but liberationist, she is outspoken in her opposition to all forms of "political" education. She sharply challenges the view that a republican or democratic (or any other particular form of) political regime is warranted in instituting a mode of education designed to serve its political character and purposes.

Arendt believed that, under the influence of sinister figures such as Rousseau and Robespierre, Europe had come to view early education as a political instrument and political activity itself as a means of educating adults to the duties of citizenship (1954, "The Crisis in Education," p. 176). I have been claiming, with Arendt, that this view remains powerfully influential among us. Notwithstanding her republican or participationist proclivities, however, Arendt insisted that this outlook involves a doubly disastrous misconception. As to politics as a mode of education, "Education can play no part in politics, because in politics we always have to deal with those who are already educated," with persons who stand as "equals in assuming the effort of persuasion, and running the risk of failure." Having earlier appropriated Arendt's thoughts, let me now quote her words. "Whoever wants [by means of politics] to educate adults really wants to act as their guardian and prevent them from political activity. The word 'education' has an evil sound in politics; there is a pretense of education, when the real purpose is coercion without the use of force" (p. 176).

Matters are worse regarding the project of teaching children beliefs and skills necessary to political participation in this or that regime. Hoisting her antiliberationist colors, Arendt asserts that without education children cannot become human beings as distinct from mere *Homo sapiens*. Unable to educate themselves, they must be taught by adults who have superior knowledge of what the world now is like (p. 195). Education is conservative not in the impossible sense of maintaining the status quo but in that its purpose is "conservation"; its "task is always to cherish and protect something—the child against the world, the world against the child, the new against the old, the old against the new" (p. 192).[32] By teaching children how the world now is (which requires teaching them how it had been), adults make it possible for children to make for themselves a "home" on an earth from which they would otherwise be forever estranged.

Eschewing details while railing against "progressive education," Arendt insists that students must "acquire the normal prerequisites of a standard curriculum" (p. 183), one taught by adults who are competent in their subject matters (p. 189), have a deep respect for the past (p. 192–93), and are accorded full authority to direct school activities. Insofar as education has a forward-looking end, it is to assist the process by which children become persons of cultivated "taste" and "judgment" in the enlarged sense that Arendt appropriates from Kant (see pp. 225–26 in Arendt, 1954, "The Crisis in Culture"). "Professional training," so far from contributing to these objectives, places insuperable obstacles in the path of achieving them (pp. 195–96).

Education is pertinent to an ennobling politics exclusively in that such a politics presupposes already educated participants. To act politically is to initiate, to begin anew. It requires the "capacity for" judgment as to how to effect change. But because political activity transforms the circumstances from which it begins, it cannot proceed from judgments that one has previously been taught. Above all, it requires qualities of character. The foremost such quality is the courage to act in the absence of reliable knowledge of how others will respond. It also requires magnanimity toward other participants and fidelity to promises. In the absence of these characteristics there can be no politics worthy of the name. Persons with no education, with no world that is theirs and no "common sense," will not have these qualities. But the preparation that education effects cannot itself instill these politically necessary *virtùs*.

Accordingly, "we must decisively divorce the realm of education from all the others, most of all from the realm of public, political life" (p. 195).

VI

Given that Arendt shares their view that politics is a distinctively valuable activity, republican-participatory-democratic-civic-educationists might well take pause from her arguments that their political objectives are *disserved* by specifically civic education. But Arendt is surely correct that thinking about education (as, in her view, is true of virtually all recent thinking) has for some time been relentlessly instrumentalist and teleocratic. The second of the two questions raised earlier is therefore the more pressing. Insofar as politics and governance are regarded as the royal road not only to stability and order but to community, virtue, and humanity, there will be assiduous efforts to use institutionalized education to shape citizens to the needs of politics and governance. As with so much of her thinking, Arendt spits her demand that we divorce education from political life into the winds of modern life.

Offensive as many will find it, we owe to no less than Aristotle the understanding that citizenship is an office, a position of authority in the polis. There is no such thing as citizenship (except in the mostly sentimental sense of a "citizen of the world") apart from a politically organized and governed society. It is political society that creates, defines the authority of, and distributes the office of citizen. To become a citizen is to submit to political rule; it is to yield to rule that aims to make one into what the regime wants one to be.[33]

Our Aristotelian inheritance also includes the notion that citizens rule and are ruled in turn, a formula radicalized by participatory democrats for whom all citizens are to rule all of the time. These views appear to draw the sting of the submission that is involved in acquiring the office of citizenship; they claim to give something of surpassing value in return for that submission.

There are excellent reasons for doubting the extent to which either of these formulas has described actual political arrangements and practices. Leaving aside the fact that citizenship has been far more frequently denied than accorded, there is abundant evidence that most of the ruling has been and continues to be done by a very small proportion of the citizenry. The role of most of those who hold the office of citizen consists in the further submission, dressed up in the moraline language of legitimacy and obligation, that is obedience to an "elite."

There are two reasons why I invoke these historical facts with reticence and ambivalence. The least important of these is that much of the evidence for them has been assembled, in a celebratory spirit, by political scientists who promote rather than regret "elite" rule and "mass" political docility. Instead of taking their empirical findings as reason for a wary stance toward politics and governance, theorists of "stable" democracy favor political rule that ranges as widely and intrudes as deeply as that promoted by the least chastened theorists of active democracy.[34]

Given this depressing circumstance, it might be thought that prudence obliges liberals not only to extend the rights of citizenship as widely as possible (which they surely ought to do) but to enlist in the company of those who would, through civic education, make citizenship and its activities our primary self-identification and commitment.

From Thucydides to Hobbes, from Nietzsche to Oakeshott, it has been objected that this strategy is badly misguided. Even if we succeed in ridding ourselves of elite rule, when we identify ourselves first and foremost as citizens we conscript ourselves to the state that creates that office; in making the activities of citizenship our primary commitment we risk adding the force of our thinking and acting to the authority and power of the state. To the extent that politics becomes avidly participatory and government widely popular, political rule extends its range and deepens its penetrations. Prudent self-regard, while forbidding political indifference or withdrawal, counsels us to maintain what Nietzsche calls a "pathos of distance" vis-à-vis the state and politics.

Lurking in this wise but incomplete counsel are powerful objections against the most insistent demands and the proudest claims of civic and participatory theories. The demand is that all citizens be equal partners in the activity of ruling. The claim is that when political inequalities have been eliminated *we* will be ruling ourselves and *I* as part of that *we* will be ruling *myself.*

Taken together, the requirement and the ideal entail a dangerous and offensive inequality of another and worse kind. Those who find ruling—officeholding and official duties, imposing and being imposed upon by others—distasteful, diminishing, or merely distracting from preferred pursuits thereby become alien and threatening figures, become enemies of the regime. As with all ideals that are "for everyone" (Nietzsche), the participatory ideal excludes and must combat all ideals that challenge its hegemony. As thinkers otherwise as diverse as Tocqueville and Mill, Nietzsche and James, Oakeshott and Foucault have tried to teach us, such demands and ideals, even if they do not become specifically political in the sense of being adopted and enforced through government, are deeply oppressive. To the extent that we accept or submit to them, we become pervasively ruled by monotonic and monolithic cultures and regimes.

In the hands of civic, republican, and participationist theorists, the demand and ideal become political several times over. The demand can be met and the ideal realized only if there is active participation in those quintessentially political activities that are inseparable from governance. Whether or not political participation is legally required, through civic education such participation is promoted as at once a stern duty and a peerless advantage. The ideal (in a sense that, unintentionally, resonates with the irony with which Nietzsche invested the notion) is "for everyone." Civic education aims to engender pride in those who are accorded standing as citizens and who participate vigorously in the activities of this office, guilt in those who have but default on its duties, and perhaps shame on the part of those who are denied this honorific standing and are deprived of its inestimable benefits. In this circumstance, and under the authority and power of civic, republican, and democratic educators who have moralized the ideals (and themselves) with notions of good, right, and obligation, the prospects of the "enemies" of the regime are less than bright.

It is therefore hardly surprising that proponents of this ideal champion rigorously civic education. Aware that their ideal conflicts with numerous others, and—at their occasional best— recognizing that it is tarnished to the extent that citizens must be conscripted and ruled by force rather than conviction, these proponents correctly infer that their project depends on the beliefs and values of citizenries. They may well believe that the politics and governance they foster would themselves be profoundly educative, that the grandeur and nobility of such a politics would transform the believing and thinking of those who participate in them. But their self-identification as proponents of a lost or largely unrealized ideal requires them to acknowledge that few if any such political opportunities are now actively on offer. In this situation their best hope is the leverage afforded by institutionalized education. They look to schooling to discredit conflicting ideals and to inculcate the beliefs and values essential to the political regime they champion.

Political educationists tell us, and more particularly would teach our children, that subscription and fidelity to certain quite definite political beliefs and values are conditions of a full, satisfying, noble or humane life. Republican/civic/democratic political educationists teach that some of us, and participatory-democratic educationists that all of us, can achieve such a life only if we actively participate in the political processes through which suitable beliefs and values are identified, disseminated, and enforced. To the extent that they succeed in this teaching, there will be a sense in which they thereby validate the premises from which they proceed. Having been brought by the training they have given us to believe that life in a regime that satisfies their requirements is full, rich, and noble, if such a regime is made by or for us we are likely to experience it in exactly this way.

Gratified and contented with ourselves we may well be. Nevertheless, our institutionalized civic, republican, or democratic training will have enclosed us in a set of beliefs that conceals and excludes a rich array of sensibilities, self-understandings, and ways of being and becoming. I can therefore end my discussion of civic as opposed to liberal education where I began it, that is, with Humboldt: civic or democratic political education might produce "a tranquil, peaceable, prosperous State," but the citizens of such a state "would always seem to me a multitude of well-cared-for slaves" (1993, p. 79).

VII

It would be disingenuous to pretend that liberal education is, by contrast, unqualifiedly liberating or antiseptically apolitical. We have seen that proponents of liberal education insist on distinctions between proper versus improper methods and procedures and between commendable versus objectionable objectives and purposes. Although they seek means of diminishing the role of hierarchy and authority, direction and discipline, they accept that education requires these elements. Opposed as they are to the notion that education should yield a standardized "product" in the shape of persons with a fixed inventory of skills, abilities, and values, their ideal of civil, literate, cultivated, humane, or self-enacting persons is nevertheless a something not an anything or a nothing. The attraction of these ideals resides importantly in the fact that civility or liberality can take numerous forms, that one can be literate or cultivated in many ways and about numerous subject matters, and that there is reason to expect that the selves the liberally educated enact will be diverse by various criteria. Yet each of these desiderata is paired with opposite or contrasting notions signaling educational outcomes that liberal education aims to prevent or avoid. Just as liberal political theory at its best is enticed by but cannot fully embrace anarchist or antinomian thinking, so liberal education must reject the liberationist notion that, in education, "anything goes."

From a political perspective, liberal education is regime nonspecific. The qualities of character that it hopes to cultivate are not chosen to service the objectives of anarchism or libertarianism; of liberal, participatory, or other forms of democracy; of aristocratic, bureaucratic, or other authoritarian polities. Accordingly, there is no secure basis for inferring that those who are liberally educated will be loyal or obedient to rather than disaffected from or disruptive of their politically organized societies. Features internal to the notion of liberal education might give us hope that the responses of the liberally educated will depend primarily on the quality of the political regimes in which they find themselves. If the regime is "good," those who have had a liberal education will realize this and will be keen to be supportive of the regime and perhaps keen to participate constructively in its affairs. If it is "bad," they will recognize this and will withdraw their support from the regime. But there is both reason and evidence against these expectations. Because politics is no more than one among the many languages that liberal education teaches, in reason those who are liberally educated may elect to converse or not in the language of politics. In fact, the liberally educated have been among those supportively participant in, actively antagonistic to, and stubbornly withdrawn from regimes widely judged to be "good" and others judged to be "bad."

None of this is to say that liberal education is irrelevant to political life. Mill was overly sanguine concerning the effects of liberal education on the quality of government and politics. The refined sensibility that he promoted is no guarantee of a refined and intelligent participation in politics and governance. But—given that there are no such guarantees—this is hardly reason to lurch to no education at all and certainly no ground for embracing vocational, civic, or other illiberal forms of education.

A fundamental political insight informing liberal education (albeit one often blurred by liberal uses of the distinction between public and private) is that politics and governance, distinctive as they are, are continuously interwoven with the other domains and dimensions of human affairs. This is sufficient reason to agree with Mill and Arendt that there can be politics and governance—as distinct, say, from chaos or a brutally imposed order—only if there is "a general knowledge of the leading facts of life, both moral and material," only where those involved in politics and governance have acquired that "common sense" that depends on familiarity with how the world has been and now is. However organized and conducted, liberal education is contributive to all politics and governance because it aims to satisfy this requirement, because it recognizes that no vocational, regime-specific civic education can meet this necessary condition.

There are yet more important contributions that liberal education can make to politics and governance, contributions that can be identified only if we at once sustain and qualify the distinctions between the cognitive and the conative, between knowing and doing, that are drawn too sharply in the previous paragraph and that have been in tension throughout this essay.

These distinctions are both necessary and dangerous. We must sustain the cognitive or knowledge-transmitting components of education both for Arendtian and more specifically political reasons. However differently they come to acquire their knowledge, and however differentially they construe and employ it, human beings can think and act only if they know a good deal about their world. Thinking and acting are (almost) always in a language and interactive thinking and acting are possible only for those who already know a language in which to think and act. Thinking is always about some facts or ideas and acting always occurs in a setting that it seeks to sustain or to alter. If we could imagine persons who have acquired no information, hold no beliefs, and are familiar with no ideas, we would have to say that they could not think and could not form the intentions or make the instrumental decisions that are integral to action.

The most specifically political reason for a cognitive component of education, accentuated by Mill and Durkheim but obscured by Arendt, is that there is something in particular that everyone should know about how matters stand with politics and government. While interwoven with other human concerns and activities, in our world politics and governance are distinctive first and foremost in that they are widely accorded a dominant standing vis-à-vis all other domains and dimensions. In the name of notions such as sovereignty and the rule of law, it is widely accepted that decisions reached through politics and adopted by government take precedence over all others. Some polities place constitutional limits on the range of permissible governmental actions, and some of these polities leave room for dissent and may accord honored standing to dissent and disobedience. But the predominant view is that governments are entitled, as they judge necessary, to enforce their decisions by coercion and physical violence. Citizens can and often must learn these facts about the world for themselves. Regrettably, in this as in other regards, direct experience is a harder school than the vicarious learning provided by the classroom or the study. If it is part of the purpose of education to acquaint students with the "general principles" discernible in human affairs, these are surely among the lessons education ought to teach.[35]

It is in part because of this immensely hazardous circumstance that exclusive emphasis on the cognitive or knowledge-transmitting function of education is both inadequate and dangerous. It is dangerous when it is pretended that the world is or ought to be some one way in all significant respects and that it is the task of education to assure that all students hold one set of beliefs about and values concerning their world. Such an exclusive emphasis is inadequate because it treats students as receptacles into which knowledge and information can and should be poured. It denies the activating emotional, attitudinal—they might better be called spiritual—characteristics that distinguish each student from all others and that allow education to be part of rather than merely preparation for self-making.[36]

As Mill and Durkheim, Nietzsche and Oakeshott insist, education that cultivates these individuating capacities enables the at-once instrumental and final goods, namely, freedom and self-enactment, in the name of which cognitive education must be justified. Such education also advantages politics and government. In societies that accord jural and moral privilege to authoritative governance, education to civility and other adverbial *virtùs* takes on great importance. Whatever ends persons educated in this way might pursue, whatever policies they might encourage their governments to adopt, their educations will dispose them to discipline their own and their government's actions by these adverbial constraints.

The most important contribution that liberal education can make to politics is to engender the disposition to a stance that is wary of politics and government. Liberal education is not training. Even at its infrequent best, it is far from a sufficient condition of citizens with this admirable characteristic. With so much else working relentlessly against this *virtù*, education to critical conversability in our political languages does the most and the best that education can do for politics, for governance, and for civility and humanity.

Notes

Introduction

1. For Oakeshott's distinctions and his reflections concerning them, see Oakeshott (1966, especially pt. III; 1983, essays I–III; 1991, "The Activity of Being an Historian"). I of course deny neither the value of historical studies nor a certain limited availability of what Oakeshott calls the "past past" as distinct from the practical and the historical pasts.

2. Oakeshott is not ordinarily classified as a genealogist, but I think this is a perfectly apt characterization of the third essay in his 1975 collection and of several of the essays in his 1991 volume.

3. Historically, few if any self-styled anarchists have taken this position in the unqualified form stated above. They have denied that these or those rules and norms, and hence these or those institutions—typically the institutions that constitute the state—can deserve authoritative standing, but they readily accord such standing to some number of other institutions, such as the family, the church, and the syndicate. In its categorial formulation, the position stated above goes beyond anarchism to antinomianism and perhaps beyond the latter to some form of (passive) nihilism. But the list of confirmed and consistent antinomians is much shorter than the list of anarchists, and the only living and breathing passive nihilist with whom I am familiar is the Russian Nechaev.

4. I am inclined to make something of an exception in this regard of the thinking of Proudhon. But because I have yet to study his thinking closely, thus far this remains no more than an inclination or temptation.

1 / Strains in and around Liberal Theory:
An Overview from a Strong Voluntarist Perspective

1. The bibliography of a recently published work on liberal political theory, restricted primarily to books, runs to well over one hundred items (Johnston, 1994). The bibliography of a survey of recent political theory, most of which is in or in the vicinity of liberal theory, runs to twenty-seven closely packed pages (Galston, n.d.).

2. Recent histories of liberalism include works by Arblaster (1991), Clarke (1978), Collini (1978), Freeden (1978, 1986), and Holmes (1984).

3. In the traditional distinction, they are Pyrrhonic rather than academic or dogmatic skeptics.

4. "The words 'good' and 'evil' are ever used with relation to the [desires or passions of the] person that useth them: there being nothing simply and absolutely so; nor any common rule . . . to be taken from the nature of the objects themselves" (Hobbes, 1962c, chap. 6). Because Hobbes regards this as a conceptual as well as a psychological truth, for him it makes no sense to say that a desire or passion is good or evil in itself. But he thinks that having desires and passions is a necessary condition of there being goods and evils and hence gratifications and frustrations. Although it is less widely recognized in the Hobbes literature, he also holds that there are certain passions that must never be acted on, in particular the passion (often showing itself as "vainglory") that consists in denying that natural equality of all human beings that is the basis of the "Right of Nature."

5. So-called interest-group liberalism, a variant of the American version of political pluralism, and also arguments for "neutralism" such as that of (the early) Ackerman (1980) and especially of Charles Larmore (1987), are positions or tendencies of thought engagingly intermediate between my agency and virtue types. The idea that politics and government do—and *should* at least in the sense that there is no practicable alternative—respond to and service subjectively determined interests aligns these positions with agency-oriented liberalism. On the other hand, the notion that individuals can, frequently do, and in any case ought to subordinate their individual interests to the extent necessary to form groups with shared or common interests, and the further notion that there are procedural principles and rules that, because rational, are neutral to or among the competing group interests, move thinking of this kind toward virtue liberalism.

6. Without using the distinction between agency and virtue liberalism, Christopher Berry (1989, 1993) has effectively underlined differences among liberals concerning democracy.

7. The foregoing remarks, as well as my later brief discussion of rights-oriented liberalisms, underline the point that I regard the agency/virtue dif-

ferentiation as more perspicuous than the familiar distinction between deontological and teleological liberal doctrines.

8. Nietzsche in particular thought that romanticism leads to rabid nationalisms in which the "letting go" takes collectivist forms that are immensely destructive. Berlin, among other agency liberals, is endlessly ambivalent on this question.

9. This designation is misleading because "perfectionism" is commonly construed (e.g., by Rawls, 1971, pp. 325ff.) as promoting *the* perfection to be sought by or appropriate to all human beings or all of the members of a society. Strong voluntarists and willful liberals insist that all human beings must create and pursue their own ideals, must perfect themselves by their own lights. Nietzsche's characteristically pungent remarks memorably capture the spirit of this latter, distinctive, form of idealism: "Whatever kind of bizarre ideal one may follow . . . one should not demand that it be *the* ideal: for one therewith takes from its privileged character. One should have it in order to distinguish oneself, not in order to level oneself." As regards his own "strange, tempting, dangerous" ideal of free-spiritedness, the ideal "of a spirit who plays naively—that is, not deliberately but from overflowing power and abundance—with all that was hitherto called holy, good, untouchable, divine," he declares that he "should not wish to persuade anybody" of its merits (1974, pp. 346–47). Indeed, he would not "readily concede *the right to it* to anyone. My ideal is *mine*. This is what *I* am; this is what *I* want:—*you* can go to hell!" (1967, pp. 191–92; emphases added).

3 / The Good or Goodnesses of Polity and Polities à la Liberalism: Plurality Rather than Unicity, Singularity beyond Plurality

1. These difficulties are manifested in the evident tension between, on the one hand, anti-imperialism and support for self-determination of nations or peoples and, on the other, the insistence that there are certain human rights that every polity and people must respect. At the level of practice, the likelihood of eliminating or substantially reducing this tension seems low if not nil. Conceptually or ideationally, however, these ideas and ideals may be reconcilable. On the views considered thus far, the liberal planetary utopia would be a circumstance in which all polities are alike in respecting human rights. But because the members of those polities would be allowed and perhaps encouraged to put those rights to differing uses or purposes, the polities would be internally diverse and would therefore contribute to international plurality. This is an engaging ideal. Dim as its prospects no doubt are, I argue for what many will regard as the yet more distant or unachievable ideal of singularity in a third and more individuality-seeking sense, which I go on to explore.

2. See also Gray (1992b). Understandably given the recent ascendancy of neo-Kantianism, Gray's polemic is aimed primarily at this genre of liberalisms.

But his objections also apply to utilitarian liberalisms from Bentham to Sidgwick and up to R. M. Hare.

3. See also Butler (1990). Compare Gilles Deleuze and Félix Guattari's observation: "Groups and individuals contain microfascisms just waiting to crystallize" (1987, pp. 9–10). Contrary to Deleuze and Guattari, I would be inclined to insert the words "who identify strongly with groups" after "individuals" in the sentence I have quoted from them. On these points see also William E. Connolly (1991, 1995).

4. Compare Flathman (1992, pp. 81–82).

4 / Ruling, Rules, and Rule Following: Mainstay or Mirage, Miracle or Misfortune?

1. These assumptions seem to be not only credited but deepened by formalist linguistics such as Saussure's and perhaps further widened and deepened by theories of "deep" linguistic structure such as Chomsky's. They operate quite powerfully in much "analytic" or "linguistic" philosophy, albeit they are sharply qualified by Wittgenstein and Austin. Perhaps the most potent critique of them is provided by Bakhtin.

2. As noted, Hobbes did entertain the possibility that the language of geometry and perhaps other aspects of mathematics could be made entirely perspicuous. Insofar as this expectation was grounded in the belief that mathematics did not engage interests and passions other than purely intellectually, he was disabused of it by the sharply and (he thought) captiously antagonistic responses to his own mathematical formulations. There is no doubting his view that passion and interest greatly compound the uncertainties in and disputations concerning the languages of morals, politics, and law, but these are by no means the only sources of ambiguity and equivocality on which he insists. It would be difficult to reconcile his hopes for an entirely perspicuous mathematical language with his epistemology and ontology.

3. Although Hobbes himself would never countenance doing so, we might regard his account of language and all that depends on it as the projection of an ideal, one that foregrounds and seeks to promote individuality. If we do so, the passage just quoted may remind us of Friedrich Nietzsche's characterizations of his own comparable efforts: "This is what *I* am; this is what *I* want: *you* can go to hell!" (1967, para. 349, p. 191). "May your virtue be too exalted for the familiarity of names: and if you must speak of her, then do not be ashamed to stammer of her. Then speak and stammer, 'This is my good; this I love; it pleases me wholly; thus alone do *I* want the good. I do not want it as a divine law; I do not want it as human statute and need: it shall not be a signpost for me to overearths and paradises'" (Nietzsche, 1966, first part, sect. 5, p. 36).

Is this "going too far" in reinterpreting Hobbes? Consider that Hobbes ends *De Cive* with the following verse from Paul's Epistle to the Romans: "Let not him that eateth, despise him that eateth not, and let not him that eateth not, judge him that eateth; for God hath received him. One man esteemeth one day above another, another esteemeth every day alike. Let every man be fully persuaded in his own mind" (1972, p. 386).This is not a passage likely to appeal to one of a regularian temper (and it is therefore surprising to find it in Paul but not surprising to find it appropriated by Hobbes.

4. Taking "language" to mean the entire "prodigiously diverse" array of devices through or in which we think, act, and communicate with one another, it is a serviceable generalization (albeit one that requires much qualification) that "there cannot be a question whether these or other rules are the correct ones for the use of 'not' [or whatever word or words are before us]. For without these rules the word has as yet no meaning; and if we change the rules, it now has another meaning (or none), and in that case we might as well change the word too" (Wittgenstein, 1953, p. 147n.). We can go so far as to say that "the rule-governed nature of our language permeates our life" (Wittgenstein, 1977, p. 303); "there exists a correspondence between the concepts 'rule' and 'meaning'" (1969, p. 62); the "word 'agreement' and the word 'rule'... are cousins"; and "the use of... 'rule' and ... 'same' are interwoven. (As are the use of 'proposition' and ... 'true.') [hence, presumably, 'rule' and 'different,' 'proposition' and 'false']" (1953, I, pp. 224–25). The following passages, taken more or less at random from Wittgenstein's post-*Tractatus* works, are further and arguably representative examples.

In cases of speech and other actions that "involve" as distinct from merely "according with" a rule, the "symbol of the rule" forms part of the calculation, "involves" the rule that it follows in a fashion that it involves no other symbols or considerations (1964, *Blue Book* [hereafter *Blue*], p. 13). If we have taught someone the Cyrillic alphabet and how each of its letters is pronounced, and if our pupil then spells out lines from a Cyrillic script "according to the pronunciation of each letter as we had taught it, we should undoubtedly say that he was deriving the sound of every word ... [from the] *rule* of the alphabet." The rule and the pupil's knowledge of it appear to be the necessary and sufficient conditions of his pronunciation (1964, *Brown Book* [hereafter *Brown*], p. 123; compare 1953, I, p. 162). "'But surely you can see ...' ... is just the characteristic expression of someone who is under the compulsion of a rule" (1953, I, p. 231). "Disputes do not break out (among mathematicians, say) over the question whether a rule has been obeyed or not. People don't come to blows over it, for example" (1953, I, p. 240). "*Essence* is expressed by grammar" (1953, I, p. 371), that is, by a feature of human affairs that is a paradigm of rules and rule-governedness.

5. "The procedure of putting a lump of cheese on a balance and fixing the price by turn of the scale would lose its point if it frequently happened

for such lumps to suddenly grow or shrink for no obvious reason" (Wittgenstein, 1953, I, p. 142). "What we have to mention in order to explain the significance, I mean the importance, of a concept, are often extremely general facts of nature: such facts as are hardly ever mentioned because of their great generality" (1953, I, p. 142n.). Compare Quine's view that the lexicographer translating an unfamiliar language into her own is provided "an entering wedge . . . [by] the fact that there are many basic features of men's ways of conceptualizing their environment, of breaking the world down into things common to all cultures" (1963, pp. 61–62).

6. "Commanding, questioning, recounting, chatting, are as much a part of our natural history as walking, eating, drinking, playing" (Wittgenstein, 1953, I, p. 25). "Only of a living human being and what resembles (behaves like) a living human being can one say: it has sensations; it sees; is blind; hears; is deaf; is conscious or unconscious" (I, p. 281).

7. "How does a human being learn the meaning of the names of sensations?—of the word 'pain' for example. Here is one possibility: words are connected with the primitive, the natural expressions of the sensation and used in their place. A child has hurt himself and he cries; and then adults talk to him and teach him exclamations and, later, sentences. They teach the child new pain-behaviour." "So you are saying," his imagined interlocutor responds, "that the word 'pain' really means crying?" But this is a mistaken response: "The verbal expression of pain replaces crying and does not describe it. For how can I go so far as to try to use language to get between pain and its expression?" (Wittgenstein, 1953, I, pp. 244–45).

8. The following passage may be taken as drawing together the several threads of Wittgenstein's views on the foregoing questions: "If the formation of concepts can be explained by facts of nature, should we not be interested, not in grammar, but rather in that in nature which is basis of grammar?—Our interest certainly includes the correspondence between concepts and very general facts of nature. . . . But our interest does not fall back upon these possible causes of the formation of concepts; we are not doing natural science; nor yet natural history—since we can also invent fictitious natural history for our purposes.

"I am not saying: if such-and-such facts of nature were different people would have different concepts (in the sense of an hypothesis). But: if anyone believes that certain concepts are absolutely the correct ones, and having different ones would mean not realizing something that we realize—then let him imagine certain very general facts of nature to be different from what we are used to, and the formation of concepts different from the usual ones will become intelligible to him" (1953, II, xii, p. 230).

9. Many of Wittgenstein's discussions of the teaching of rules and rule-governed activities place a powerful emphasis on the physical, indeed the coer-

cive, character of the process (see, e.g., 1964, *Blue*, p. 12; 1964, *Brown*, pp. 77, 89, 123; 1956, I, pp. 34, 37, 147; 1953, I, pp. 143, 441). In the early stages of instruction the teacher often literally takes control of the learner's body and forces it to move in the desired manner, prevents it from moving in ways that go against the rules. In these respects we should speak of training and "trainability" rather than education and educability. To the extent that such training is effective, its result is behavioral regularities that "accord with" rather than "involve" the rules, and the "rule following" is, at least initially, decidedly "mechanical" in character (see 1956, I, p. 63). Moreover, as we see more fully later, Wittgenstein agrees with Hobbes that there is, finally, a "trained" and unreflective quality to most if not all rule-governed conduct. Even rule following that "involves" close and critical attention to rules is characterized or inflected by a certain "blindness."

10. One can even imagine "someone's having learnt the game without ever learning or formulating rules. He might have learnt quite simple board-games first, by watching, and have progressed to more and more complicated ones. He too might be given the explanation 'This is the king,'—if, for instance, he were being shewn chessmen of a shape he was not used to. This explanation again only tells him the use of the piece because, as we might say, the place for it was already prepared. . . . And in this case it is so, not because the person to whom we give the explanation already knows rules, but because in another sense he is already master of a game" (Wittgenstein, 1953, I, p. 31).

11. As my late and deeply missed colleague David Sachs frequently emphasized, this is one of the most radical passages in the whole of Western philosophy.

12. For various purposes these judgments might be redescribed as rules in the sense of regularities. But to think of our making such judgments as rule making or rule following would be to miss Wittgenstein's point. This is one of the largest and most important respects in which our acting is not and cannot be rule-governed. "It is [not rules but] our *acting* which lies at the bottom of the language-game" (1969, p. 204).

13. Much of our activity depends on beliefs that "lie apart from the route travelled by inquiry" (Wittgenstein, 1969, pp. 211–12). "Much seems to be fixed, and it is removed from the traffic. It is so to speak shunted unto an unused siding. . . . it gives our way of looking at things . . . their form. Perhaps it was once disputed. But perhaps, for unthinkable ages, it has belonged to the *scaffolding* of our thoughts" (p. 205).

14. For additional discussion of this and related points, see Flathman (1973, 1987).

15. It might be objected that this passage concerns a command not a rule and hence is irrelevant to rules and rule following. A first response would be that commands are usually understood (e.g., by Hayek and other theorists of

the rule of law) to be *more* particular, *more* determinant and determinative than rules. Thus by reminding us of commands or directives that are usable and consequential despite being "inexact," Wittgenstein prepares and fosters the thought (already present in the later sentences of the above passage) that the usually less particular, less determinate entities called general and prospective rules have the same combination of characteristics. A second and more direct response is provided by passages such as the following: There are rules as to what can be called a chair but they do not cover "every possible application of" the word. "But do we miss the[se further specifications] when we use the word . . . and are we to say that we do not really attach any meaning to this word" because there are cases not covered by the rules (1953, I, p. 80)?

16. On the philosophical side, see Edward H. Minar (1991). This article is a superb antidote to both the overweening and inordinately skeptical responses to the first two lessons of Wittgenstein's teaching.

17. In another work I have explored, with enthusiasm, many of the further respects in which, according to Hobbes, Wittgenstein, Nietzsche, and numerous other thinkers, thought and action are (and ought to remain) beyond or outside of rules, even including rule-governed language (see Flathman, 1992). As regards Wittgenstein, I there foreground the respects in which we are "enigmas" to one another, in which, despite sharing a language and hence a "form of life," we cannot "find our feet" with one another. I return to this theme at intervals below, but do not here reiterate the discussions of the thinkers to whom I am most indebted in the work just cited.

18. This speculation takes plausibility from the frequency with which Montaigne and Wittgenstein, in fact two of the most "radical" thinkers in our tradition, are characterized as "conservatives" and from the yet more widely distributed view that Hobbes is a regularian.

19. I would say much the same of Hobbes, and have argued for this reading of him in earlier works (see Flathman, 1992, 1993). Montaigne is a harder case, but I take him to be promoting no more than outward conformity, conformity *in foro externo* as Hobbes puts it, with the customary and the conventional. His skepticism requires this stance.

20. Here and throughout I am indebted to the late Judith Shklar's reflections concerning the ideological character of what she styles "legalism" (see Shklar, 1964).

21. The materials interjected in brackets in this quote are from Oakeshott (1983, pp. 160–61).

22. In 1975 he calls it *societas* or civil association and contrasts it with *universitas* or enterprise association.

23. Recall, in connection with this passage, my earlier remarks concerning the rules of musical composition.

24. Compare Bakhtin: "Words belong to nobody, and in themselves they

evaluate nothing. But they can serve any speaker and be used for the most varied and directly contradictory evaluations on the part of the speakers" (1986, p. 85). Bakhtin has much of importance to say on the topic of this and the following chapters. I hope to consider his views further in a subsequent work.

25. By the same token, one can speak or write grammatically or ungrammatically only by saying or writing *something*.

26. Perhaps the most astonishing qualities of antiregularian thinkers such as Montaigne, Hobbes, Nietzsche, and Oakeshott—I would add Hannah Arendt to this list—is that they so readily and powerfully imagine such a descent and yet refuse the temptations of rigidly nomian thinking.

5 / Liberalism and the Suspect Enterprise of Political Institutionalization: The Case of the Rule of Law

1. Recall Benjamin Constant's exquisitely appropriate response to Montesquieu: "No doubt there is no liberty when people cannot do all that the laws allow them to do; but laws could forbid so many things as to abolish liberty altogether" (quoted in Leoni, 1919, p. 152).

2. For an instructive analysis of the complex, fluctuating, and always problematic interaction between liberal ideals and institutions in the American case, see Huntington (1981). Huntington's formula, "Ideals versus Institutions," or the "IvI gap," expresses some of the themes I develop here. I am, however, in disagreement with his pronounced tendency to prefer institutionalism and the order *it* idealizes when there are conflicts between it and other liberal values. Of course putting the matter this way problematizes the "IvI" formula.

3. For these distinctions, see Friedman (1973); see also Flathman (1980).

4. Institutionalists sometimes deliberately arrange structures and procedures that engender competition and conflict among the several components of the overall system of institutions. Famously, some of the American Founders favored federalism, bicameralism, and the separation of powers on the ground that these devices would make it difficult for the federal government to act. In addition to the points made above, however, this strategy "succeeds" only to the extent that its motivating concern is widely shared. If there is a general desire for and expectation of vigorous and extensive use of state power, either the several centers of authority cooperate to bring it about or dissatisfaction and disaffection mount.

Institutions and institutional structures matter. As I argue throughout this and adjoining chapters, however, they matter less than institutional*ism*, less than the beliefs and attitudes, hopes and fears, that inform the thinking and acting of those whose institutions they are.

5. For example Lon Fuller, who treats his version of the requirements of the rule of law as constituting law's "inner morality," allows that "over a wide

range of issues" the morality internal to law "is indifferent toward the substantive aims of law and is ready to serve a variety of such aims with equal efficacy" (1964, p. 153). This pronounced tendency in contemporary rule of law thinking is sharply and effectively critiqued, especially in respect to legislative law, by Bruno Leoni (1991).

6. Compare the Weberian pronouncements of Franz Neumann and Bruno Leoni: "The [rule of law] doctrine clearly reveals the ambivalent position of modern man—the emphatic assertion of the autonomy of man is accompanied by the equally passionate insistence on the rule of the state" (Neumann, 1957, p. 140). "One of the paradoxes of our era is the continual retreat of traditional religious faith before the advance of science and technology, under the implied exigency of a cool and matter-of-fact attitude and dispassionate reasoning, accompanied by a *no less continual retreat from the same attitude and reasoning in regard to legal and political questions.* The mythology of our age is not religious, but political, and its chief myths seem to be 'representation' of the people, on the one hand, and the charismatic pretension of political leaders to be in possession of the truth and to act accordingly, on the other" (Leoni, 1991, p. 23). These remarks help us to understand how and why enormously complicated and internally conflicted institutions such as the U.S. government continuously produce a vast number of laws and regulations on myriad subjects.

7. In our time this view has been forcefully advanced by H. L. A. Hart (see, for example, 1983, especially pp. 81–82).

8. For a concise listing of the usual components of the ideology, expanded and much ambiguated in the pages that follow the account, see Fuller (1964, pp. 39–40).

9. Later I comment on aspects of Hayek's indebtedness to Hume. Given Hume's insistence that the laws of nature *as we know and use them* are deeply subjective, Hayek might have asked himself whether this comparison serves his purposes.

10. Franz Neumann makes meeting this requirement a condition of an independent judiciary. The law must have "a minimum of substantive content" in order that it "guarantees to the judge a minimum of independence because it does not subordinate him to the individual measures of the sovereign" (1957, p. 30).

11. I have added the italics to this quote to emphasize what seems to be implicit in Hayek's "we," namely that neither the authors nor the addressees of such laws can know or make reliable predictions concerning what the laws require, forbid, and permit.

12. As Leoni emphasizes, laws that are sufficiently particular to afford predictability nevertheless deprive their addressees of that advantage if they are frequently changed. "We are actually far from attaining . . . the ideal certainty

of the law, in the practical sense that this ideal should have for anybody who must plan for the future and who has to know . . . what the legal consequences of his decisions will be." Given the rage to legislate and administer that is rampant in the modern state, "people can never be certain that the legislation in force today will be in force tomorrow or even tomorrow morning" (1991, pp. 9–10).

13. Of course these views, although in a distinctive idiom in Wittgenstein's work, are hardly unique to him. Yet more insistent and unsettling contemporary versions of them are discussed below, but it should be remembered that they are pervasive in the thinking, from Plato to Hobbes to the present, of most of those who have given critical attention to language in the wide Wittgensteinian sense.

14. See Stanley Cavell (1979, especially part I; 1988, pp. 5, 38, 59, 85–87, 110–11, 132–33, 147–48; 1990, pp. 92–100).

15. The materials interjected in brackets are from pp. 160–61.

16. In 1975, Oakeshott calls it *societas* or civil association and contrasts it with *universitas* or enterprise association.

17. Requirements of law as such include "rules not secret or retrospective, no obligations save those imposed by law, all associates equally and without exception subject to the obligations imposed by law, no outlawry, and so on. It is only in respect of these considerations and their like that it may perhaps be said that *lex injusta non est lex*" (Oakeshott, 1983, p. 140).

6 / The Ideas, Ideals, and Practices of Liberalism and the Institutions and Institutionalisms of Police and Policing

1. As throughout Part II, my background but also overarching concern in this chapter is with the institutions and institutionalisms appropriate to the ideals of liberalism as I conceive them. For this reason, in discussing the police and policing I begin and through much of the essay operate with the commonplace understanding that the police (the public police, as I for the most part call them) and the activities of policing are distinguishable institutions and institutionalized arrangements and practices. At the level of both official conceptualization and popular culture and lore, there is much in current thinking and practice that manifests and sustains this view. Policing is an organized practice or activity that is juridically authorized by the state. As distinguished from self-help, vigilantism, mutual moral surveillance, and ethnic cleansing, and also (if less clearly) from the rapidly growing number of state-licensed but privately hired security and investigation agencies and forces, public police and policing presuppose authoritatively declared prohibitions against and requirements on conduct. (In the foregoing remarks I have in mind the distinction between legally established prohibitions and the requirements established, or alleged to be established, of the *sensus communis* or com-

munal mores or morality). As I for the most part use the terms, police and policing also presuppose formally identified corps or cadres the uniformed or otherwise credentialed and identified members of which have the duty of enforcing juridically established prohibitions and requirements. The Los Angeles Police Department, the New York City Police Department, the Military Police, possibly even the operatives of the CIA are in principle distinguishable from the Ku Klux Klan, the SPCA, the Moral Majority, and so on. Police and policing thus institutionally differentiated are the primary focus of my concern.

As the qualifiers in the foregoing paragraphs begin to indicate, it is important to bear in mind that, both empirically and conceptually, these differentiations are matters of degree, rarely of kind. J. S. Mill speaks of the "powerful police" and the severe "penalties" that "opinion" does and apparently in his judgment should exercise over and impose upon "those vices" (e.g., "gambling or drunkenness, or incontinence, or idleness") that "the law" (due partly to its "imperfections") leaves unregulated (1951, *On Liberty*, chap. 4). This is a theme that, their respective valorizations aside, links Mill to Nietzsche and most especially to Foucault. As Shklar among others has emphasized, institutionalizations in the formal sense are empty or merely formal in the absence of institutionalisms that enliven and give them purpose, and there are institutionalisms that are powerful despite or even because they have not been formally institutionalized (1964).

There is nevertheless an important difference between institutionalisms (e.g., racisms, sexisms) that are institutionalized and those that are not. The plight of blacks, Jews, gays, Muslims, communists and anticommunists, and so on is dramatically worsened where the institutionalized public police and the police power are formally authorized and otherwise empowered to act against them. To initiate a minor disagreement that I have with Michel Foucault, the monarch may have lost her head, but she continues to throw her weight around.

2. This Weberian theme is cogently reiterated in Gray and Skolnick (1975, see especially II, p. 3). There are difficult questions concerning when, historically, policing in the Weberian sense became established in various countries. I touch, but only lightly, on those questions below.

3. In an interview that prefaces a French edition of Bentham's *Panopticon*, Foucault says "Les mutations economiques du XVIII siècle ont rendu necessaire de faire circuler les effets du pouvoir, par des canaux de plus en plus fins, jusqu'aux individus lex-mêmes, jusqu'a leur corps, jusqu'a leur gests, . . . a chacune de leurs performances quotidiennes. Que le pouvoir, meme avec une multiplicité d'hommes a regir, soit efficace que s'il s'exercait sur un seul" (1977).

4. It must of course be recognized that, for Foucault, dictions and rhetorics often conceal as much as or more than they reveal. The absence,

from English, of the notion of the *Polizei* and its positive tasks no more establishes that Anglophone countries do not have substantial elements of a *Polizeistaat* than does the presence of that notion in French or German prove that, in countries that speak the latter languages, there are no primarily defensive or protective police practices and understandings.

5. There is a relatively recent but rapidly growing body of scholarship, focusing particularly on the thinkers of the Scottish Enlightenment, that sharply challenges this construal of "Anglophone" thinking. Foregrounding the notions (importantly analogous to Foucault's notion of "populations") of society and especially "civil society," this literature stresses the commonalities between *Polezei* and *Polizeistaat* conceptions and the thinking of, for example, Adam Smith. In part because this tendency of thought is marginal to or, better, partly askew of, the liberal tradition as I (along with Foucault) am interpreting it, I do not pursue this literature here. Attention to it, however, would support my larger argument. I am indebted to John Pocock, James Wiley, and especially Jeffrey Lomonoco for calling these developments to my attention.

6. Later I consider the views of the more pronouncedly individuality- and freedom-oriented of the protoliberal Hobbes and the analogous thinking of liberals such as Constant, Berlin, and Hampshire. Hobbes, a pre-*Polizeistaat* thinker, thought that the second—if not the first—most serious threat to freedom and individuality was that form of lèse-majesté that consists of fomenting civil war. He nevertheless went beyond Bentham and his utilitarian or liberal successors and accorded to every person a natural right, a right that cannot be annulled by any justification for the exercise of the police power, to resist the sovereign and the sovereign's authorized agents whenever she judges those activities threatening to her life or well-being.

7. I discuss Mill's educational views in Chapter 7.

8. Hiring bodyguards and private security forces can be viewed as a response to the perceived failure of both the directly deterrent/protective and the more generally educative activities of the public police (and of course of other "policing" and educative agencies in society). Owing to the failure of the latter, the tendency or disposition to criminal activity becomes so great that it overwhelms the capacity of the public police to deter it or protect against it by coercion and violence. Thus members of the public (those who can afford to do so) supplement the public police by employing protective services devoted exclusively to protecting *them*. Although there are tensions between private and public police officers, in this country at least the public police authorities, rather than viewing private police as rivals (or as examples of the still-decried phenomenon of vigilantism), welcome them as diminishing somewhat their increasingly unmanageable task.

9. The necessarily enlarged, extended, and substantially discretionary activities of those police who patrol (as opposed to administrators, detectives,

and so on) are vividly described in the now very extensive literature concerning policing. Among any number of examples, see Bent and Rossum (1976), Gray and Skolnick (1975), Skolnick (1966), Slovak (1986), Cohen and Feldberg (1991), and Wilson (1975).

10. Wilson sharply contests the view that crime is "caused by" poverty, unemployment, and the like but offers the equally sweeping analysis that it stems from the "breakdown of community." I discuss the latter of his arguments below.

11. In the work I am primarily discussing, Wilson claims to support many policies of the kinds just mentioned. Some among them are valuable in their own right, regardless of their effects or lack thereof on rates of crime (see 1985, especially chap. 13).

12. The understanding must be tempered, as from time to time it is in Wilson's writings, by the recognition that societies often disable significant numbers of their members from such self-responsibility or self-overcoming and hence ought to seek ways—as best they can consistent with a "decent respect for the opinions of [hu]mankind"—to relieve or diminish these as it were iatrogenic maladies.

Wilson's several discussions of the "rehabilitation" of those already incarcerated or otherwise in the toils of the criminal justice system are pertinent to this theme. His emphasis falls on what he takes to be the empirical evidence—provided primarily by rates of recidivism—that most attempts at rehabilitation fail and hence that we must look primarily to deterrence and incapacitation to prevent or reduce crime. But there are brief moments at which he recognizes both the case for and the epistemic and normative arrogances of rehabilitationist outlooks and programs.

13. For a valuable development and critique of the mode of conservative thinking that, in company with Straussians and other republicans and communitarians, Wilson represents, see Robert Devigne (1994). The index locates Devigne's several discussions, to which I am indebted, of Wilson's views.

14. He in effect adopts the notion, invented by Hillel Steiner (1974–75) of "throffers," that is, incentives that are at once threats and offers.

15. Thus, ontologically, this is something that *I* can do only in the sense of the initial resignation or submission. *I* cannot do it in any continuing sense because, as regards my relation to them, *I* no longer exist. This formulation is hyperbolic in that it reduces me, all of me so to speak, to the entity that is "submitting" to the other. But the formulation captures what is most important in, for example, Mill's argument against voluntary self-enslavement.

16. The remarks about "I," "self," and other in this paragraph are not much more than a gloss on Hobbes's argument for the right of nature. The further remarks about looking to police and policing for, as it were, supplementary assistance in protecting the self are also much indebted to him.

17. I do not deny that there are human events, call them behaviors, that transgress the law but that do not have these characteristics at all or have them only in minimal degree. (There are of course many more such events or behaviors that do not transgress the law.) I have no wisdom to offer concerning how to respond to such behaviors, but insofar as we treat them as such we threaten to make irrelevant the question of justifying, to those whose behaviors they are, the ways in which we respond to them.

7 / Liberal versus Civic, Republican, Democratic, and Other Vocational Educations: Liberalism and Institutionalized Education

1. The relationship between "basic" and "liberal" education is complex in ways that prefigure issues central to this chapter. Common between the two conceptions is the idea that education differs from vocational training in that it prepares students for a wide variety of activities and styles of life rather than for particular vocations or professions. Commonly, however, proponents of basic education are confident that they have identified the skills and bodies of knowledge—in some cases also the attitudes and values—that are essential to all worthwhile activities or perhaps to any life that is worth living. Numerous self-styled liberal educators (most obviously those who promote "core curricula" and related notions) participate in this conceit. A major issue here is whether or in what respects liberal education, especially liberal *political* education, can or should be "basic" by the latter criterion or at least in the sense that its tuitions are necessary to living well in all or a generously defined range of regime types. I return an affirmative but narrowly qualified answer to this question.

2. The leading recent proponents of this conception of liberalism are John Rawls (see especially 1971), Charles Larmore (1987), and Bruce Ackerman (1980). In some cases later works by these authors amend or otherwise depart from the arguments of the works just cited. Also relevant are the numerous writings of Jürgen Habermas.

3. See Rawls's recent arguments for a "reasonable" pluralism (1993). As I argue in Chapter 6, there is a serious question whether Rawls's and related arguments are consistent with the claim to neutrality among conceptions of the good.

4. Aspects of a liberal education might in fact service, for example, careers of criminal activity, but no liberal educators known to me intend or would endorse such a use of their tuitions.

5. Rawls, to take a leading example, is hardly neutral toward those persons and doctrines that he characterizes as "unreasonable." When he and others claim that their views are neutral among competing values or objectives they are expressing the belief—perhaps more likely the hope or wish—that in fact no one will openly disagree with their ideas and proposals.

6. Recall the passage from José Ortega y Gasset discussed earlier: "Liberalism ... is the *supreme* form of generosity; it is the right by which the majority concedes to minorities and hence it is the noblest cry that has ever resounded on this planet" (1932, pp. 83–84).

7. In the concluding section of this essay I discuss, nervously, the respects in which (insofar as there is or could be such a thing) this is true of liberal *political* education.

8. I am thinking primarily of the *Meno*. As Tracy Strong has emphasized to me, however, my remarks thus far, and the larger argument of this essay, raise a wider issue. Addressed most directly by Plato in the *Protagoras*, this is the question of whether each of us comes into the world already provided, at least nascently or in potential, with abilities and understandings sufficient to participate appropriately in politics. In the latter view, attributed to Protagoras and combatted by Socrates, the learning, wisdom, or judgment necessary to political activity must be provided by nature and political experience themselves, not by purposefully political education. I agree with Protagoras in opposing education that is political in the sense of inculcating beliefs and values thought to be necessary to conduct in this or that particular regime. I also agree that much of the learning contributive to political thinking and activity is in fact acquired inadvertently rather than through institutionalized education. I argue, however, that purposive but regime-nonspecific liberal education concerning politics can contribute valuably to political understanding and activity.

9. Educational "liberationists" such as Ivan Illich are sensitive to these concerns. They agree that virtually all extant institutionalized educational arrangements and practices are paternalistic and impositional, but they argue that students could and should be accorded a much larger role in setting the priorities and procedures of their own educations. In this respect, educational liberationism stands to liberal education much as libertarianism, anarchism, and antinomianism stand to moral and political liberalism as here conceived. Educational liberalism rejects liberationism, and moral and political liberalism rejects libertarianism, anarchism, and antinomianism. But the best proponents of both of the former are haunted by the latter.

10. See Oakeshott (1989, 1991, especially "Political Education" and "The Study of Politics in a University").

11. The latter tendency of thought is pronounced in the work of Amy Gutmann (1987). The tendency is most commonly associated with conservative and communitarian thinking, but Gutmann is by no means the only liberal thinker who is attracted to it.

12. I briefly discuss Rousseau in the following paragraphs and Arendt in more detail later in the essay. For Durkheim, see his attack on "the malady of infinite aspiration" and his argument that children undisciplined "from the

outside" are despots (1961, especially pp. 40–49, 130–34, 185–89, 226–30. See also Dewey (1990, especially pp. 48ff., 191–96). For a more recent attack on liberationist views, see Battistoni (1985).

13. Locke makes it clear that his primary concern is with the education of "young gentlemen," that is, of the gentry. His sparse remarks concerning daughters of the gentry and boys and girls of lower classes make it clear that he thinks that their educations—it would be better to call them their trainings—should be conducted on quite different principles. There is every reason not to follow him in these prejudices.

14. It is partly for these reasons that the work arouses the animus of civic educationists such as Battistoni (1985, pp. 33-36) and Thomas Pangle (1992, pp. 146–47, 166–69) and why commentators such as Nathan Tarcov (1984) and Rogers Smith (1986) admire *Thoughts* primarily for its rationalist moralism.

15. In the setting in which Locke advanced them, these arguments were of course importantly political in the sense (emphasized to me by John Pocock) that Locke hoped/aimed to prepare the emergent gentry to play a diverse and supple part in national life—more specifically, to deplace the aristocracy and the clergy that had theretofore predominated.

16. A little earlier, while arguing that the Ten Commandments and the Lord's Prayer should be learned by heart, Locke opines that much of the Bible makes poor reading for young children (see pp. 68–69).

17. From Kant to T. H. Green and Leonard Hobhouse up to Rawls and Gutmann, thinkers who identify themselves as liberals have advocated the educational objectives and practices that Battistoni claims are alien to Lockean and related expressions of liberalism. I mention recent examples below, but see especially Rawls (1993, pp. 71, 86, 200, 269, 277).

18. Mill's "liberal" and "humane" are "wider" than Locke's civility in that Mill uses them to promote the acquisition of skills and bodies of knowledge that Locke regards as peripheral to the civility of the gentleman. If we associate "civility" with character and sensibility as distinct from learning, we might say that this feature of Mill's thinking moves him in an instrumental and hence a less liberal direction. There is a genuine and persistent tension here. Mill is aware of this tension and tries to reduce it by arguing that there are general abilities and bodies of knowledge that contribute to character and sensibility.

19. Here Mill enters upon difficult but fecund terrain. He insists that each of us needs to be educated by others who have already achieved some degree of mastery of the abilities and bodies of knowledge essential to successful performance in society as it has come to be. In this dimension of his thinking he employs the active verb "to make" primarily in discussing educators whose task is to transmit past achievements or accomplishments to those not yet in command of them. Accordingly, in discussing educatees he uses the passive

construction "being made into" "capable and sensible men." It quickly becomes clear, however, that in Mill's view this process of transmission is likely
to "take" only if students participate actively in it. Becoming educated in the
sense of assimilating information and abilities is no more than (in Nietzsche's
phrase) preparatory. "Making" a person "capable and sensible" is valuable because doing so enhances the prospects that she will go on to "make" and "remake" herself in ways that her teachers could not have anticipated.

20. To let a child grow up without such "instruction and training for its
mind, is a moral crime" (Mill, 1951, *On Liberty*, p. 216). From the perspective of
education for "making something of themselves," Mill favorably estimates the
value of familiarity with general truths that have become widely accepted in
the history of civilization. This view, which echoes Humboldt and anticipates
Nietzsche and Oakeshott, is grounded in the conviction that we "make" ourselves not *de novo* or from materials that are entirely of our own invention but
by continuously reconfiguring the facts, beliefs, and values—what Oakeshott
calls the "languages"—that we have inherited. Self-making requires knowledge of how other human beings have made or unmade themselves. Contrary
to proponents of core curricula or a fixed "canon," precisely which parts of
that inheritance should be transmitted neither requires nor allows of authoritative determination. What matters is that students become fluent in a diverse
array of the "languages" that make up human cultures and hence able to appropriate and adapt those languages to their own ends and purposes (see pp.
216–17). Mill is reaching for Oakeshott's view that "languages" are instruments
needful in order to compose and to play one's own tune but are not determinative of the particular tunes to be played.

21. "The rule [of discipline], because it teaches us to restrain and master
ourselves, is a means of emancipation and freedom. Above all in democratic
societies like ours it is essential to teach the child this wholesome self-control.
For . . . there remains only moral discipline to provide the necessary regulatory
influence" (Durkheim, 1961, p. 49).

22. With France in mind, Durkheim remarks: "The nature of political
life is such that we take part in it only intermittently. The State is far away. We
are not directly involved in its activities" (p. 233). He regrets this situation and
wants schools to do something to remedy it. But he is a pluralist not a statist
and his most serious charge against French political society is that "with the
exception of the school, there is no longer . . . any society intermediate between the family and the state. All the groups of this kind . . . have been totally
abolished or at least survive only in very attenuated form." The monarchy
began this process of destruction and "the Revolution continued and completed the work of the monarchy" (p. 232). Durkheim's primary objective was
to revive and enrich "intermediate society," not to intensify activities that are
political in the sense of accentuating the office (trade? vocation?) of citizen

and that enmesh or embroil citizens in the state. As here conceived, liberalism certainly should embrace this thought but then move (echoing the subtitle of Chapter 3 of this volume) "from unicity to plurality and on to singularity."

23. Posing questions that every teacher must ponder, Durkheim asks: "Is there not at the core of pedantry—that trait so characteristic of our professional makeup—a kind of megalomania? When one is continually in relationship with subjects to whom he is morally and intellectually superior, how can he avoid developing an exaggerated self-conception, expressed in gesture, attitude, and language?" An attitude of this sort "readily gives rise to violent expression; for any behavior which offends it easily takes on the character of sacrilege. . . . There is . . . in the situation of school life itself, a predisposition to violent discipline." Where there is no counter to these tendencies they "become increasingly influential to the degree that the school develops and is organized. For as the teacher's . . . professional character is emphasized, the force of professional sentiment cannot fail to grow in parallel fashion" (1961, pp. 194–95). Institutionalized education becomes a powerful engine of imposition.

(We are all familiar with the argument that graduate programs, aiming as they do to prepare students for careers as teachers, ought to include instruction on how to teach. I have resisted these arguments. There are as many good ways to teach as there are good teachers; one learns to be a good teacher by example and practice. But if I were to offer a course on pedagogy to prospective teachers, the featured item on my reading list would be this passage from Durkheim.)

24. J. W. Burrow's remarks concerning "a dilemma in liberal culture itself" are perspicuous: "How are you to make people aware of the tradition which can both shape their energies into something coherent and by its plurality open to them new possibilities of freedom unless you in some sense first impose it upon them? Humboldt, even when he became a minister, wanted education kept pluralistic so far as possible, but the dilemma remained. Only an educated people can take full advantage of . . . freedom, but any educational system . . . involves taking vital decisions affecting the very character structures of people not yet in a position to choose" (1993, p. xvii).

25. The possibilities I canvass and reject in the following paragraphs depend on a conflation of "liberal society" or "liberal politics" and "liberal education." Because I partially effect such a conflation in my concluding section, I am poorly placed to reject it categorically. It is nevertheless a conflation to be resisted. Liberal education can contribute to a liberal politics, but liberal education and liberal politics are different things.

26. Rawls does not directly discuss formal or institutionalized education, but his *Political Liberalism*, with its persistent emphasis on "the wide role of a political conception as educator" (1993, especially p. 86) is a leading example of the latter tendency.

27. I expect the gratitude of theorists of civic, republican, and democratic education for resisting the temptation to liken their views to those of proponents of, for example, Puritan, "Orwellian," Stalinist, Fascist, or Maoist educational objectives and schemes.

28. We should honor Durkheim for acknowledging that his insistence on disciplinary moral education "has necessarily darkened the child's life, rather than drawing him spontaneously to instruction as Tolstoy claimed" (1961, p. 189).

29. Even if politics is regarded—as in the "interest group liberalism" now so widely disdained by participationists and virtue-oriented liberals—as a trade and governing as a way of making a living, it might be inferred that, as with other forms of "enterprise," something akin to business school training, for example, the kinds of training proffered by schools of public affairs, will enhance one's prospects of success in them.

30. Recent examples include Barber (1992), Gutmann (1987), Galston (1991), Macedo (1990), and Rawls (1971, 1993).

31. See also Oakeshott (1989, 1991, especially "Political Education" and "The Study of Politics in a University").

32. Whereas Durkheim agonizes over the darkening of childhood inflicted by megalomaniacal pedagogues, Arendt worries little if at all about this tendency and objects rather to the ways in which liberationists deny childhood by treating the young as already responsible for the mature judgment expected of adults. Both concerns are warranted by the documented excesses to which the two theorists respectively respond. Durkheim's thinking is the more nuanced and persuasive of the two. Arendt thinks of education as a process through which adults, already knowledgeable and capable of judgment, instill these qualities in "newcomers" who lack and must passively receive them. Durkheim agrees with this but thinks that adults also have a lot to learn and that they ought to respect the active and otherwise affirmative characteristics of those who come under their tutelage.

33. However we assess Aristotle's conception of the "good man" as opposed to the "good citizen," attention is owed to his (and Humboldt's) argument that the two coincide, if at all, only under improbable circumstances.

34. I have assessed these theories of democracy in previous work (see Flathman, 1989, chap. 3).

35. I acknowledge that this argument is from a liberal perspective as I conceive it and that the facts about governance and politics that I argue education ought to teach are contestable. It can therefore be objected that in making my argument I have betrayed my own distinction between liberal and civic or political education. Regarding liberal education generally, my claim is that it enables self-enactment and hence does all that education can do to encourage a diversity of styles and sensibilities. In respect to the general political

principles I am claiming education ought to teach, my assertion is that they are pertinent to all political societies and hence that appreciation of them will be valuable to citizens or subjects regardless of the character of the regime under which they live. In a world in which no one can find entire refuge from politics and governance, the species of political education for which I contend deserves to be regarded as "basic."

36. Although I endorse Arendt's hostility to regime-specific political education, on the issues now under discussion I disagree with her educational thinking. She is correct that a chief aim of education is to acquaint students with the world and hence that it presupposes some who know the world and its history and others who thus far are comparatively deficient in such knowledge. Oddly, given her otherwise perspectivalist views (to say nothing of her actual practice of the art of writing history!), she thinks that there should be a standard curriculum the teaching of which is the exclusive object of institutionalized education. She also insists that the *virtùs* she thinks essential to politics, and the self-disclosing she hopes from political activity, can develop and take place only in the course of political action itself. She underestimates the active character of learning and diminishes the respects in which we become persons of sensibility through becoming educated. Her educational views have a passive and a "first this, then that" character. First be taught by others how the world is, then act to disclose yourself in the course of making the world other than it has been.

Bibliography

Ackerman, Bruce (1980). *Social Justice in the Liberal State.* New Haven, Conn.: Yale University Press.

———— (1989). "Constitutional Politics/Constitutional Law." *Yale Law Journal* 99: 453–547.

Arblaster, Anthony (1991). *The Rise and Decline of Western Liberalism.* Oxford: Basil Blackwell.

Arendt, Hannah (1954). *Between Past and Future.* New York: Viking.

———— (1963). *Eichmann in Jerusalem.* New York: Viking.

Aristotle (1953). *Nichomachean Ethics.* Harmondsworth: Penguin.

Aron, Raymond (1957). *The Opium of the Intellectuals.* Garden City, N.Y.: Doubleday.

Avinieri, Shlomo (1972). *Hegel's Theory of the Modern State.* Cambridge: Cambridge University Press.

Bakhtin, Mikhail M. (1986). *Speech Genres and Other Late Essays.* Austin: University of Texas Press.

Barber, Benjamin R. (1992). *An Aristocracy of Everyone: The Politics of Education and the Future of America.* New York: Ballantine.

Battistoni, Richard M. (1985). *Public Schools and the Education of Democratic Citizens.* Jackson: University Press of Mississippi.

Bent, Alan E., and Rossum, Ralph A. (1976). *Police, Criminal Justice and the Community.* New York: Harper & Row.

Bentham, Jeremy (1977). *Le Panoptique.* Paris: Pierre Belfond.

Berlin, Isaiah (1969). *Four Essays on Liberty.* London: Oxford University Press.

Berry, Christopher (1989). *The Idea of Democratic Community.* New York: St. Martin's.

———— (1993). "Shared Understanding and the Democratic Way of Life." In John Chapman and Ian Shapiro (eds.), *Democratic Community.* New York: New York University Press.

Burrow, J. W. (1993). "Editor's Introduction." In Wilhelm von Humboldt, *The Limits of State Action.* Indianapolis: Liberty.

Butler, Judith (1990). *Gender Trouble: Feminism and the Subversion of Identity.* New York: Routledge.

————. (1993). *Bodies That Matter: On the Discursive Limits of Sex.* New York: Routledge.

Cavell, Stanley (1979). *The Claim to Reason.* Oxford: Oxford University Press.

———— (1988). *In Quest of the Ordinary.* Chicago: University of Chicago Press.

———— (1990). *Conditions Handsome and Unhandsome.* Chicago: University of Chicago Press.

Charvet, John (1981). *A Critique of Freedom and Equality.* Cambridge: Cambridge University Press.

Cixous, Hélène, and Clément, Catherine (1986). *The Newly Born Woman.* Minneapolis: University of Minnesota Press.

Clarke, Peter (1978). *Liberals and Social Democrats.* Cambridge: Cambridge University Press.

Cohen, Howard S., and Feldberg, Michael (1991). *Power and Restraint: The Moral Dimension of Police Work.* New York: Praeger.

Collini, Stefan (1978). *Liberalism and Sociology.* Cambridge: Cambridge University Press.

Connolly, William E. (1991). *Identity/Difference.* Ithaca, N.Y.: Cornell University Press.

———— (1995). *The Ethos of Pluralization.* Minneapolis: University of Minnesota Press.

Constant, Benjamin (1988). *Political Writings.* Cambridge: Cambridge University Press.

Cowling, Maurice (1963). *Mill and Liberalism.* London: Cambridge University Press.

Deleuze, Gilles, and Guattari, Félix (1987). *A Thousand Plateaus: Capitalism and Schizophrenia.* Minneapolis: University of Minnesota Press.

Derrida, Jacques (1992). "Before the Law." In *Acts of Literature*, Derek Attridge, ed. New York: Routledge.

Devigne, Robert (1994). *Recasting Conservatism*. New Haven, Conn.: Yale University Press.

Dewey, John (1927). *The Public and Its Problems*. New York: Henry Holt.

———— (1990). *The School and Society* [and] *The Child and the Curriculum*. Chicago: University of Chicago Press.

Dicey, A. V. (1992). *Introduction to the Study of the Law of the Constitution*. Indianapolis: Liberty Classics. (Originally published 1915)

Durkheim, Emile (1961). *Moral Education*. Glencoe, Ill.: Free Press.

Dworkin, Ronald (1977). *Taking Rights Seriously*. Cambridge: Harvard University Press.

———— (1978). "Liberalism." In Stuart Hampshire et al. (eds.), *Public and Private Morality*. Cambridge: Cambridge University Press.

Elster, Jon (1979). *Ulysses and the Sirens*. Cambridge: Cambridge University Press.

Finnis, John (1980). *Natural Rights*. Oxford: Clarendon.

Fishkin, James (1983). *Justice, Equal Opportunity and the Family*. New Haven, Conn.: Yale University Press.

Flathman, Richard E., ed.(1973). *Concepts in Social and Political Philosophy*. New York: Macmillan.

———— (1980). *The Practice of Political Authority*. Chicago: University of Chicago Press.

———— (1987). *The Philosophy and Politics of Freedom*. Chicago: University of Chicago Press.

———— (1989). *Toward a Liberalism*. Ithaca, N.Y.: Cornell University Press.

———— (1992). *Willful Liberalism*. Ithaca, N.Y.: Cornell University Press.

———— (1993). *Thomas Hobbes: Skepticism, Individuality, and Chastened Politics*. Newbury Park, Calif.: Sage.

Foucault, Michel (1977). "L'Oeil du Pouvoir." In Jeremy Bentham, *Le Panoptique*. Paris: Pierre Belfond.

———— (1979). *Discipline and Punish*. New York: Vintage Books.

———— (1980). *Power/Knowledge*. New York: Pantheon.

———— (1988). "The Political Technology of Individuals." In Luther H. Martin, Huck Gutman, and Patrick Hutton (eds.) *Technologies of the Self*. Amherst: University of Massachusetts Press.

Freeden, Michael (1978). *The New Liberalism*. Oxford: Clarendon.

———— (1986). *Liberalism Divided: A Study in British Political Thought 1914–1939.* London: Oxford University Press.

Friedman, Richard B. (1973). "On the Concept of Authority in Political Philosophy." In Richard E. Flathman (ed.), *Concepts in Social and Political Philosophy.* New York: Macmillan.

Fuller, Lon (1964). *The Morality of Law.* New Haven, Conn.: Yale University Press.

Galston, William (1991). *Liberal Purposes.* Cambridge: Cambridge University Press.

———— (n.d.). "Political Theory in the 1990's: Perplexity Amidst Diversity." Unpublished manuscript.

Gewirth, Alan (1978). *Reason and Morality.* Chicago: University of Chicago Press.

Gray, John (1992a). "Against the New Liberalism." *Times Literary Supplement,* July 3, 1992, 13–15.

———— (1992b) *Liberalism.* Minneapolis: University of Minnesota Press.

Gray, Thomas C., and Skolnick, Jerome H., eds. (1975). *Police in America.* Boston: Educational Associates.

Green, T. H. (1986). *Lectures on the Principles of Political Obligation and Other Writings.* Cambridge: Cambridge University Press.

Griffin, James (1986). *Well-Being.* Oxford: Clarendon.

Gutmann, Amy (1980). *Liberal Equality.* Cambridge: Cambridge University Press.

———— (1987). *Democratic Education.* Princeton, N.J.: Princeton University Press.

Habermas, Jürgen (1984). *The Theory of Communicative Action* (2 vols.). Boston: Beacon.

Hampshire, Stuart (1983). *Morality and Conflict.* Cambridge: Harvard University Press.

———— (1989). *Innocence and Experience.* Cambridge: Harvard University Press.

Hare, R. M. (1981). *Moral Thinking.* Oxford: Clarendon.

Hart, H. L. A. (1962). *The Concept of Law.* Oxford: Clarendon.

———— (1983). *Essays in Jurisprudence and Philosophy.* Oxford: Clarendon.

Hayek, Friedrich A. (1944). *The Road to Serfdom.* Chicago: University of Chicago Press.

———— (1960). *The Constitution of Liberty*. Chicago: University of Chicago Press.

Hegel, Georg W. F. (1942). *Philosophy of Right*. Oxford: Clarendon.

———— (1977). *Phenomenology of Spirit*. Oxford: Oxford University Press.

Hobbes, Thomas (1962a). *De Corpore*. In Richard S. Peters (ed.), *Body, Man, and Citizen: Selections from Hobbes's Writings*. London: Collier.

———— (1962b). *Elements of Law*. In Richard S. Peters (ed.), *Body, Man, and Citizen: Selections from Hobbes's Writings*. London: Collier.

———— (1962c), *Leviathan*, Michael Oakeshott, ed. London: Collier.

———— (1972). *De Cive*. In *Man and Citizen*, Bernard Gert, ed. New York: Anchor.

Hobhouse, Leonard (1964). *Liberalism*. New York: Galaxy.

Hohfeld, Wesley (1923). *Fundamental Legal Conceptions*. New Haven, Conn.: Yale University Press.

Holmes, Stephen (1984). *Benjamin Constant and the Making of Modern Liberalism*. New Haven, Conn.: Yale University Press.

Honig, B. (1993). *Political Theory and the Displacement of Politics*. Ithaca, N.Y.: Cornell University Press.

Humboldt, Wilhelm von (1993). *The Limits of State Action*, J. W. Burrow, ed. Indianapolis: Liberty.

Huntington, Samuel P. (1981). *American Politics: The Promise of Disharmony*. Cambridge: Harvard University Press.

Illich, Ivan (1970). *Deschooling Society*. New York: Harper & Row.

Irigaray, Luce (1985). *This Sex Which Is Not One*. Ithaca, N.Y.: Cornell University Press.

James, William (1968). *The Writings of William James*. New York: Modern Library.

Johnston, David (1994). *The Idea of a Liberal Theory*. Princeton, N.J.: Princeton University Press.

Kant, Immanuel (1948), *Groundwork of the Metaphysic of Morals*. London: Hutchinson.

Kateb, George (1992). *The Inner Ocean*. Ithaca, N.Y.: Cornell University Press.

Kelman, Mark (1987). *A Guide to Critical Legal Studies*. Cambridge: Harvard University Press.

Kymlicka, Will (1989). *Liberalism, Community and Culture*. Oxford: Oxford University Press.

Larmore, Charles (1987). *Patterns of Moral Complexity*. Cambridge: Cambridge University Press.

Leoni, Bruno (1991). *Freedom and the Law*. Indianapolis: Liberty Fund.

Locke, John (1759). *Some Thoughts Concerning Education*, In *The Works of John Locke* (6th ed.). London.

———— (1960). *Two Treatises of Government*. Cambridge: Cambridge University Press.

Lowi, T. J. (1979). *The End of Liberalism*. New York: W. W. Norton.

Lyotard, Jean-François (1991). *The Inhuman*. Stanford, Calif.: Stanford University Press.

Lyotard, Jean-François, and Thebaut, Jean Loup (1992). *Just Gaming*. Minneapolis: University of Minnesota Press.

Macedo, Stephen (1990). *Liberal Virtues*. Oxford: Oxford University Press.

MacIntyre, Alasdair (1971). *Against the Self-Images of the Age*. New York: Schocken.

———— (1981). *After Virtue*. Notre Dame, Ind.: University of Notre Dame Press.

MacIver, R. M. (1914). "Institutions as Instruments of Social Control." *Political Quarterly* 2: 109 ff.

McIlwain, C. H. (1939). *Constitutionalism and the Changing World*. Cambridge: Cambridge University Press.

Mill, John Stuart (1951). *Utilitarianism, Liberty and Representative Government*. New York: E. P. Dutton.

———— (1971). "Inaugural Address." In Francis W. Garforth (ed.), *John Stuart Mill on Education*. New York: Teachers College Press.

Minar, Edward H. (1991). "Wittgenstein and the 'Contingency' of Community." *Pacific Philosophical Quarterly* 72: 203–34.

Montaigne, Michel de (1959). *In Defense of Raymond Sebond*. New York: Ungar.

Mouffe, Chantal (1993). *The Return of the Political*. New York: Verso.

Neumann, Franz (1957). *The Democratic and the Authoritarian State*. Glencoe, Ill.: Free Press.

Nietzsche, Friedrich (1955). *Beyond Good and Evil*. Chicago: Henry Regenry.

———— (1956). *The Genealogy of Morals*. Garden City, N.Y.: Doubleday.

———— (1966). *Thus Spoke Zarathustra*. New York: Penguin.

———— (1967). *The Will to Power*. New York: Vintage Books.

———— (1974). *The Gay Science*. New York: Vintage Books.

Nozick, Robert (1974). *Anarchy, State and Utopia*. New York: Basic Books.

Oakeshott, Michael (1966). *Experience and Its Modes*. London: Cambridge University Press.

———— (1975). *On Human Conduct*. Oxford: Oxford University Press.

———— (1983). *On History and Other Essays*. Totowa, N.J.: Barnes & Noble.

———— (1989). *The Voice of Liberal Learning*. New Haven, Conn.: Yale University Press.

———— (1991). *Rationalism in Politics*. Indianapolis: Liberty.

Ortega y Gasset, José (1932). *The Revolt of the Masses*. New York: W. W. Norton.

Paine, Thomas (1953), *Common Sense and Other Political Writings*. Indianapolis: Bobbs-Merrill.

Pangle, Thomas (1992). *The Ennobling of Democracy*. Baltimore: Johns Hopkins University Press.

Peters, R. S. (1967). "What Is an Educational Process?" In R. S. Peters (ed.), *The Concept of Education*. New York: Humanities Press.

Pocock, J. G. A. (1985). *Virtue, Commerce and History*. London: Cambridge University Press.

Proust, Marcel (1992). *Albertine Disparu*. Paris: Gallimard.

Quine, Willard van Orman (1963). *From a Logical Point of View*. New York: Harper & Row.

Rawls, John (1971). *A Theory of Justice*. Cambridge: Harvard University Press.

———— (1993). *Political Liberalism*. New York: Columbia University Press.

Raz, Joseph (1986). *The Morality of Freedom*. Oxford: Clarendon.

Rorty, Richard (1989). *Contingency, Irony, and Solidarity*. Cambridge: Cambridge University Press.

Sandel, Michael (1982). *Liberalism and the Limits of Justice*. Cambridge: Cambridge University Press.

Scanlon, T. M. (1982). "Contractualism and Utilitarianism." In Amartya Sen and Bernard Williams (eds.), *Utilitarianism and Beyond*. Cambridge: Cambridge University Press.

Sen, Amartya (1987). *On Ethics and Economics*. Oxford: Basil Blackwell.

Shklar, Judith N. (1964). *Legalism: Law, Morals and Political Trials*. Cambridge: Harvard University Press.

———— (1984). *Ordinary Vices*. Cambridge: Harvard University Press.

Skolnick, Jerome (1966). *Justice without Trial*. New York: John Wiley.

Slovak, Jeffrey S. (1986). *Styles of Urban Policing*. New York: New York University Press.

Smith, Rogers (1986). *Liberalism and American Constitutional Law*. Cambridge: Harvard University Press.

Steiner, Hillel (1974–75). "Individual Liberty." *Proceedings of the Aristotelian Association* 75: 33–50.

Tarcov, Nathan (1984). *Locke's Education for Liberty*. Chicago: University of Chicago Press.

Taylor, Charles (1979). *Hegel and Modern Society*. Cambridge: Cambridge University Press.

———— (1989). *Sources of the Self*. Cambridge: Harvard University Press.

Truman, David (1957). *The Governmental Process*. New York: Alfred A. Knopf.

Unger, Robert Mangabeira (1986). *The Critical Legal Studies Movement*. Cambridge: Harvard University Press.

Urmson, J. O. (1958). "Saints and Heroes." In A. I. Melden (ed.), *Essays in Moral Philosophy*. Seattle: University of Washington Press.

Walzer, Michael (1983). *Spheres of Justice*. New York: Basic Books.

Williams, Bernard (1985). *Ethics and the Limits of Philosophy*. London: Fontana.

Wilson, James Q. (1975). *Varieties of Police Behavior*. Cambridge: Harvard University Press.

———— (1985). *Thinking about Crime*. New York: Vintage Books.

Wilson, James Q., and Herrnstein, Richard J. (1985). *Crime and Human Nature*. New York: Simon & Schuster.

Wittgenstein, Ludwig (1953). *Philosophical Investigations*. New York: Macmillan.

———— (1956). *Remarks on the Foundations of Mathematics*. Cambridge: MIT Press.

———— (1964). *The Blue and Brown Books*. Oxford: Basil Blackwell.

———— (1965). "Wittgenstein's Lecture on Ethics." *Philosophical Review* 74: 3–26.

———— (1969). *On Certainty*. Oxford: Basil Blackwell.

———— (1977). *Remarks on Colour*. Berkeley: University of California Press.

Wyschograd, Edith (1990). *Saints and Postmodernism*. Chicago: University of Chicago Press.

Index

Ackerman, Bruce, 11, 131, 153, 166, 179
anarchism, xv–xvii, 6–7, 35, 79–80, 84, 115, 128, 131, 135, 161, 165, 180
antinomianism, xvi–xvii, 6–7, 77, 79–80, 84, 128, 131, 135, 161, 180
Aquinas, xiii
Arblaster, Anthony, 166
Arendt, Hannah, 19, 89, 142, 155–57, 162–63, 173, 182, 184–85
Aristotle, xiii–xiv, xix, 19–20, 83–84, 87, 155, 157–58, 184
Aron, Raymond, 4, 8, 22
authority, xv, 49, 82, 115
Avinieri, Shlomo, 9

Bacon, Francis, xv
Bakhtin, Mikhail, 76, 168, 172–73

Barber, Benjamin, 153, 184
Battistoni, Richard, 145–46, 153, 181
Bentham, Jeremy, xiii, xv, 20, 106, 114, 116–17, 131, 153, 168, 177
Berlin, Isaiah, 4, 8, 13–14, 22, 32, 34, 36, 38, 45, 167, 177
Berry, Christopher, 166
Bork, Robert, 25
Burrow, J. W., 183
Butler, Judith, 42–43

Cavell, Stanley, 28, 94, 175
Charvet, John, 11
Chomsky, Noam, 168
Cicero, 26, 53, 145
Cixous, Hélène, 16
Clarke, Peter, 166
Clément, Catherine, 16
Cohen, Howard S., 178

Collini, Stefan, 166
communitarianism, and republi-
    canism, 18, 20, 22, 41,
    125–27, 153
Connolly, William E., ix, xiv, 14,
    168
Constant, Benjamin, iv, xv, xvi,
    4–5, 8, 13, 32, 34–36, 38, 45,
    103, 114, 173, 177
Cowling, Maurice, 119

de Man, Paul, 26
Deleuze, Gilles, 168
Derrida, Jacques, xviii, 52, 57,
    68–71, 75, 92–95, 100
Descartes, René, 67
Devigne, Robert, 178
Dewey, John, 9, 142, 181
Dicey, A. V., 89
Durkheim, Emile, 23, 141–42,
    147–51, 153, 163, 180, 182,
    184
Dworkin, Ronald, 7, 12, 20, 25,
    36, 91, 115–18

education, liberal versus voca-
    tional, xix; "basic, "137–38,
    141–42, 179; civic, 139,
    149, 157, 159; liberationist,
    142–43, 153, 156, 180
education, political, 138–39,
    147, 151–64
Elster, Jon, 5
Emerson, Ralph Waldo, 103
Empiricus, Sextus, 26, 53
equality, 7, 9, 159–60

Feldberg, Michael, 178
Finnis, John, 91

First Amendment rights, 24–25
Fishkin, James, 9
Flathman, Richard E., xvii, 7, 15,
    31, 80, 168, 171–73, 184
Foucault, Michel, xiv, 13, 26,
    108–15, 117, 122, 176–77
Freeden, Michael, 9, 166
Friedman, Richard B., 173
Fuller, Lon, 83, 89, 91, 96,
    173–74

Galston, William, 10–11, 13, 20,
    34, 36, 110, 131, 166, 184
genealogy, xiv
Gewirth, Alan, 11–12
Gray, John, 37–39, 42–43,
    167–68
Gray, Thomas, 176, 178
Green, T. H., 7, 10–12, 20, 23,
    32, 34, 36, 115–16, 131, 154,
    181
Griffin, James, 5, 11
Guattari, Félix, 168
Gutmann, Amy, 10–11, 13, 20,
    36, 110, 131, 153, 180–81, 184

Habermas, Jürgen, 10–11, 13,
    20, 36, 68, 131
Hampshire, Stuart, 4–5, 8, 22,
    38, 177
Hare, Richard, 5, 168
Harrington, James, 153
Hart, H. L. A., 4, 8, 62–63,
    100–101, 174
Hayek, Friedrich, xviii, 52, 68,
    71, 81, 83, 85–91, 96, 115–16,
    171, 174
Hegel, G. W. F., xiii, 7, 9, 12, 34,
    111–15, 122, 127

Heidegger, Martin, 45
Hobbes, Thomas, xiii, xix, 4–6,
  8, 12–14, 34–35, 38, 49,
  52–57, 67–68, 77, 80–82, 84,
  100–101, 103, 114, 116, 158,
  166, 168–69, 171–73, 175, 177
Hobhouse, Leonard, 7, 10, 34,
  36, 115–16, 131, 181
Hohfeld, Wesley, 12
Holmes, Stephen, 166
Honig, Bonnie, 11
Humboldt, Wilhelm, 8, 13, 36,
  38, 114, 137, 148, 150, 160,
  182–83
Hume, David, 26, 52, 62, 71, 77,
  90, 174
Huntington, Samuel, 173

ideals and idealisms, xii–xiii, 16,
  131, 140, 159
idiosyncrasies, idiolects and singularities, xvii–xviii, 167 (see
  also chapters 2–3)
Illich, Ivan, 142
individuality, xviii, 4, 6, 14, 23,
  35–37, 42–45, 50, 83, 103,
  115–16, 153, 177
institutions, institutionalizations,
  and institutionalisms, xiii–xiv,
  xviii–xix, 173–75, 183
Irigaray, Luce, 16

James, William, 14, 19, 38, 103,
  115
Johnston, David, 166

Kant, Immanuel, 8–12, 20, 36,
  71, 77, 80, 92, 116, 131
Kateb, George, 8, 11

Kelman, Mark, 97
Kymlicka, Will, 8, 11

language and language games,
  169–72 (see also chapter 4)
Larmore, Charles, 166, 179
legal positivism, 84, 97
Leoni, Bruno, 173–74
liberal democracy, 80–81,
  137–40, 152–56
liberalism: agency-oriented,
  virtue-oriented, voluntarist
  and willful, xvii, xix–xx, 17,
  20–22, 128, 131–33, 167;
  ideals of, xiii, xvi, xvii, 4, 31,
  41–46, 49–50, 79–80, 106–7,
  128, 137; varieties of theories
  of, 17–20, 105, 128, 131
libertarianism and liberationism,
  14, 35, 131
Locke, John, 9, 11, 20, 34, 36,
  80, 115–16, 131, 143–45,
  147–48, 151, 181
Lomonoco, Jeffrey, 177
Lowi, Theodore, 83, 89
Lyotard, Jean-François, 6, 8, 16,
  26

Macedo, Steven, 10–11, 20, 131,
  184
Machiavelli, Niccolò, xiv, xvi,
  15, 19, 153
MacIntyre, Alasdair, 18–22, 115
MacIver, Robert, 79
Marx, Karl, xiii–xvi
McClure, Kirstie, ix
McIlwain, C. H., 89
Mill, John Stuart, 4–6, 8–9, 13,
  20, 22, 32, 34, 36, 38, 103,

108, 115–19, 128–30, 132,
146–47, 151, 155, 162–63,
176–77, 181–82
Minar, Edward, 172
modus vivendi, 37–38
Montaigne, Michel de, xiii, xv,
xvi, 8, 14, 19, 26, 35, 49,
52–57, 67–68, 172–73
Montesquieu, xiv, xv, xvi, 81, 83
Mouffe, Chantal, 14, 23, 36

Neumann, Franz, 89, 97, 101, 174
Nietzsche, Friedrich, xiii, xiv,
xvi, 13–16, 19, 26, 38, 42, 77,
103, 114–15, 142, 153,
158–59, 167–68, 172–73, 182
Nozick, Robert, 11

Oakeshott, Michael, xiv, xvi,
xviii, 4, 7, 13–14, 19, 38, 42,
44–46, 52, 57, 62, 71–77, 89,
95, 142, 153–55, 158–59, 163,
165, 175, 180, 184
Ockham, William, 49
Ortega y Gasset, José, xvii,
19–23, 41–42, 180

Paine, Thomas, 11
Pangle, Thomas, 153, 181
Pascal, Blaise, 26
perfectionism, 167
Peters, Richard, 140
Plato, xiii, 53, 67, 83–84, 141,
143, 175, 180
pluralism and plurality, 4, 6, 14,
23, 27, 83, 115, 148–50
Pocock, J. G. A., 18–19, 177
Polanyi, Michael, 52, 90
police and policing, conceptions

of, xviii–xx, 175; Anglo-
phone versus Continental,
107, 110, 116, 119–24, 129,
133, 177; *Polizeistaat* versus
Die Politik, 111–14, 118, 124,
126, 177
police, private, 120–22, 177
political theory and theorizing,
tasks of, xi–xvi, 37–38, 44,
133
Proudhon, Joseph, 165
Proust, Marcel, xvii, 26–30

Quine, Willard van Orman, 170

Rawls, John, 7–10, 12–13,
20–22, 26–27, 32, 35–36, 68,
80, 83, 110, 115–18, 129–31,
142, 151, 167, 179, 181,
183–84
Raz, Joseph, 5, 11, 110
regularianism, 173 (see also
chapters 4–5)
republicanism, and communitarianism, 18, 20, 22, 41, 125–27,
153
Right of Nature, 7, 12, 166
rights, 11–12, 19–20, 24–26
romanticism, 14, 167
Rorty, Richard, 5, 21, 26–27,
130–31
Rothbard, Murray, 115
Rousseau, Jean-Jacques, 9, 35,
86, 142–43, 148–49, 153–55
rule of law, xviii, 173–75 (see
also chapter 5)
ruling, rules, and rule following,
xv, xviii, 170–73 (see also
chapters 4–5)

Sachs, David, 171
Sandel, Michael, 11, 34
Scanlon, Thomas, 5, 11
Schmitt, Carl, 122
self-making and self-enactment, xvi–xvii, 14–15, 141–42, 164
Sen, Amartya, 5, 11
Shklar, Judith, 5–6, 97, 101, 106, 172, 176
skepticism, 4, 6–7, 55, 67, 80, 82, 141, 166, 172
Skolnick, Jerome, 176, 178
Slovak, Jeffrey, 178
Smith, Rogers, 181
stability, 36
Steiner, Hillel, 178
Strong, Tracy, 180

Tarcov, Nathan, 181
Taylor, Charles, 9, 11, 34
Tocqueville, Alexis de, 32, 34, 38, 106, 154

tolerance, 20, 22, 27, 140
Truman, David, 23

Unger, Roberto, 97
Urmson, J. O., 21

virtues and *virtus*, 7, 10–12, 15, 17, 19–20, 22, 24–25, 30, 44–46, 49, 151, 157, 164
voluntarism, 12–16

Walzer, Michael, 11
Weber, Max, xix, 14, 89, 106–7, 176
Wiley, James, 177
will and willfulness, 12–16, 49
Williams, Bernard, 4
Wilson, James Q., 110, 123–27, 130, 134–35, 178
Wittgenstein, Ludwig, xvii–xviii, 3, 15, 17, 26–30, 50–52, 57–68, 71, 90–94, 100, 105, 168–72, 175

Richard E. Flathman is the George Armstrong Kelly Memorial Professor of Political Science at the Johns Hopkins University. His numerous books include *Willful Liberalism* (1989), *The Philosophy and Politics of Freedom* (1987), *The Practice of Political Authority* (1980), and *The Practice of Rights* (1976).